BBC RADIO 3

90—93 FM

The BBC presents the 117th se[ries of]
Promenade Concerts, broadca[st]
and in high-definition sound at

CW00409395

Wherever you are this summer, the BBC Proms are available for you to enjoy —
across BBC Radio, Television and online. And you can listen and watch again for
seven days after broadcast at bbc.co.uk/proms and via the BBC iPlayer. **BBC iPlayer**

The Proms 1895–2011

The Proms was founded to bring the best of classical music to a wide audience in an informal and welcoming atmosphere. From the very outset, part of the audience has always stood in the 'promenade'. Prom places originally cost just a shilling (5p); today, standing places at the Royal Albert Hall cost only £5.00, and over 500 tickets go on sale for every concert there from two and a half hours beforehand. Programmes have always mixed the great classics with what Henry Wood, the first conductor of the Proms, called his 'novelties' – in other words, rare works and premieres.

1895 The 26-year-old Henry Wood launches the Promenade Concerts at the newly opened Queen's Hall, Langham Place; Wood conducts the Proms throughout their first 50 years **1927** The BBC takes over the running of the Proms **1930** The new BBC Symphony Orchestra becomes the orchestra of the Proms **1939** Proms season abandoned after only three weeks following the declaration of war **1941** The Proms moves to the Royal Albert Hall after the Queen's Hall is gutted in an air raid **1942** The season is shared between two orchestras for the first time: the BBC Symphony Orchestra and the London Philharmonic **1947** First televised Last Night **1961** First complete opera heard at the Proms: Mozart's *Don Giovanni*, given by Glyndebourne Festival Opera **1966** First foreign orchestra at the Proms: the Moscow Radio Orchestra, under Gennady Rozhdestvensky **1970** First Late Night Prom: cult pop group The Soft Machine **1971** First 'world music' Prom: sitar-player Imrat Khan **1994** The Proms celebrates its 100th season with a retrospective of past premieres **1995** The Proms celebrates its centenary year with a season of new commissions **1996** First Proms Chamber Music series; first Prom in the Park **1998** First Blue Peter Family Prom signalling a new commitment to music for families **2002** The Proms goes digital on BBC Four; on-demand listening begins online **2003** Proms in the Park reaches out to all four nations of the UK with the unique festive atmosphere of the Last Night **2005** Proms Chamber Music moves to Cadogan Hall **2008** Proms Plus expands to precede every main evening Proms concert **2009** The Proms Family Orchestra makes its Proms debut **2010** Paul Lewis becomes the first pianist in Proms history to play all five Beethoven piano concertos in a single season; Henry Wood Day celebrates the Proms' founder-conductor; Basil Brush makes history as he becomes the first fox to present a Prom

24
30
92
88
62
36
48
52

BBC Proms 2011

CONTENTS

FSC
www.fsc.org
MIX
Paper from
responsible sources
FSC® C003270

Printed using vegetable-based inks on FSC-certified paper. Formed in 1993 as a response to concerns over global deforestation, FSC (Forest Stewardship Council) is an independent, non-governmental, not-for-profit organisation established to promote the responsible management of the world's forests. For more information, please visit www.fsc-uk.org.

Cover illustration: Justin Krietmeyer/Premm Design. **This page:** Musée Carnavalet, Musées de la Ville de Paris/Archives Charmet/Bridgeman Art Library (Liszt); Brahms Museum, Styria, Austria (Brahms); Fine Arts Museum of San Francisco/Bridgeman Art Library (Eiffel Tower); Royal Academy of Music/Lebrecht Music & Arts (Bridge); The Harold and Esther Edgerton Foundation/Palm Press, Inc./Bridgeman Art Library (bullet & apple); RKO Radio Pictures Inc./akg-images (Astaire & Rogers); Chris Christodoulou/BBC (girl with violin); Phoebe Ling/NYCGB (girl singing)

Welcome to the 2011
BBC Proms

Memories of the 2010 festival are still fresh in my mind as I write this and I hope that we can repeat the success of last year's record-breaking season. There are so many characteristics of the Proms which, over the past 116 years, have made it what it is, but the single most important driving factor in building a festival on this scale is to offer two months of exceptional music-making at the lowest possible prices. Promming tickets are still £5.00 (even cheaper if you buy a Season Ticket), continuing our founder-conductor Henry Wood's original ambition of bringing the best classical music to the widest possible audience. The BBC's commitment since 1927 in organising and funding the Proms has

ROYAL ALBERT HALL

developed this ambition exponentially, bringing the festival to many millions on BBC Radio 3, BBC Television and online.

With so many great artists and events – 74 concerts at the Royal Albert Hall, 12 at Cadogan Hall (including a series of Saturday Matinees devoted to contemporary music), daily introductory Proms Plus events at the Royal College of Music and the nationwide Proms in the Park celebrations on the Last Night – the scale of the BBC Proms remains unparalleled anywhere in the world.

Every Sunday this season is devoted to choral masterpieces, beginning with Havergal Brian's monumental 'The Gothic' Symphony, which receives its Proms debut (and its first outing in the UK since 1980) in a unique performance featuring two BBC orchestras and 10 choirs. Among other highlights in the series are the great *Requiems* by Mozart and Verdi, Mendelssohn's *Elijah*, Beethoven's *Missa solemnis*, Mahler's *Das klagende Lied*, and choral music by Benjamin Britten in a recreation of a Prom that Britten himself conducted in 1963. Thousands of choral singers – including many amateurs and young people – will take part in the Choral Sundays and you can join in too: each Sunday afternoon there will be a Proms Plus Sing workshop (*see pages 92–99*). The choral spirit also spills over into the Last Night, offering participatory fun as the nation unites for ambitious mass singalongs around the UK.

In addition to the leading British orchestras, international visitors arrive from Australia, France, Germany, Hungary, Italy, Israel, the Netherlands, Russia, Sweden, Switzerland and the USA. The last, alphabetically, is from Venezuela, as Gustavo Dudamel returns for Mahler's 'Resurrection' Symphony. We welcome back many of the world's foremost soloists – Martha Argerich, Angela Hewitt, Stephen Hough, Nigel Kennedy, Lang Lang, Yo-Yo Ma, Anne-Sophie Mutter, Viktoria Mullova and Maria João Pires, to name but a few – and there are notable Proms debuts from brilliant young performers Alice Sara Ott, Yuja Wang and the British pianist Benjamin Grosvenor, who kicks off our Liszt bicentenary celebrations on the First Night and returns later with the National Youth Orchestra to play Britten's Piano Concerto.

The Liszt bicentenary celebrations include performances of the piano concertos at the First and Last Nights, recitals from Marc-André Hamelin and current BBC Radio 3 New Generation Artist Khatia Buniatishvili and much of his important orchestral music. It's also good to shine the spotlight on composers who do not have particular birthdays, but whose music we have chosen to feature nonetheless – not least, Bartók (whose three piano concertos all appear for the first time in one season), Frank Bridge (who richly deserves to be better known) and Brahms. In the tradition of the single-composer nights reintroduced with last year's Beethoven Night, Brahms has two evenings devoted to his music, in which Bernard Haitink conducts the Chamber Orchestra of Europe and Emanuel Ax plays the two piano concertos. In fact you will be able to hear all of Brahms's concertos this year, including one he didn't write! Croatian pianist Dejan Lazić, making his Proms debut, performs his fascinating arrangement for piano and orchestra of Brahms's Violin Concerto.

Including all the Brahms concertos means a welcome performance of his unusually scored Double Concerto for violin and cello. This in turn encouraged us to look at other atypical concertos – hence Beethoven's Triple Concerto for violin, cello and piano, Pascal Dusapin's string quartet concerto, Simon Holt's *Centauromachy* for clarinet and flugelhorn, Glière's Concerto for Coloratura Soprano and ▶

Lang Lang | Viktoria Mullova | Bernard Haitink | Maria João Pires | Gustavo Dudamel

BBC Symphony Orchestra

Jiří Bělohlávek Chief Conductor

CONCERTS
2011—12

A season of distinctive concerts from the BBC Symphony Orchestra featuring an extraordinary range of music from the great Romantic symphonies to thrilling premieres from today's leading composers.

Sibelius Symphony Cycle
All seven symphonies with conductors including Neeme Järvi, Sakari Oramo and Jukka-Pekka Saraste

The BBC SO at the Movies
Live accompaniment of Anthony Asquith's 1928 silent thriller *Underground*

A Night at the Opera
Jiří Bělohlávek conducts Dvořák's romantic comedy *The Jacobin*

Total Immersion
Celebrations of the music of Jonathan Harvey, Brett Dean and Arvo Pärt

English Oratorios
Walton's *Belshazzar's Feast* and Tippett's *A Child of Our Time*, conducted by Edward Gardner and Sir Andrew Davis

Thrilling Premieres
Including concertos by Einojuhani Rautavaara and Kalevi Aho

'…an orchestra playing with the precision, bounce and colourful glow that only the best possess.' The Times

BBC RADIO 3

90 – 93 FM

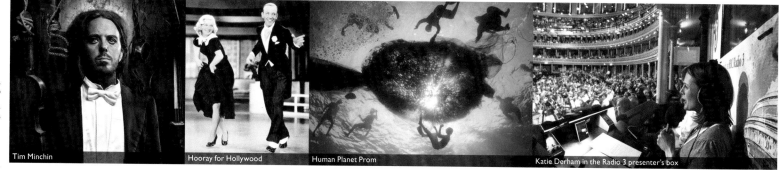

Tim Minchin   Hooray for Hollywood   Human Planet Prom   Katie Derham in the Radio 3 presenter's box

Gabriel Prokofiev's Concerto for Turntables and Orchestra. This little strand is just one example of the way in which concerts are built organically with ideas feeding into each other, as well as of our desire to keep the programming fresh with new and less familiar work.

To add to the sense of celebration we have two specially commissioned festive opening pieces to frame the season, by Judith Weir and Sir Peter Maxwell Davies, which open the First and Last Nights respectively. And, as ever, at the heart of the Proms, there's a huge range of new, often specially commissioned music from an array of British and international composers.

A focus on French music since 1900 throws light on how three major figures of contemporary French music – Henri Dutilleux (95 this year), Pascal Dusapin and Marc-André Dalbavie (who both have major premieres this season) – have extended the traditions of Debussy, Ravel and Messiaen. There are also two major 'French' operas: Antonio Pappano and the Orchestra and Chorus of Academy of Santa Cecilia from Rome give the first complete Proms performance of Rossini's *William Tell*, and Sir John Eliot Gardiner's Orchestre Révolutionnaire et Romantique and Monteverdi Choir introduce Berlioz's version of Weber's *Der Freischütz*, created for the Opéra de Paris.

In the great Proms tradition of wide-ranging programmes we welcome back John Wilson and his hand-picked orchestra for a Hollywood celebration,

while comedy meets classical music for the first time at the Proms, when a variety of musically inventive comics take to the stage for what promises to be a hugely entertaining Saturday-night Comedy Prom.

Blockbuster scores by the late John Barry, centenary composer Bernard Herrmann and the great John Williams are at the heart of the Film Music Prom and are followed by a Late Night Prom featuring the Spaghetti Western Orchestra, which brings its unique approach to the film scores of Ennio Morricone. In another light-hearted late night, with the Budapest Festival Orchestra, conductor Iván Fisher will invite members of the audience to pick the pieces they perform in their unique Late Night Prom.

There's a major collaboration with CBBC's *Horrible Histories*, which brings a free Prom for families, and in another major TV collaboration we invite world musicians from all corners of the globe for the Human Planet Prom, presented by John Hurt. Other 'alternative' highlights feature a World Routes Academy Prom, celebrating the music of Southern India, and a Late Night Prom to mark the centenary of jazz legend Stan Kenton. Plus, this year we've introduced a Proms Plus Late series of informal post-Prom music and poetry in the Royal Albert Hall's Elgar Room, with a late bar.

There are so many other concerts and events that you can read about in this Proms Guide and there's even more on our new-look Proms website.

Booking for tickets opens on 7 May and it's worth using the Proms Planner online beforehand

to give yourself the best chance of getting the tickets you want. One other tip: if you find that a concert is sold out, or that seats in your preferred seating area are no longer available, it's worth returning later to the new-look Proms website, as tickets do become available and you may find more on offer nearer the time. Or why not Prom on the night (*see pages 18–21*)?

I hope you find plenty to whet your appetite in the following pages, and that you enjoy an unforgettable summer of music-making at the 2011 BBC Proms.

Roger Wright

Roger Wright
Director, BBC Proms

EDINBURGH INTERNATIONAL FESTIVAL

12 August – 4 September 2011

Influences and Inspirations
Europe and Asia Explored

Shanghai Peking Opera Troupe / Strauss's *Die Frau ohne Schatten* /
Schumann's *Das Paradies und die Peri* / Rossini's *Semiramide* /
Mariinsky Opera / Massenet's *Thaïs* / **Seoul Philharmonic Orchestra** /
Haydn's *Orlando paladino* / **Valery Gergiev** / Mahler's Symphony No 2 /
Kent Nagano / **Orchestre symphonique de Montréal** / Martha Argerich /
Tonhalle Orchestra / Murray Perahia / **Jonathan Nott** / Philadelphia
Orchestra / **Bamberg Symphony Orchestra** / BBC Scottish Symphony
Orchestra / **Bo Skovhus** / Charles Dutoit / **Philip Glass** / David Zinman /
Ravi Shankar / Scottish Chamber Orchestra / **The Sixteen** /
Amjad Ali Khan / **Belcea Quartet** / Philharmonia Orchestra /
Simon Keenlyside / Sir Roger Norrington / **Orchestra of the
Age of Enlightenment** / Xuefei Yang / **Karita Mattila** / Yundi

For your free brochure call +44 (0)131 473 2000 or visit eif.co.uk

Supported by the City of Edinburgh Council
and Creative Scotland. Charity No SC004694.

All around the Proms

There's more to the BBC's Proms broadcasts than bringing the concerts to you, wherever you are. With offstage access to artists, lively presenters and a plethora of media platforms, the multi-layered coverage can be truly immersive. Helen Wallace dives in.

The Proms on BBC Radio 3

- BBC Proms broadcast live on BBC Radio 3 (90–93FM)
- Many Proms repeated during *Afternoon on 3* (weekdays, 2.00pm), plus a series of repeats over the Christmas period
- Listen Again for seven days after broadcast via bbc.co.uk/proms
- Proms-related programmes during the season, including *Breakfast* (daily, 7.00am) and *In Tune* (weekdays, 5.00pm)

Did you know that you could watch a Prom from a camera angle fixed on the conductor? Or on the principal oboe? Listen to any Prom, whenever you like, for a whole week after the broadcast? Follow an artist into their dressing room after a performance and find out how they're feeling? These are just some of the possibilities available this year, from BBC Radio 3, BBC Two, BBC Four, via the red button or online.

'Our aim,' says Edward Blakeman, Radio 3's Proms Editor, 'is to make the Proms as much a broadcast festival as it is a concert festival. We are here for the vast majority of people who can never come to the Royal Albert Hall in person during the season, and we are also here for audience members on the nights when they aren't at the concerts, but still want to be part of the Proms. We want to take everyone to the Proms! To let them feel the atmosphere before the concert, to give them context during it – a personal guide to the music – and to take them behind the scenes with opportunities to hear directly from the artists themselves. We offer a whole summer of listening.'

No stone has been left unturned: you can hear Proms artists chatting and playing chamber music on the weekday drivetime programme *In Tune*, and you can follow rehearsal dramas on the Proms blog. You can read in-depth programme notes on the Proms website before the concert or enjoy selected Proms accompanied by a blow-by-blow commentary via the red button. Equally, you can pose questions to the Director of the Proms, share your own video via social media (*eg* Facebook) or post a review of the previous night's performance.

THREE'S COMPANY

In terms of breadth and depth, Radio 3 has a pretty unbeatable propositon. The network not only broadcasts every single Prom on radio and in high-definition sound

via the website, but provides context and insight throughout the day during the whole season. Live listening is a striking feature of the Proms season, and the figures really do spike during those summer evenings. But there has also been a steady increase in internet listening as a new generation of music-lovers tunes in. Although each concert is available online for seven days after broadcast, Blakeman finds it telling that the majority of internet listening still happens live, rather than time-shifted: 'In a way it's surprising, but I think there's a strong sense of wanting to feel part of the event in the hall. So we get listeners emailing us from New Zealand to say that they are up at 4.00am listening to a Proms Saturday Matinee, or from California saying they've heard an evening concert at lunchtime. They want to share in the moment.' Veteran Radio 3 presenter Sean Rafferty puts it down to the special attention required of the radio listener: 'There's something about the Proms on radio that just communicates: instead of that rather deferential murmur you hear before some other concerts, there's an electric atmosphere an almost feral sense of anticipation among such a mass of people. And that has an indescribable sound and an energy which comes palpably through the airwaves. During the performance, the radio listener has to engage so intensely; it sharpens your imagination, and you become part of the creative process.'

A DAY AT THE PROMS, AT HOME

The Proms day begins with *Breakfast*, as Edward Blakeman explains: 'You wake up to *Breakfast*, the start of your Proms day as we give the latest updates and news about the season. We'll also play music related to the concert that night or feature artists who are appearing. *Classical Collection* will have a Proms strand through the season, as will *Composer of the Week* – and on ▶

Sean Rafferty presents the Proms on BBC Radio 3 and Radio 3's *In Tune*

Presenting *In Tune*, I'm lucky to have a preview of each Prom. There's this incredible procession of great performers hurtling into London, and I have the privilege of a conversation and an intimate concert from them in our own studio before the main event.

It's a great opportunity to get to know them, and very often once I've heard them play I drop everything to try to get to the concert at the Royal Albert Hall the next day. The interviews can have that effect on the *In Tune* audience too: they hear these artists talking with such passion, humility and honesty, and it puts a whole new light on the forthcoming concert. What was a mere listing of a concerto suddenly has a new flavour, a personal angle, and they rush to get a ticket. The downside of presenting *In Tune* is that I always miss the first part of the Prom: I've developed various subterfuges to sneak in for the main work, all deadly secret! On the First Night last year I could be found running like hell from the Proms Preview at the Royal College of Music to make it to the hall in time for the start of the concert.

I love presenting the Last Night of the Proms for Radio 3: people are sometimes a bit sniffy about it, but for me it's about jubilation, not jingoism. We've had all those weeks of queuing, listening, all that commitment and energy, and then it's time to let your hair down and have a party. I always sing along lustily to the songs, even to 'Land of Hope and Glory' – it's wonderful to see so many different national flags waving so harmoniously in the hall.

Croatian pianist Dejan Lazić *(left)* in the *In Tune* studio with presenter Sean Rafferty: a procession of Proms artists appears on the live drivetime show during the summer

Saturday mornings *Summer CD Review* also links to the Proms. Our Monday-lunchtime chamber concert comes direct from Cadogan Hall (and is repeated on Saturday afternoons). On weekday afternoons we have Proms repeats – 40 in all during the season, plus another series at Christmas. Then we come to drivetime and *In Tune*, in which you'll hear from artists who'll be playing in the next day or two. Finally, in the evening, comes the Prom itself.'

A recent innovation is the series of Proms Plus pre-concert events at the Royal College of Music and a selection of these are broadcast as mini radio features. 'The Music Intros proved so popular,' says Blakeman, 'that we're doing more of them this year. Concert-goers really liked hearing an enthusiastic presenter talking you through the works in that evening's Prom – getting under the skin of the music – with recorded examples as well as live performance and talk from some of the musicians you will be hearing later that evening. And brand-new this year is a special series of eight Proms Plus Intros for the Choral Sundays, broadcast live each week at 5.15pm. You'll have a 45-minute talk on Verdi's *Requiem*, or Mendelssohn's *Elijah*, or Beethoven's *Missa solemnis*, leading into the Prom at 7.00pm.'

Other Proms Plus events will be recorded for broadcast as intervals in the concerts. These include contextual talks in which experts discuss aspects of a composer's cultural milieu. 'They might be looking at aspects of Mahler's personality, or politics, or Hungary at the time of Liszt, for instance.' Some of the Proms Plus Literary series will focus on Proms artists and their tastes in poetry and prose: 'This is a sort of Private Literary Passions for musicians. So we'll be asking a performer such as Stephen Hough to choose his favourite extracts of

fiction and poetry. We know him as a pianist, but here we'll discover what he reads, what he really cares about in terms of ideas and literary style.' There will also be a new series on instruments featured in literature, alongside events exploring the connections between music and literature.

SHARING THE TALENT

Given the number of interviews taking place during the broadcasting of the Proms, it's amazing there are never any clashes, repetitions or, let's face it, fisticuffs between the radio and television presenters – how do they achieve that? 'We do look ahead and work out who is going to be where, and what works for radio doesn't necessarily work for television,' explains Edward Blakeman. 'For radio, we'll often grab a performer just after the rehearsal, when their minds are still buzzing with the music, and record the interview then, whereas there's an appeal for the television audience to see an artist actually coming off stage and into their dressing room immediately after the performance. Presentation style on both radio and television aims to be engaging and informal, and several presenters – notably Suzy Klein, Katie Derham, Petroc Trelawny and Sara Mohr-Pietsch – will be seen on BBC Two or BBC Four and heard on Radio 3 during the 2011 Proms.'

The Proms on BBC Television

- 24 Proms broadcast across BBC One, BBC Two, BBC Four and BBC HD
- Regular Saturday-evening broadcasts on BBC Two and BBC HD
- Two Proms each week on BBC Four
- Maestro Cam and Player Cam, along with expert audio commentary, available for selected Proms via the red button
- The Last Night of the Proms on BBC HD, first half on BBC Two and second half on BBC One – plus Proms in the Park events around the country via the red button

One of the discreet Q-Ball cameras, employed in recent Proms TV broadcasts

SEEING IS BELIEVING ...

As viewers will have been aware, the television coverage of the Proms has changed in recent years to a less formal, more in-the-moment approach, particularly on BBC Four. Oliver Macfarlane, Editor, Classical Music TV, explains: 'There has been a step-change in the way we cover Proms in recent times, away from static, formal presentation and towards a more lively, free-flowing style.' One memorable example of this from last year was the presentation of Mahler's Third Symphony from the backstage area, which caused controversy when it was first proposed. Presenter Petroc Trelawny recalls the night itself: 'That was breaking new ground. There was concern that we would be distracting the musicians just at the moment they needed to prepare mentally for an epic work like that. We were under strict instructions to take up certain positions and not stray from them, and I was instructed not to look conductor Donald Runnicles in the eye before he went on. The funny thing was, he absolutely understood that this was as much a television event as a live one, and he came over to talk to me, relaxed as anything. He knew what was needed, and led the whole interview ▶

Suzy Klein presents the Proms on BBC Four and BBC Radio 3
I love the fact that my role as presenter has been freed up, allowing us to move around the hall into the backstage areas and Green Room, as well as delivering more traditional presentation from the box. The aim is for the TV audience to feel that the event is unfolding right in front of them. For me, last year's most memorable moment was the performance of Wagner's *The Mastersingers*: I'd always found Wagner thorny, but I had this major conversion as I listened. I was totally overwhelmed and there was a real tension between the emotion I felt as a listener and the need for a cool head as a presenter. I also loved the two Berlin Philharmonic Proms – you really felt that people had been queuing around the block, desperate to get in.

Having produced Proms broadcasts in the past, I maybe know a bit too much about the process, and am always aware of who might be talking in my earpiece, what kind of headsets and battery packs are needed … I have to try to let go of that and enjoy presenting, which is less of a job and more of a privilege: it gives me the excuse to talk to extraordinary artists, composers and performers!

My biggest challenge last year was presenting two concerts back to back for both radio and TV: the first was a BBC Symphony Orchestra Prom for Radio 3, featuring Barber's Violin Concerto and Sibelius's Second Symphony, the other was Jamie Cullum and the Heritage Orchestra for BBC Four. I had to do the first concert and then immediately get changed, put on another microphone and try to convey the utterly different atmosphere of the late-night show. The gear change was quite something!

until the point where I became worried the whole orchestra was waiting for him! In the end I shook his hand and practically pushed him on stage. The whole thing worked: it was a complete integration of a live and broadcast event.'

Macfarlane points out that such intimate filming is possible thanks to technical advances: 'The cameras have moved things forward. We can now present the concerts more from the point of view of the musicians without compromising their work.' He's referring to the small, remote-controlled Q-Ball and SMARThead cameras that enable a constant view of the conductor or an individual player (the 'Maestro Cam' or 'Player Cam' features, via red button). 'These cameras can get into very interesting places in the orchestra without distracting the players and also give the general audience a different, and often illuminating, new point of view.' A Towercam, operated on a vertical rig at the back of the hall, gives a good perspective and sense of scale from above, while a jib arm 'allows us to swing over the orchestra and creates movement and drama'.

This highly versatile technology opens the door to a myriad of creative possibilities, but it doesn't eliminate all the practical challenges of televising the Proms, as Macfarlane knows all too well, especially this year with a packed programme of big choral events such as Verdi's *Requiem* and Beethoven's *Missa solemnis*: 'We cover a complex live concert, sometimes with hundreds of participants, before an audience of 5,000 in a big and complicated building – and we share the coverage with radio, so, yes, it does take a lot of planning!' He's determined that

they should continue opening out the experience, however: 'We want to build on what we've already developed: to get closer to the musicians, to talk to members of the orchestra, to get backstage and to rove all over the hall, the Gallery, the Green Room, the Arena. We'll be as lively and out-of-the-box as possible on BBC Four, continuing that flavour on BBC Two, but with perhaps some additional pre-recorded interviews.'

Another developing feature of the television coverage has been the range of commentators involved in each broadcast, from performers, to composers, experts and other interested celebrities. What does Macfarlane look for in his talking heads? 'We are always widening the pool of contributors. We look for experts, or practitioners, who have something to say, who speak engagingly, enthusiastically and – importantly for this sort of live event – who have the ability to be brief!'

The Proms Online

- Every performance available online as audio or video for seven days after broadcast; share with friends via Facebook and Twitter
- Search for Proms by composer, artist or genre (eg concertos) – plus searchable archive
- Read the Proms blog, view photos and video about the artists. Glean backstage insights from people working on the Proms
- In-depth programme notes for every concert

- Discover the music – audio and video analyses of selected works
- Proms newsletter and daily text alerts
- Digest of press reviews plus editor's picks of reviews written by the audience
- Text or email your review to Radio 3's *Breakfast* (daily, 7.00am)
- Download interviews with Proms performers, conductors and composers from Radio 3's *In Tune* (weekdays, 5.00pm)

On site for online: the Proms website features specially recorded audio and video offering insights into composers and works featured during the season

Macfarlane is interested in developing more interaction with the audience this year: 'We welcome the audience sending in comments and questions and we feed those into our interviews – the more the better. That characterises our presentation, I think – the fact that there's a two-way conversation with the audience – and our presenters act as the interlocutors.'

OPENING UP THE TREASURE TROVE

Audience emails and texts are fed through the Proms website and, when it comes to interactivity, online is where the real dialogue starts. Listeners can add their own concert reviews, or comment on others' reviews or on blog posts. You can share experiences and even photos and videos via social media or put questions to Proms Director, Roger Wright. You can also sign up for the newsletter and daily text alerts.

After the success of the new Proms online booking service last year, the website has had a complete redesign for 2011, which is much more than a facelift, as Interactive Editor, Gabriel Gilson, explains: 'The most significant new feature this year is that we've integrated the Radio 3 website's archive with the Proms website, which represents a very rich resource. It means that you will not only be able to access in-depth programme notes on the site itself, but cross-refer to information on key composers, analyses of works of music – that might have appeared, for instance, on *Discovering Music* or *Composer of the Week* – or look at the *Building a Library* archive to find out more about recordings of a work you've just heard.' So anyone who wants to tell apart their Bruch from their Bruckner, or discover the back-story to Janáček's *Glagolitic Mass* can browse at will.

The web team have responded to last year's feedback by ensuring that each individual Prom concert is findable via Google, and that Proms can be searched for by type: 'As well as searching by composer or performer,' says Gilson, 'you can search by category, including

choral Proms, family-friendly concerts or Baroque and Early Music. And we are promoting the Listen Again feature: many people don't realise you can listen to every single Prom for seven days after broadcast. Nor do they realise they can probe the Proms Archive for details of every concert since the Proms began in 1895. You can also watch the televised Proms again by going to the Proms website.'

Added to this will be weekly podcasts compiled from *In Tune* and *Lebrecht Interview*, a Proms Quiz and photos and videos to relive big events such as Human Planet, Horrible Histories, Hooray for Hollywood and the Comedy Prom. The Proms buzz will be reflected on social media with updates on Facebook and Twitter, and you'll be able to browse and listen via your mobile phone. So, wherever you go this summer, you need never be more than a click away from the Proms. ●

Helen Wallace is Consultant Editor of *BBC Music Magazine* and a former editor of *The Strad*. She has written histories of the music publishers Boosey & Hawkes and of the Orchestra of the Age of Enlightenment, and is a regular critic for BBC Radio 4's *Front Row*.

Petroc Trelawny blogs for the Proms website and presents the Proms on BBC Radio 3 and BBC Four
You get something direct and immediate from a blog as opposed to a piece of writing in print. I like the sense of sharing a stream of consciousness, there's an honesty to it. I find myself turning to blogs for all sorts of up-to-the-minute commentary on food, restaurants, travel and opinion. When blogging for the Proms, I'll be trying to bring that sense of the inside track, of inviting the audience into the engine room of the festival. The difference between radio presentation and blogging is really the time frame: while I'm presenting live on air, I'm focusing on vital, basic information, but on a blog you've got the space to tell behind-the-scenes stories, mention artists' comments which never got on air, offer a view from the orchestra. Looking ahead, I'll have four different perspectives from which to blog this summer: I'll be presenting *In Tune*, so there's always more to share when chatting with artists off air; then I'll be down in Cornwall for a few days, experiencing the Proms as a radio listener; I'll be presenting televised Proms, and, again, there's so much going on that viewers never see, I can give a wider picture; lastly, I'll be blogging from the point of view of simply being in the hall, attending rehearsals and concerts. The essential thing is that blogs enhance the experience of the music, give audiences closer access to the making of a performance. It's also an exciting way of having a dialogue: I can feed back comments and questions into my presentation. Of course, although it's a rapid way of communicating, I don't just press 'send'. The blogs go to Graeme Kay, who edits the Proms site, adds pictures, links, all the context – and deals with my appalling apostrophes!

Adrian Weinbrecht/BBC (p14, Klein); Des Burkinshaw (above left); Adrian Weinbrecht/BBC (Trelawny)

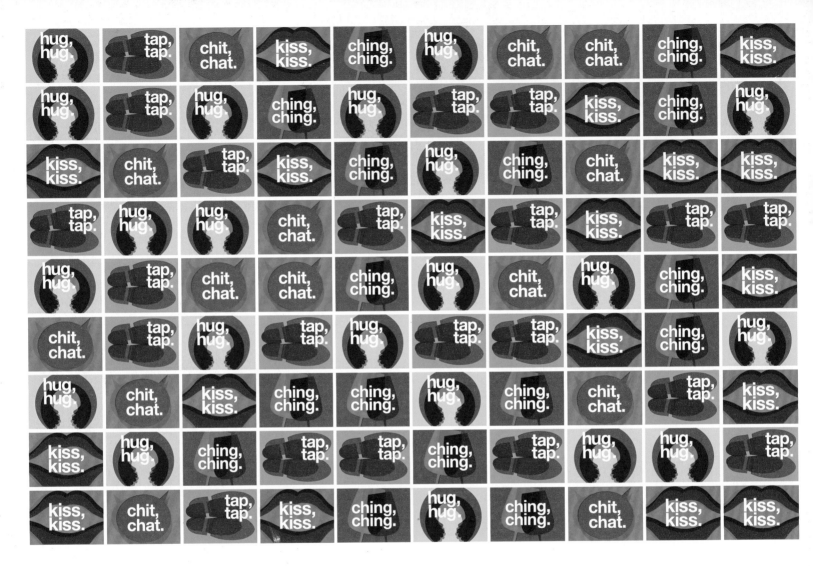

BBC Concert ORCHESTRA

Some of the things people do at BBC Concert Orchestra events

Join us...

Call Freephone **0800 096 1616**. We are always happy to chitchat, or tap tap to visit **bbc.co.uk/concertorchestra**

Follow us on Twitter – **twitter.com/bbcco**, or become a fan on Facebook – **facebook.com/bbcconcertorchestra**

Virtuoso
Performance

A powerful iPod/iPhone dock with best-in-class audio, Contour brings your iTunes library to life with an open soundstage that's dynamic and detailed. And with digital, FM and internet radio, and music streaming direct from your Mac or PC there's always something good to listen to, whether it's high-quality classical music from over 300 classical stations worldwide, news, sports, music by location or genre, podcasts or listen again programmes. **Now it's easy to find the listening you like... And it sounds stunning.**

www.pure.com   0845 148 9001

PURE

HOW TO PROM

'Prommers do it standing up!' was the message emblazoned on Proms T-shirts one year, but Jenny Beeston delves deeper into the time-honoured Proms tradition of standing up for music, to offer an easy-to-follow Promen-aid.

Where should I queue? And when? And why did the crowd just seem to shout at the piano? Promming can seem an odd mix of formality and informality, of laid-back behaviour and mysterious unwritten rules. But it's the cheapest and best way to get up close and personal with the vast array of top-class musicians who visit the BBC Proms each year, and a popular choice for younger people.

Being only a few feet away from some of the best orchestras in the world for just a few quid (five, to be exact) sounds almost too good to be true, and of course there are some small catches. You can expect to be standing most of the time, for one thing, but luckily there's no dress code, so comfortable clothing – particularly shoes – makes obvious sense (the flags and amusing hats only come out for the Last Night). However, there's usually enough space in the Arena (the larger Promming space, directly in front of the stage) to sit on the floor beforehand and during the interval, if you want to rest your feet. At less packed concerts there can even be room to stretch out on the floor at the back – a wonderful way to enjoy the special acoustic qualities of the Royal Albert Hall.

People tend to associate Promming with the Arena, but there's also the Gallery, the uppermost balcony, way up, just beneath the roof. This is the best choice if you want more space and don't mind being further away from the action.

Queuing is a vital part of the Promming experience and, with a bit of advance planning, it doesn't need to be a tedious one either. Some regulars turn it into a sort of party, complete with picnic hampers. You might not want to go that far, but a sandwich and drink is a good idea for a long wait. An entertaining companion can come in useful to pass the time, or you can browse the

Being only a few feet away from some of the best orchestras in the world for just a few quid (five, to be exact) sounds almost too good to be true

internet on your mobile or bring a good book. But why not chat to your neighbours? Marriages have resulted from being in the Proms queues, so you never know …

You can avoid queuing by buying a Season Ticket in advance (*see page 21*). This guarantees entry up to 30 minutes before the concert begins, and the cost potentially works out at less than £2.60 per concert. If the idea of a Season Ticket brings on a fear of commitment, there's also a Weekend Promming Pass (*see page 158*), but the footloose alternative is to turn up and queue for a £5 ticket on the day. Hundreds of these are available

for every Royal Albert Hall Prom (there are fewer for concerts at the smaller Cadogan Hall), even if the seats are completely sold out. All you have to do is turn up on the day and join the appropriate queue, signposted for either Arena or Gallery Day Promming.

If you arrive early, the Royal Albert Hall stewards will hand you a numbered ticket which marks your place. This means you don't lose your position in the queue if you attend a Proms Plus event before the concert – just a stone's throw away, at the Royal College of Music – or if you need a short break (half an hour).

Admission begins 45 minutes before the performance (30 minutes before late-night concerts). It's advisable to arrive earlier, though, especially for the more popular concerts, in case there aren't enough spaces to meet demand. A tip: the Gallery queue is generally shorter than that for the Arena, making it more likely you'll get in on a busy day.

The earlier you start queuing, the wider the choice of spots you'll have once you're inside. A place near the front of the Arena brings you within spitting distance of the performers, but it's easier to secure a space towards the rear, or up in the Gallery.

All these hows and wheres are straightforward. What at first seems more mysterious are the Prommers' chants. Anyone can join in. When the piano lid is lifted before a piano concerto, the Arena cry 'Heave!', and the Gallery respond with 'Ho!' Following a little collective preparation in the Arena, foreign orchestras are often greeted in their own language, generally to their great delight. But the repartee can be more inventive, such as

All right at the back? Young Prommers relaxing at the rear of the Royal Albert Hall's Arena

when the Arena Prommers once pointedly asked the assembled choirs, anxiously awaiting their orchestral colleagues before a performance of Mahler's 'Resurrection' Symphony: 'Do you know the *a cappella* version?'.

After the interval you'll hear the Prommers announce their post-Prom collection for musical charities. This is your cue to remember what a bargain your ticket was and drop a coin or two into the bucket on your way out – every year Proms audiences raise scores of thousands of pounds for good causes, proving that the Prommers are nothing if not public-spirited.

Jenny Beeston is a regular Prommer and writes about opera for Whatsonstage.com.

Chris Christodoulou (all photos)

Handcrafted Perfection

Steinway & Sons pianos are individually created, which gives them their own unique characteristics and incomparable sound. Suffice to say that those at the top of their profession, as well as those who simply want the best, invest in nothing less.

"STEINWAY & SONS IS THE ONLY PIANO ON WHICH THE PIANIST CAN DO EVERYTHING HE WANTS, AND EVERYTHING HE DREAMS"

VLADIMIR ASHKENAZY

STEINWAY & SONS

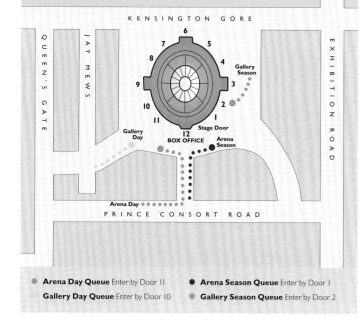

KENSINGTON GORE

QUEEN'S GATE

JAY MEWS

EXHIBITION ROAD

PRINCE CONSORT ROAD

Gallery Season
Gallery Day
Stage Door
BOX OFFICE
Arena Season
Arena Day

- **Arena Day Queue** Enter by Door 11
- **Gallery Day Queue** Enter by Door 10
- **Arena Season Queue** Enter by Door 1
- **Gallery Season Queue** Enter by Door 2

Justin Knietemeyer/Premm Design (illustration, far right)

WHAT IS PROMMING?

The popular tradition of Promming is central to the unique and informal atmosphere of the BBC Proms at the Royal Albert Hall.

Up to 1,400 standing places are available for each Proms concert at the Royal Albert Hall. The traditionally low prices allow you to enjoy world-class performances for just £5.00 each (or even less with a Season Ticket or Weekend Promming Pass). There are two standing areas: the Arena, located directly in front of the stage, and the Gallery, running round the top of the Hall. All spaces are unreserved.

DAY PROMMERS

Over 500 Arena and Gallery tickets (priced £5.00) are available for every Prom. These tickets cannot be booked in advance, so even if all seats have been sold, you always have a good chance of getting in (though early queuing is advisable for the more popular concerts). You must buy your ticket in person, and must pay by cash.

A limited number of Arena tickets will usually be sold to the Day Queue from two and a half hours before each performance (from 9.45am for 11.00am concerts). The remaining Day Promming tickets will then be sold from Door 11 (Arena) and Door 10 (Gallery) from 45 minutes before the performance to those queuing. Tickets for Late Night Proms are available only on the doors, from 30 minutes before the performance. Arena and Gallery tickets are available only at Door 11 and Door 10, not at the Box Office.

Wheelchair-users who wish to Prom (Gallery only) should queue in the same way but will be redirected to Door 8 once their ticket is purchased. For further information for disabled concert-goers, see page 164.

If you are in doubt about where to go, Royal Albert Hall stewards will point you in the right direction.

SEASON TICKETS

Frequent Prommers can save money by purchasing Arena or Gallery Season Tickets covering either the whole Proms season (including the Last Night) or only the first or second half (ie Proms 1–37 or Proms 38–73, excluding the Last Night).

Season Ticket-holders benefit from:

- guaranteed entrance (20 minutes before each concert)
- great savings – prices can work out at less than £2.60 per concert
- guaranteed entrance to the Last Night for Whole Season Ticket-holders and special access to a reserved allocation of Last Night tickets for Half Season Ticket-holders (see page 159)

Important information: Season Ticket-holders arriving at the Hall less than 20 minutes before a concert are not guaranteed entry. They will be asked to join the back of the Day Queue.

Season Tickets are non-transferable and two passport-sized photographs must be provided before tickets can be issued. Season Tickets are not valid for concerts at Cadogan Hall.

For further details and prices of Season Tickets, see page 161. You can also buy Weekend Promming Passes (see page 158).

PROMS AT CADOGAN HALL

For Cadogan Hall Day Seats, Proms Chamber Music Series Pass and booking information, see page 163.

BBC National Orchestra of Wales

Get closer to the music

2011-12 concert season

Aberystwyth / Bangor / Brecon / Bristol / Caerphilly / Cardiff
Cheltenham / Haverfordwest / Llandudno / London / Marlborough
Newtown / St Asaph / St Davids / Swansea / Wrexham

Call FREE for further details

BBC cymru wales

BBC RADIO 3
90 – 93 FM

Cyngor Celfyddydau Cymru
Arts Council of Wales

Noddir gan
Lywodraeth Cynulliad Cymru
Sponsored by
Welsh Assembly Government

BBC National Orchestra of Wales Audience Line:
0800 052 1812　　bbc.co.uk/now

RCM
LONDON

EXTRAORDINARILY TALENTED PEOPLE

ROYAL COLLEGE OF MUSIC, LONDON

020 7591 4300
www.rcm.ac.uk

A Lust for Liszt

Malcolm Hayes argues that it's time to look beyond the sparkle of the virtuoso poster boy to consider Liszt's achievements as a visionary composer and an artist of wide-ranging inspiration and unswerving resolve

Nothing succeeds like success. Or does it? Liszt's status as one of the 19th century's great composers was strangely embattled even during his lifetime. It has remained so ever since – far more than his reputation as possibly the greatest pianist who has ever lived. This is a composer whose music it is still considered smart to despise in many academic, critical and pianistic circles. Happily, the same is not true of the listening and CD-buying public. But, even allowing for the demands of conformist fashion, the anti-Liszt mood that prevails in much of the professional musical world seems bizarre. How can it have come about?

The central reason is a simple one: the magnitude of the Liszt phenomenon is of a kind that resists categorisation. Besides the music – around 1,300 items,

CONCERT
by
Franz Liszt

Saal der Gesellschaft der Musikfreunde, Vienna
Thursday 5 March 1846, 12.30pm

Works by Schubert, Chopin & LISZT

grouped into nearly 700 numbered works – there is the life story, an astonishing epic in itself. Liszt was the only son of a manager (and talented cellist) working for the Esterházy estates, located on the cusp of the German- and Hungarian-speaking lands of the Austro-Hungarian Empire. Resigning his job, Adam Liszt took his fantastically gifted and already deeply religious young son Franz to study in nearby Vienna, then to Paris. By the time Adam died in 1827, the teenage Liszt was an international celebrity whose piano-playing had the power to haunt the memory of whoever heard it.

Over the next 20 years Liszt pursued a travelling career that saw him giving concerts across the whole of Europe. There was also a sizeable interlude, when he eloped from Paris in 1835 with the older and already married Countess Marie d'Agoult, first to Switzerland, then to Italy; their three children, Blandine, Cosima and Daniel, were born in these years. Encouraged by Marie's literary interests, Liszt read widely, immersing himself in the Romantic and pre-Romantic worlds of Byron, Dante and Petrarch. He also composed the early versions of what

This is a composer whose music it is still considered smart to despise in many academic, critical and pianistic circles.

became, after later revision, some of his greatest piano works. Then in 1847, with his relationship with Marie effectively over, he withdrew from the concert platform – partly out of jaded exasperation at the circus-like adulation surrounding his recitals, partly from a deeper need to make time to compose. He was still only 36 years old.

Small wonder, then, that the wider musical world shared the misunderstanding of the concert promoter who, in 1874, tried to coax Liszt out of his early retirement with the question: 'How is it possible for you *not* to be a pianist?' Liszt replied to him:

Dear Sir, Your friendly communication is based on a harmless mistake. You do not seem to know that for 26 years past I have altogether ceased to be regarded as a pianist; I have for a long time not given any concerts,

Liszt the pedagogue with his pupils in Weimar: among them, on the front row, Rachmaninov's cousin Alexander Siloti (*second from left*), Emil Sauer (*third from right*) and Moriz Rosenthal (*second from right*)

and have only very occasionally played the piano in public … to aid some charity or to further some artistic object, and then only in Rome, Hungary (my native country) and in Vienna – nowhere else. And on these rare and very exceptional occasions no-one has ever thought of offering me any remuneration in money. Excuse me therefore, dear Sir, that I cannot accept your invitation to the Liverpool Music Festival, inasmuch as I cannot in any way think of wearying the public with my 'erstwhile' piano-playing.

As Liszt said, he was still prepared to appear for what he considered to be the right cause. The next year, in Budapest, he played Beethoven's 'Emperor' Concerto at a fund-raising concert for the forthcoming staging of Wagner's *Ring* cycle at Bayreuth. Part of the concert was conducted by Wagner himself, who announced afterwards to his wife – Liszt's second daughter, Cosima – that her father's piano-playing 'annihilated everything else'. (The day before, Liszt had cut one of his fingers and therefore gave this evidently devastating performance using only the remaining nine.) ▶

Countess Marie d'Agoult, whom Liszt met aged 22 and who bore him three children during their 12-year relationship

Liszt conjuring a
storm from the piano
in a French caricature
from 1845

and the dark and turbulent *Dante Symphony*, inspired by the 'Inferno'
and 'Purgatorio' parts of Dante's *Divine Comedy*.

When Liszt and Carolyne's long-planned marriage in Rome
was thwarted by the intrigues of Carolyne's former husband and
his relatives, Liszt stayed on in the city, living for several years in a
monk's cell in a church in the surrounding hills. In 1865 he took minor
Catholic orders, becoming the black-cassocked 'Abbé Liszt' who
now completed his large-scale oratorios *St Elisabeth* and *Christus* –
expressions of a religious faith which, during his years as the travelling
pianist-hero of Romantic legend, had never left him. From the late
1860s he divided his teaching and composing activities between Rome,
Weimar and Budapest in the restless *vie trifurquée* ('trifurcated life')
of his old age. Some of the music of his last years was composed in a
pre-modernist idiom so advanced and dissonant that it has bewildered
later generations of listeners as much as his own.

This is the case also with some of his earlier works. Partly this
relates to the way he composed. Liszt was an improviser: amazingly
gifted in this respect at the keyboard, he naturally relied on the same
spontaneous inspiration when writing down his music. The level of

> Some of the music of his last years was composed
> in an idiom so advanced that it has bewildered
> later generations of listeners as much as his own.

that inspiration, by its nature, was therefore uneven – a situation for
which Liszt has been much criticised. But a deeper reason for the
affliction of Liszt Resistance Syndrome is the composer's radical streak.
This was the quality that ran into entrenched opposition from those
hostile to the progressive 'New German School' of composing seen to
be centred around Liszt in Weimar. He himself, on the contrary, was
much more open-minded. In 1853 he invited a rising new talent called
Johannes Brahms to his Weimar home. Welcoming Brahms good-
naturedly, he sight-read one of his young colleague's piano works, and
then played his own Sonata in B minor – during which Brahms nodded
off to sleep. Further overtures were not made; and the conservative-
leaning Brahms always made out that he detested Liszt and his music.
To be fair, it isn't difficult to understand why the wildly dramatic
Totentanz ('Dance of Death') for piano and orchestra might not have
been Brahms's cup of tea: the anti-lyrical ferocity of its opening bars
prefigures the wilder extremes of most 20th-century modernism by
almost a century (the music was first drafted in 1839).

And yet, since 1847, Liszt had essentially renounced this side of his
life to devote himself to composing – first in Weimar, where for a decade
he was 'Kapellmeister in Extraordinary', conducting concerts and opera
there (he premiered Wagner's *Lohengrin* in 1850), and living in another
unmarried relationship with Princess Carolyne Sayn-Wittgenstein,
whom he had met in her native Ukraine. Liszt now set about bringing
earlier versions of his music into their final form – among them the
coruscating First Piano Concerto, sketched as early as 1832, and now
condensed into a radical single-movement design. Besides an all-new
Second Concerto, these years also saw the creation of the brilliantly
bold and inventive *A Faust Symphony*, based on Goethe's verse play,

piano, and itself existing in several versions. Liszt's bold development of the single-movement symphonic poem as a vehicle for the aspiring Romantic imagination was a fruitful example for later generations, including composers as different as Sibelius, Smetana and Richard Strauss. And the idea of the multi-movement choral-orchestral symphony, as in the *Faust* and *Dante* symphonies, was to be a central influence on Mahler.

If a composer defies the categories into which his work is supposed to fit, then it's reasonable to assume that there is something wrong with the categorising process itself. Instead, let's celebrate on its own terms the rich and ceaselessly colourful heritage of this unique and extraordinary musician – Liszt the Romantic dreamer and lover, the prophetic composer, literary connoisseur, Hungarian patriot and unofficial musical ambassador, pianistic magician, devout Catholic, inspirational teacher, and the exceptionally dedicated supporter of musical causes besides his own (those of Berlioz and Wagner particularly). He also remains the only great composer to have written a book about another. Liszt's *Life of Chopin* is a posthumous tribute to the former friend whose musical and artistic values he deeply admired, for all their temperamental differences. The words with which he introduced his fellow-artist to his readers apply equally to himself.

If it has been often proved that 'no-one is a prophet in his own country', is it not equally true that the prophets, the men of the future, who feel its life in advance, and prefigure it in their works, are never recognised as prophets in their own times? It would be presumptuous to assert that it can ever be otherwise. In vain may the young generations of artists protest against the 'Anti-Progressives', whose invariable custom it is to assault and beat down the living with the dead. Time alone can test the real value, or reveal the hidden beauties, either of musical compositions, or of kindred efforts in the sister arts. ●

Malcolm Hayes is a composer, writer, broadcaster and music journalist who contributes regularly to *BBC Music Magazine*. His book on Liszt was published earlier this year.

Faust and Mephistopheles (painting by Charles Buchel, 1872–1950): a scene from the verse play by Goethe, which inspired Liszt's dramatic *A Faust Symphony*

The same resistance to pigeon-holing resurfaces in another way as well, in that many of Liszt's works exist in versions for different genres. For all the scintillating pianism of the *First Mephisto Waltz*, the music's first incarnation was for orchestra, as *Der Tanz in der Dorfschenke* ('The Dance in the Village Inn') as part of the *Two Episodes from Lenau's 'Faust'*. The situation is reversed in *La notte* ('Night'), the second of the orchestral *Three Funeral Odes*: this is an extended version of *Il penseroso* ('The Thinker') from the earlier Book 2 of Liszt's piano cycle *Années de pèlerinage* ('Years of Pilgrimage') – a brooding statement inspired by a Michelangelo sculpture on the tomb of Lorenzo de' Medici in the church of San Lorenzo in Florence. And the symphonic poem *Mazeppa* began life as one of the *Études d'exécution transcendante*, also for

Switch on.

Listen to the BBC Singers on BBC Radio 3 (90–93FM)

bbc.co.uk/radio3

Turn up.

Come to a BBC Singers concert

bbc.co.uk/tickets

Join in.

Get involved in our learning activities

bbc.co.uk/singers

BACK TO BRAHMS

Though once revered as one of 'the Three Bs', Brahms in recent decades seems to have fallen from grace. Stephen Johnson returns him to the pedestal

J.S. BACH

JOHANNES BRAHMS

LUDWIG VAN BEETHOVEN

Once upon a time there were 'the Three Bs'. For the best part of a century, Johann Sebastian Bach, Ludwig van Beethoven and Johannes Brahms formed a Holy Trinity of German music – and not just of German music, many would say. Of course, Brahms is still highly popular today: it's hard to find an orchestral season anywhere that doesn't feature at least one of his symphonies or solo concertos. But he does seem to have suffered a downwards shift in status, beginning some time after the Second World War. These days, if people talk in Trinitarian terms about classical music, the three sacred names are much more likely to be Bach, Beethoven … and Mozart – with the newcomer often singled out for special reverence.

So what has happened to change our valuation of Brahms? Some have argued that the ideal of *Meisterschaft* ('mastery') that Brahms was once held to embody has dropped right out of fashion. At a London conference on Beethoven last year a prominent musicologist argued that the concept of mastery was 'deeply oppressive' for many.

Of course, Brahms is still highly popular today … But he does seem to have suffered a downwards shift in status, beginning after the Second World War

And yet *every night* of that same week, what did we find in a primetime BBC One slot but the cookery-contest series *Masterchef*? In sport, too, the word 'master' is still a badge of distinction, while the radical edge of modern dance music teems with self-styled 'spinmeisters' and 'dubmeisters'.

Perhaps the truth is that, as our knowledge of Brahms – the man and the composer – has increased, he has become a more complex, enigmatic, at times even unsettling figure. The classical pedestal begins to look too small and too crude to hold him. Our view of musical history has changed too. Once there was a clear evolutionary scheme into which Brahms, the 'Third B', slotted comfortably. Brahms was held aloft as the triumphant inheritor of the two noblest musical mantles. From Bach he had learnt that structure, far from being a mere scaffold or container for musical thoughts and feelings, could enhance and deepen their meaning. And, in his symphonic works, Brahms alone had met the challenge thrown down by Beethoven. If Bach embodied the ideal of 'Classical' objectivity, and Beethoven that of Promethean Romanticism, then Brahms was the great Classical-Romantic, the emotionally intelligent intellectual – fusing ideal form with intense lyricism.

One thing was clear, however: if Brahms was the pre-eminent Classical-Romantic, it was the Classical, objective, intellectual aspect of his achievement – the traditionally 'masculine' attributes of *Meisterschaft* – which were held up for special veneration. The Romantic part of the equation, it seems, could speak for itself – or, better still, remain discreetly in the shadows. This process began well within Brahms's own lifetime. One of the composer's most prominent allies, the hugely influential critic Eduard Hanslick, notoriously used Brahms as a stick with which to beat down Wagnerian and Lisztian Romantics, who responded by branding Brahms a 'reactionary'. Brahms's scholarly interest – very unusual for its time – in the music of what was then considered the remote past (the early Classical, Baroque and even Renaissance periods) was taken as further proof of nostalgic neophobia. And yet, viewed from today's perspective, Brahms's rejection of the 19th-century Religion of Progress and his intensely creative fascination with the music of other ages look curiously modern – or perhaps one should say, Postmodern.

At the same time, however hard some of Brahms's champions may have tried to play down the Romantic aspect of his nature, it remained there beneath the surface – hidden, one might say, behind the civic-dignitary corpulence and that iconic patrician beard. And, like Mrs Rochester in *Jane Eyre*, it has been growing increasingly restless in recent years. Deepening interest in the arch-Romantic Robert Schumann, especially during his bicentenary celebrations last year, has inevitably flushed out a lot of information about Brahms – who, during their short but intense friendship, adopted Schumann as musical father-figure, and also fell lastingly in love with Schumann's wife Clara. Schumann's traumatic suicide attempt in 1854, his subsequent incarceration in a mental asylum and Brahms's intense but understandably confused passion for Clara left emotional scars on several works begun around that time. The slow movement of the First Piano Concerto (1854–9) was either partly or wholly conceived as a ▶

A caricature from 1890 in which Brahms's ally, the critic Eduard Hanslick, is shown venerating the composer

requiem for Schumann. A 'slow scherzo' originally included in an earlier version of the score was eventually transferred to *A German Requiem* (1865–8), where it finds a text clearly suited to its original inspiration: 'For behold, all flesh is as grass.' And generally the concerto's turbulence, its anguished dissonances and often abrasive scoring sound like the product of a mind wrestling with demons. No wonder the audience at its Leipzig premiere hissed it, and that the only praise in the musical press should have come from the avant-garde.

And what of Brahms's famous two-decade-long struggle to produce his First Symphony (1855–76)? This is usually ascribed to feelings of massive inferiority before Beethoven: 'Have you any idea how hard it is with such a giant marching behind you?' Brahms agonised to a friend. But it's equally probable that there were more acutely personal emotional problems here too. The darkly impassioned character of the first movement surely owes a great deal to Brahms's own desperate state at the time he conceived it (he first showed its theme to Clara in 1855). Schumann was still alive, but in a desperate condition, mentally and physically, while Clara was grappling with her own complex feelings about her husband – and very likely about Brahms too. Years later, when Brahms had at last worked up the nerve to write the symphony's finale, he incorporated a striking horn figure that he'd once sent as a greeting to Clara in a letter. The 'Clara' horn figure emerges after a timpani thunderclap has dramatically dispelled the murky minor-key darkness that has so far dominated the music. A little later, the main movement strides out confidently with a magnificent tune clearly intended as a salute to the 'Ode to Joy' theme in Beethoven's Ninth. Brahms has found the courage to face down the giant – but, the music seems to say, it is the 'Clara' horn theme that has provided the deliverance from pain and doubt. As so often in Wagner and Liszt, redemption is provided by an ideal female beloved: pure Romanticism – even if Brahms is characteristically less explicit about it than his 'progressive' contemporaries.

If Clara Schumann appears as a spirit of light in the finale of the First Symphony, the more troubling image of her husband casts a shadow in the opening movement of the Third (1883). The first three wind chords, spelling out the notes F–A–F, which for Brahms spelt out the German motto *Frei aber froh* ('free but happy'), yield to a downwards-thrusting violin theme, marked *passionato*, taken directly from the first movement of Schumann's Third Symphony, the 'Rhenish'. More intriguing still is the way the return of this theme is prepared: the momentum flags, sombre descending scales in the deep bass instruments apparently invoke an early funeral cantata, *Begräbnisgesang* ('Burial Song'), composed immediately after the Schumann-haunted First Piano Concerto. The music seems to have lost any pretension to being 'free but happy', but then F–A–F rouses itself twice, and the original Schumann theme surges forward again. A highly charged personal crisis seems to be enacted here – and again one may ask what any of this has to do with Classicism?

The shock of Schumann's terrible end, and the sadness and hopeless longing (not only for Clara) that ensued, were themes that continued to haunt this acutely sensitive, vulnerable, lonely and depressively inclined man right through to the end. The Fourth Symphony (1884–5) includes in its first movement an eerie reference to Brahms's own 'Oh death, how bitter you are' from the cycle *Four Serious Songs* – while the finale theme is taken from a Bach cantata,

Joseph Joachim, for whom Brahms wrote his Violin Concerto, accompanied by Clara Schumann, who became Brahms's muse and confidante

Nach dir, Herr, verlanget mich, BWV 150 ('I long for you, O Lord'), which similarly grapples with mortality. Here's another fascinating paradox: in this finale Brahms revives a long-forgotten musical form, the passacaglia, in which a whole movement is built up on repetitions of a bass theme outlined at the beginning. On one level, the music is intricately crafted, both in its fine detail and as an overarching structure; on another, it is explosively passionate. It brings to mind the famous last lines from Dylan Thomas's *Fern Hill*: 'Time held me, green and dying, though I sang in my chains like the sea.'

And here, surely, we come close to the heart of the Brahmsian paradox. When one contemplates his painstaking use of abstract, 'archaic' musical devices, it can seem that Brahms is fashioning chains for himself. And perhaps he needed them. Brahms's obsession with form, with the intellectual scaffolding of his works, closely resembles that of his contemporary, Anton Bruckner. Like Bruckner (another death-haunted, intensely lonely bachelor), Brahms needed reassuringly

Like Bruckner (another intensely lonely bachelor), Brahms needed reassuringly strong structures to contain his wildest and most troubling thoughts

strong structures to contain his wildest and most troubling thoughts. And yet, also like Bruckner – and the young Dylan Thomas – Brahms is still able to 'sing', magnificently, in those chains. There's hardly a major work of Brahms that doesn't contain at least one of those long-breathed, endlessly unfolding, ripely sensuous melodies that seem to throw their arms around us, only to put us down whole minutes later. The embrace can be tender, as in the slow movement solo cello theme of the Second Piano Concerto, or can draw us irresistibly onwards, like the great waltz tune that forms the Second Symphony's first big idea. At times the expression moves from song-without-words to opera-without-words, as in the gorgeous duet for the two soloists at the heart of the Double Concerto's central slow movement. Even the pre-eminent British anti-Brahmsian George Bernard Shaw had to concede, in the midst of a fairly typical diatribe, that Brahms was capable of 'delicious musical luxuries'. If delight in creating these sometimes grates or chafes against the *Meister*-ly will-to-order, this surely makes Brahms more, not less, interesting – and very, very human. ●

Stephen Johnson has written regularly for *The Independent*, *The Guardian* and *BBC Music Magazine*, and is the author of books on Bruckner, Mahler and Wagner. He is a regular presenter of BBC Radio 3's *Discovering Music*.

Brahms at his lodgings in Vienna – overlooked, tellingly, by a bust of Beethoven

Brahms at the Proms

Academic Festival Overture
Prom 1, 15 July

Clarinet Quintet
Proms Chamber Music 2, 25 July

Concerto in A minor for violin and cello
Prom 6, 19 July

Intermezzos, Op. 117 – Nos. 1 & 2; Piano Quartet in G minor (orch. Schoenberg)
Prom 48, 19 August

Symphony No. 1 Prom 51, 22 August

Symphony No. 2
Prom 27, 4 August

Symphony No. 3; Piano Concerto No. 1
Prom 47, 19 August

Symphony No. 4; Piano Concerto No. 2
Prom 49, 20 August

Violin Concerto Prom 32, 7 August

'Piano Concerto No. 3'
(arr. Lazić, after Violin Concerto)
Prom 37, 11 August

BBC Philharmonic

Saturday 24 September, 7.30pm
Mahler Symphony No. 2

New Chief Conductor
Juanjo Mena's opening concert
at The Bridgewater Hall, Manchester.

*"Juanjo Mena and the BBC Philharmonic
perform with a thrilling brilliance
and engagement"*

Gramophone Magazine, March 2011

bbc.co.uk/philharmonic

Inspiration with every note **BBC**

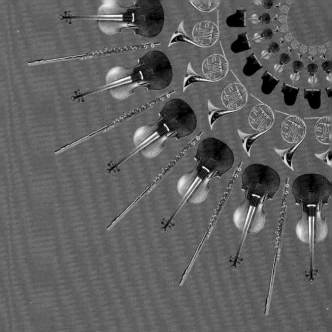

BOX OFFICE
0121 780 3333
www.thsh.co.uk

THSH
TOWN HALL BIRMINGHAM   SYMPHONY HALL BIRMINGHAM

Birmingham International Concert Season 2011/12

On sale soon

Artists include...

Leif Ove Andsnes, Renaud and Gautier Capuçon, Kronos Quartet with Philip Glass, Lang Lang, The Orchestra and Chorus of the Royal Opera House with Antonio Pappano, András Schiff, St Petersburg Philharmonic Orchestra with Yuri Temirkanov, Bryn Terfel, Sir John Tomlinson, Mariinksy Theatre with Valery Gergiev, Orchestre National du Capitole de Toulouse with Tugan Sokhiev, Vienna Philharmonic with Sir Simon Rattle

For full details on all the season's events please visit: www.thsh.co.uk/bics-2011-12

Information correct at the time of going to press.

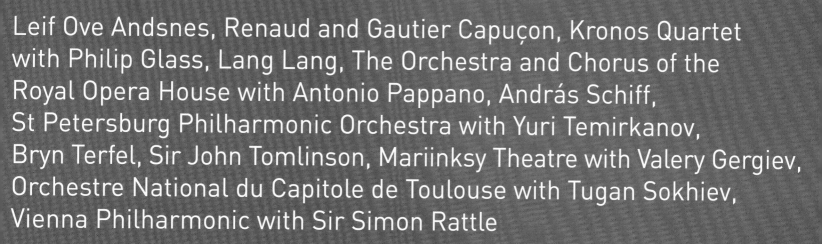

f search 'Town Hall Symphony Hall'   @THSHBirmingham

Supported by
Birmingham City Council

Town Hall renovation also funded by
LOTTERY FUNDED
PROJECT PART-FINANCED BY THE EUROPEAN UNION

French Connections

As the Proms marks the 95th birthday of Henri Dutilleux, **Julian Anderson** discovers that the French fascination for sensuous harmonies and alluring tone-colours remains as strong today as it was in Debussy's time, a century ago

Claude Debussy
(1862–1918)

These days it's probably harder than ever to discern national characteristics in art music. The internet enables us to keep abreast of the latest international developments and arts news spreads quicker than bird flu. In today's global culture it seems absurd to think of stereotypes of national musical character, whereas a hundred years ago everyone had a clear idea of what French music was like – or they thought they had. It was decorative, colourful, sometimes witty, sensuous, harmonically exotic yet transparent, brilliantly orchestrated and subtly elusive. Sceptics duly accused French music of being pretty but superficial, lacking the emotional or structural depth of the finest Austro-German achievements. Those accusations, too, have died hard.

The sceptics' attitude was fuelled by the unfortunate use of the term 'Impressionism', previously applied to some later 19th-century French paintings, to describe the mature music of Debussy – such as the short but revolutionary *Prélude à L'après-midi d'un faune* or the elaborate symphonic seascape *La mer*. In reality this music was largely not contemporary with its supposed visual counterpart and was certainly not inspired by it. *Prélude à L'après-midi* was prompted by a poem by Debussy's Symbolist friend Stéphane Mallarmé, while part of *La mer* was completed at a prosaic hotel in Eastbourne. Certainly many now agree the term 'Symbolist' comes far closer to the truth of Debussy, whose music evokes natural phenomena but does not usually depict them, and who took great pains to suggest emotional implications rather than describe them outright. Thus his two books of piano *Préludes* have titles placed at the *end* of each piece, and within brackets, rather than at the top. Even those pieces that seem to deal more directly with visual stimuli trace a cunning path between programme music (conveying a particular narrative or image) and semi-abstract sound

canvases. The orchestral triptych *Images* is the clearest example: we may hear castanets and typically 'Spanish' melodic roulades in its central 'Ibéria' movement, but the harmony is frequently disruptive, its turns always unexpected. Orchestral colour is here aplenty, but self-indulgence is not: every sound has a distinct function and takes its place in the larger shape of the piece.

So far, so bad: our stereotypes of French music don't seem to hold up. But there are other Frances: the France of French Catholicism, for example – an intimate, personal faith characterised by near-cloying devotional intensity, which has given rise to music as varied as the chromatic post-César Franckist *Cortège et litanie* for organ and orchestra by virtuoso Marcel Dupré (1886–1971), and the more innovative colours of his flamboyant pupil Olivier Messiaen (1908–92), for instance in *Les offrandes oubliées*. Then too there is the France of order, symmetry, the gardens

A hundred years ago everyone had a clear idea of what French music was like – or they thought they had.

of Versailles, which had its musical counterpart in the works of Lully and Rameau. There is the France of émigrés, the country which welcomed into its culture the Russian Igor Stravinsky, the Spaniard Manuel de Falla and the Greek Iannis Xenakis for shorter or longer periods. Yet French culture has not always recognised its own, as shown by the curious history of Hector Berlioz, the most original French composer for generations either before or since, who had a German, not French, publisher and was far more celebrated in Germany, Great Britain and Russia than in his homeland, where he eked out a living as a music journalist.

Many of these contradictory Frances came together in the music of Debussy's younger contemporary, Maurice

Ravel (1875–1937) – a composer equally at home in Spain (*Rapsodie espagnole*, *Alborada del gracioso*) as in Vienna (*La valse*) or mythical ancient Greece (*Daphnis and Chloë*). Ravel's chameleon-like ability to morph himself while remaining musically distinctive produced a unique output that earned lasting admiration, even from comparative Francophobes such as Arnold Schoenberg. Acutely conscious of his own heritage (*Le tombeau de Couperin*), while keeping a sharp eye on international musical developments, Ravel was even able to integrate his varied manners within single pieces. Thus the Piano Concerto in G major combines Spanish modal inflections and blues figuration in its first movement, Classical harmonic simplicity and tenderness in the slow waltz of its second, with neo-Classical keyboard toccatas and sophisticated modern dissonance in its Finale. Yet the result is anything but haphazard: every chord and orchestral colour is wholly typical of Ravel and no-one else.

Inasmuch as the vivid harmonic colours and crystalline instrumentation of Pierre Boulez's mature music represent another flowering of supposedly typical French musical characteristics, Iannis Xenakis's music – tough as nails and instrumentally extreme – is a complete contradiction of everything that Frenchness in music might be. Nevertheless the French took him to their hearts (at the height of his career he was almost a pop celebrity in France) and one of the most important recent figures in French music, Pascal Dusapin (born 1955), studied closely with him. Dusapin is a fluent composer with a large output, but there is nothing superficially French about his music. It is relatively austere, even Northern-sounding in its lean orchestration and limpid modal harmonic style. A fan of Sibelius as well as of jazz, Dusapin has cultivated a highly personal musical evolution, whose expressiveness and dramatic impact have brought him in high regard with audiences internationally. This year he has two UK premieres at the Proms: *Morning in Long Island* for orchestra and his String Quartet No. 6, which also features an orchestra.

Equally independent from all passing fads is the work of Henri Dutilleux – aged 95, the grand old man of French music. A late developer, he was nearly 50 before he found his direction as a composer. He found it by focusing upon what he terms 'the joy of sound' – lush, vivid orchestral colours and subtle orchestration chosen with an infallible ear and paced with masterly sureness. Yet, like Berlioz, his music has found its readiest appreciation outside France. Most of his works have been commissioned by orchestras from the USA, or composed for major international soloists such as Russian ▶

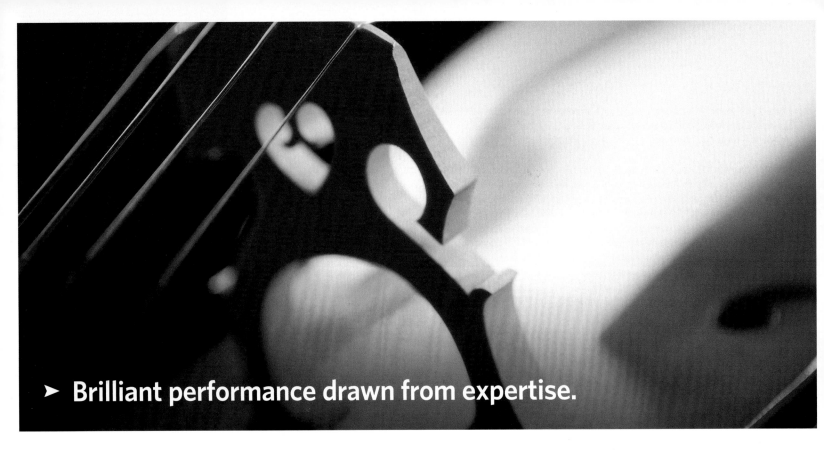

➤ **Brilliant performance drawn from expertise.**

The world over, people are uplifted, inspired and motivated by music. That is why it is our great pleasure to support the Pittsburgh Symphony Orchestra's 2011 European Festivals Tour.

5 & 6 September 2011
Royal Albert Hall, London

BNY MELLON

bnymellon.com

Léon Bakst's aptly Symbolist costume design for Diaghilev's ballet version of Debussy's *Prélude à L'après-midi d'un faune*

quickly acquired strong international reputations (both taught in the USA for some years). The music of Murail's leading pupil, Marc-André Dalbavie (born 1961), featured at the Proms in 2002 (his beautiful orchestra piece *Color*) and 2005 (the BBC co-commissioned Piano Concerto, as well as the chamber works *Trio* and *Axiom* in a preceding Proms Composer Portrait concert), and this year we hear the first London performance of his sparkling Flute Concerto, composed for Emmanuel Pahud. As with much Dalbavie, simple repetitive figures and agile, changeable polyphony are interwoven into a seamless flow of mostly fast music. Listeners will have little trouble in identifying the building blocks of this piece as they are presented with such transparency. Their gradual changes through the music are quirky, surprising and delightful. Dalbavie is clearly a major voice in French new music.

With his renewed focus on sound-colours and their structure, Dalbavie – along with the Spectral composers – appears to represent the latest manifestation of what we have come to regard as typically French concerns in music. Perhaps those old stereotypes were accurate after all. ●

Julian Anderson was Professor of Composition at Harvard University (2004–7) and is currently Senior Professor of Composition at the Guildhall School of Music & Drama. The London premiere of his *Fantasias* was given at the BBC Proms last year.

cellist Mstislav Rostropovich (the cello concerto *'Tout un monde lointain …'*) or American violinist Isaac Stern (the violin concerto *L'arbre des songes*). With its specially poetic atmosphere, its evocation of radical 19th-century French poets (the cello concerto was inspired by Baudelaire) and its avoidance of Classical forms, Dutilleux's profoundly original music betrays an underground kinship with the music of Debussy. He may write little, but each work is of high quality and remains in the repertory.

In the early 1970s a major new current emerged among younger French composers, focusing on the acoustic nature of sound itself. 'Spectral' music (as it came to be known) provided fresh, colourful insights into the most familiar musical materials, such as consonant harmony and regular pulse. Composers Gérard Grisey (1946–98) and Tristan Murail (born 1947), the founders of this new trend,

French Music since 1900 at the Proms

Jehan Alain Litanies Prom 3, 17 July

Georges Aperghis Champ–Contrechamp
BBC commission: world premiere
Proms Saturday Matinee 2, 20 August

Marc-André Dalbavie Flute Concerto
London premiere Prom 18, 28 July

Debussy Images Prom 10, 22 July; La mer Prom 19, 29 July; Prélude à L'après-midi d'un faune Prom 26, 3 August

Dupré Cortège et litanie Prom 34, 9 August

Pascal Dusapin Morning in Long Island (Concert No. 1) *BBC co-commission with Radio France: UK premiere* Prom 5, 18 July; String Quartet No. 6, 'Hinterland' ('Hapax' for string quartet and orchestra) *BBC commission: UK premiere* Prom 16, 27 July

Henri Dutilleux L'arbre des songes Prom 52, 23 August; Les citations Proms Saturday Matinee 1, 13 August; Slava's Fanfare Prom 52, 23 August; Sonatine Proms Chamber Music 6, 22 August; 'Tout un monde lointain …' Prom 26, 3 August

Messiaen Les offrandes oubliées Prom 5, 18 July

Ravel Alborada del gracioso Prom 10, 22 July; Boléro Prom 26, 3 August; Daphnis and Chloë Prom 26, 3 August; Rapsodie espagnole Prom 10, 22 July; Shéhérazade Prom 53, 24 August; La valse Prom 72, 8 September

Debussy's heirs: (*left to right*) Olivier Messiaen (1908–92), Henri Dutilleux (born 1916), Pascal Dusapin (born 1955) and Marc-André Dalbavie (born 1961)

BBC Symphony Chorus

Stephen Jackson Director

JOIN THE BBC SYMPHONY CHORUS

The BBC Symphony Chorus is one of the UK's finest and most distinctive amateur choirs. In its appearances with the BBC Symphony Orchestra, the Chorus performs a wide range of challenging repertoire, most of which is broadcast on BBC Radio 3.

As resident chorus for the BBC Proms, the BBC Symphony Chorus takes part in a number of concerts each season, including the Last Night. This year's appearances include Britten's *Spring Symphony* and Janáček's *Glagolitic Mass* under Jiří Bělohlávek and Verdi's *Requiem* alongside the BBC National Chorus of Wales and the London Philharmonic Choir under Semyon Bychkov.

Highlights of the 2011–12 Barbican season include Tippett's *A Child of Our Time* with Sir Andrew Davis, Walton's *Belshazzar's Feast* with Edward Gardner and Stravinsky's *Symphony of Psalms* with David Robertson.

Would you like to join us?
If you are an experienced choral singer who would like to work on new and challenging repertoire, as well as standard choral works, then the BBC Symphony Chorus would like to hear from you. Membership is free and includes individual vocal training.

To find out more about the Chorus, or to apply for an audition, visit **bbc.co.uk/symphonyorchestra** or contact the Chorus Administrator.
Email: bbcsc@bbc.co.uk | Tel: 020 7765 4715

BBC RADIO 3

90 – 93 FM

look what the romans did for us

then roam across the wadi rum

The world's greatest Roman ruins are not actually in Rome. They're in Jerash in the Kingdom of Jordan, home to some of the most majestic historic sites that you will ever see. With the best preserved Roman city on the planet, a visit to Jerash will take you back thousands of years. And the beauty of Jordan is its contrasts, mixing the chance to visit 'once in a lifetime' monuments like Jerash and Petra with the awesome experience of a camel trek across the Wadi Rum, the spectactular setting for David Lean's masterpiece, 'Lawrence of Arabia'.

For more information call 020 7223 1878
or visit www.visitjordan.com/uk

visit Jordan

As all three of Bartók's piano concertos appear in a single Proms season for the first time, Paul Griffiths outlines their varied creative impulses, while three generations of pianists reflect on the works prior to performing them at the Proms

Bartók Piano Concertos

E veryting we know about Bartók points to a man of extreme privacy (everything we know, that is, apart from his music). He seems to have led a reserved life even within his immediate family and, as a pianist, he preferred accompanying violinists or giving piano-duo recitals with his second wife, Ditta Pásztory, to making solo appearances. But in his early forties a special combination of circumstances led him to project himself very publicly as a concerto soloist – these included a growing international reputation, perhaps the wish to prove himself and, certainly, financial need.

The high rate of inflation in early-1920s Hungary encouraged him to seek sources of income outside his country and he had an obvious opportunity to do so as a pianist-composer, at a time when others – Prokofiev, Rachmaninov, Stravinsky – were travelling the same roads. Unlike those colleagues, however, he had nothing suitable in his catalogue to perform with an orchestra. His *Rhapsody*

A special combination of circumstances led Bartók to project himself very publicly as a concerto soloist – including … financial need.

(1905) was an old piece from his early twenties; playing it now, two decades later, only convinced him he needed something new. He therefore, in 1926, wrote himself a proper concerto and gave its first performance the following year, at the International Society for Contemporary Music festival in Frankfurt, conducted by Wilhelm Furtwängler.

Bartók appeared in that forum as one of the most esteemed composers alive, alongside Carl Nielsen (whose Fifth Symphony was on the same programme), Alban Berg and others, and he seems almost to have designed the concerto to help him live up to the role. Like Stravinsky's piano concerto of 1923–4 – or like Berg's *Chamber Concerto*, heard the day after Bartók's premiere – it strongly features the combination of piano and wind. There is a more particular nod to Stravinsky in the contrapuntal vitality and insistent pulse – features understood at the time as neo-Bachian – while the use of emphatic rotating figures suggests the factory aesthetic of other contemporaries: the Italian and Russian Futurists. Jazz, too, is sometimes just over the horizon. All musical life of the mid-1920s is there, in a massive, highly individual synthesis that also embraces – partly through Bartók's long and deep study of folk songs – features from the distant musical past, and whose dynamism stems from Beethoven.

Bartók in 1930 with his second wife, Ditta, a former piano student; in his last year (1945) he wrote his elegiac Third Piano Concerto for her impending widowhood

Bartók Piano Concertos at the Proms

Piano Concerto No. 1
Prom 15, 26 July
(Jean-Efflam Bavouzet *piano*)

Piano Concerto No. 2
Prom 43, 16 August
(Yuja Wang *piano*)

Piano Concerto No. 3
Prom 9, 21 July
(András Schiff *piano*)

The First Piano Concerto is one of the great pianistic challenges and at the time it also proved challenging for orchestras. A performance was scheduled with the New York Philharmonic near the start of Bartók's first US tour, in the winter of 1927–8, but had to be cancelled for lack of rehearsal time and, though the composer did get to play his concerto in Carnegie Hall, a couple of months later with the Cincinnati Symphony, he decided he needed something that would go down a little more easily with orchestras – and, indeed, with audiences. Perhaps it is easier now than it was then to appreciate the force and granite roughness of the First Concerto, but we can be thankful that ▶

JEAN-EFFLAM BAVOUZET on Piano Concerto No. 1

The First Piano Concerto represents a crucial step in Bartók's writing. At this time (1926) he was finding a 'new' style, mixing percussive treatment of the keyboard with lyrical simplicity. Percussion plays a major role in this concerto. Who can resist its rhythmical vitality? At times it sounds almost like rock and roll to our modern ears!

With all its metric changes, the First is by far the most difficult of the three concertos as regards the balance between the soloist and the orchestra. Bartók himself was aware of this and would try to simplify his rhythmic language in his Second Concerto.

The first time I heard it was with the late Claude Helffer. Although I was just a young teenager at the time, I still have a vivid memory of the little gesture of his right hand imitating the motif of the snare drum. My generation grew up with the legendary Géza Anda recording, which remains inspiring to this day. Interestingly, this seems deliberately to ignore Bartók's own metronome mark in the second movement. How we would love to know why! However, in this repertoire, my heart and sensibility stay with the style of Zoltán Kocsis.

Bartók performing in a piano-duo concert with his wife Ditta in 1938

YUJA WANG on Piano Concerto No. 2

I first heard the Second Piano Concerto in the amazing recording by Zoltán Kocsis of all three concertos. I liked especially the First and Second. The primitive energy, the sometimes exotic and other-worldly atmosphere really grabbed my attention, especially as, at the time, I was extremely fascinated by Stravinsky – *The Rite of Spring*, *The Firebird*, *Petrushka* and so on. Bartók's Second Piano Concerto, for me, is almost like Stravinsky with Hungarian spice.

Bartók's structure is so meticulously clear, very mathematical, and the writing is constantly contrapuntal – perhaps as a tribute to Bach. Technically it is probably the most difficult piece I have encountered, with ninth chords everywhere, thirds, very fast, bizarre scales and complex rhythms with the orchestra. But, in the end, it's the colours he is trying to create, the night-time mysteries, the joyful kicks in the folk dances that make the work so much fun.

Overall, Bartók's Second Piano Concerto is a boisterous Hungarian festival. Kocsis's recording was very impressive, and later I discovered Géza Anda's recording, which is also very interesting and amusing.

ANDRÁS SCHIFF on Piano Concerto No. 3

Bartók's Third Piano Concerto is an extraordinary piece of music. It's like a swansong: after the radically dissonant First and the brilliantly virtuoso Second, this is a wise man's farewell, full of resignation. Bartók wrote it for his wife, Ditta Pásztory, a fine pianist. He was very ill, having lived through the war in the USA in difficult circumstances. The new concerto would create performing opportunities for Ditta, and also some income.

Bartók – himself a wonderful pianist – was too frail to perform at this time. He knew that the end was near and yet he wanted to live; he didn't want to depart 'with a full suitcase', as he wrote to his son, Péter. The first movement is gentle, full of homesickness. The second, Adagio religioso, recalls Bach as well as Beethoven's String Quartet Op. 132. This is symbolic: Bartók, close to death, turns to religion for solace.

In the central section we hear sounds of nature. The murmur of insects is interrupted by birdsong. Bartók heard these birds during his holidays in Vermont. Many years later, at the Marlboro Music Festival, at my house in the woods, I was delighted to be woken by these identical calls.

Bartók's dissatisfaction – not with the work itself but with the resistance to it – impelled him to write a successor that runs in parallel (three-movement form, with the fast finale symmetrically balancing the first movement in its speed and basic ideas), only to show itself almost diametrically different in many respects: major in tonality rather than minor, diatonic rather than chromatic; positive, jovial.

Five and a half years after the premiere of the First Concerto, Bartók was back in Frankfurt to introduce No. 2, this time with Hans Rosbaud conducting. A few months afterwards there was a performance in Vienna, under Otto Klemperer, whose recollection offers a rare insight into the composer as concerto soloist: 'The beauty of his tone, the energy and lightness of his playing were unforgettable. It was almost painfully beautiful.'

The Second Concerto proved, indeed, more popular than the First, but now Bartók's timing was off, because a week after his return to Frankfurt a new German government was sworn in under Adolf Hitler. Bartók refused to play in Germany again and banned performances of his works in Fascist-ruled territories – a darkening sphere that included more and more of Europe. There was no incentive for another concerto.

In the spring of 1940 Bartók left for his second US tour and this time he stayed. He made a concerto for two pianos out of his Sonata for two pianos and percussion (1937), intending the piece for himself and Ditta, though they found no opportunity to play it. Not until the last year of his life, 1945, did he commit himself to a new solo concerto, working now under conditions very different from those that had governed the earlier two. This Third Concerto had no radio stations and festivals of contemporary music to nurture it, but would have to make its way in the more commercial world of the USA. Perhaps for that reason, or perhaps because Bartók was no longer rooted in his native environment, there was a change of style: a new simplicity that might better be construed as a new purity, and a fragility of exile.

Also contributing to the Third Concerto's grace was the fact that Bartók, now succumbing to leukaemia, was no longer writing for himself but for Ditta, providing for her widowhood. To the extent that piano concertos have sexes, this one is female. And it was designed to be heard in a world its composer had left. Bartók had given his best in his first two concertos; now he also gave his last. ●

A critic for over 30 years, including for *The Times* and *The New Yorker*, Paul Griffiths is an authority on 20th- and 21st-century music. Among his books are studies of Bartók, Boulez, Cage and Stravinsky as well as *A Concise History of Western Music*; he also writes novels and librettos.

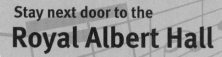

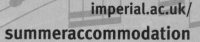

Out OF THE Shadows

Seventy years after his death, Frank Bridge is
remembered largely for being Benjamin Britten's
teacher. Anthony Payne reappraises one of England's
most significant composers, whose move away from
conservative Romanticism alienated him from his peers

When, in 1941, Frank Bridge finally succumbed
to the heart disease which had clouded the last
ten years of his life, this country was fighting
for its very existence against the Nazi axis and in no state to
celebrate the work of a recently deceased composer – let alone
one whose reputation at home had, for a variety of reasons,
already begun to slip. Only in the USA, where his patroness Elizabeth
Sprague Coolidge had long worked devotedly on his behalf, was the
passing of this bravely radical figure recognised. A splendid recital was
staged at the National Library of Congress, which presented the
Second String Quartet and String Sextet in outstanding performances
that were perpetuated on acetate discs, giving us a moving impression
of the performing style of the era.

It was some time before the work of Bridge, one of this country's
most significant composers, was to become known and valued by more
than a limited number of specialised music-lovers. Just after the
Second World War, for instance, a number of his pieces were
rejected by a BBC new music panel, which raises interesting
questions about the prevailing taste of the time. What did
people have against this music, which is now widely
admired? We know that Bridge's transformation from
an English late-Romantic into a more cosmopolitan
modernist in mid-career – creating ties with such
figures as Scriabin, Bartók and Berg – baffled many
listeners. The likes of Vaughan Williams and Holst,

however, might have been expected to take Bridge's side. Yet Vaughan Williams, in a note to Holst, famously said: 'I wonder how much a composer ought to know of instrumental technique … of course, the deepest abyss of the result of writing "effectively" is Frank Bridge.'

Was it, perhaps, that the notion of the inspired amateur as against the earnest, possibly unimaginative professional was still cherished in this country? In the 1940s and 1950s, for instance, one often met with the opinion that the young Benjamin Britten was 'too clever by half'. Critiques of Bridge's late work similarly suggested that his newly won modernism was merely for effect and lacked artistic honesty. It took some time for these shades of opinion to meet their deserved ends and, for some 20 years following his death, performances and broadcasts were few and

Britten *(centre)* with the Bridges in Paris, January 1937

It seems to us now that the radical development of style which made his later works possible was Bridge's pain-racked response to the horrors of the First World War

far between. An honourable exception was provided by Bridge's only pupil, Benjamin Britten, who made sure that the name of his old teacher and friend did not totally disappear. We can be sure that it was not solely a sense of duty that prompted Britten's efforts, but the effect, ironically, was merely to remind us who Britten's teacher was, as was also the case in the many performances of his own *Variations on a Theme of Frank Bridge*.

Meanwhile, the work of such contemporaries as Bax, Ireland and Moeran was being systematically explored by record companies and BBC Radio, and

one would like to think that the sheer quality of Bridge's output made a resurgence of interest in it inevitable, quite apart from the absorbing historical aspects of his unique stylistic development. Whatever factors were involved, his music was certainly recorded and broadcast with increasing frequency during the 1970s. From then on, no-one needed to be ignorant of the basic outlines of Bridge's creative achievement, whether in the Romantic warmth of early pieces for orchestra, such as *Isabella* (1907), *The Sea* (1910–11) and *Summer* (1914), and such contemporary chamber works as the Piano Quintet (1904–12) and *Three Idylls* for string quartet (1906, which supplied Britten with the theme for those orchestral *Variations* as well as for a recently rediscovered earlier set of piano variations); or in the dark ambivalence and increasing modernism of many later works, including the Third String Quartet (1926), Second Piano Trio (1929), the wonderfully melancholic *There is a Willow Grows Aslant a Brook* (1928), and, perhaps Bridge's masterpiece, the cello concerto, *Oration* (1930), which is in effect a funeral address for the 1914–18 war dead. Indeed, it seems to us now that the radical development of style which made those later works possible was Bridge's pain-racked response to the horrors of the First World War. Yet it did not preclude the presentation of a brighter

vision. *Enter Spring* (1927), which, remarkably, is a close contemporary of *There is a Willow*, puts his newly coined language to dazzlingly contrasted use in an exuberant celebration of the Sussex landscape, which is all blue sky, birdsong and windblown downland.

Towards the end of his life, Bridge seemed to be opening a new style chapter, refining his post-Romantic, Expressionist language, to give birth to a brand of classical modernism in his magnificent Fourth String Quartet (1937). To this new manner also belongs the overture *Rebus* (1940), his last completed work, where he expands his late style to create something of a popular utterance, tight in its motivic control, as always, but tuneful in relaxed moments. Bridge was ever the explorer. ●

Composer Anthony Payne is an authority on 20th-century English music and won widespread acclaim for his elaboration of the sketches for Elgar's Symphony No. 3 (1998). He has written books on Schoenberg and Bridge, and was a critic for The Daily Telegraph and The Independent.

Bridge at the Proms

Enter Spring; Blow out, you bugles
Prom 34, 9 August

Isabella Prom 70, 7 September

Overture 'Rebus' Prom 37, 11 August

There is a Willow Grows Aslant a Brook
Prom 19, 29 July

Three Idylls – No. 2; Piano Quintet
Proms Chamber Music 5, 15 August

See also:

Britten Piano Variations on a Theme of Frank Bridge
London premiere Proms Chamber Music 5, 15 August

Britten Variations on a Theme of Frank Bridge
Prom 50, 21 August

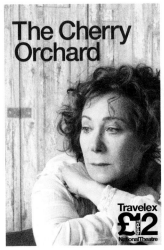

The Cherry Orchard

by Anton Chekhov
in a version by Andrew Upton
From 10 May

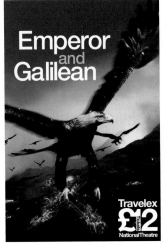

Emperor and Galilean

by Henrik Ibsen
in a new version by Ben Power
From 9 June

A Woman Killed with Kindness

by Thomas Heywood
From 12 July

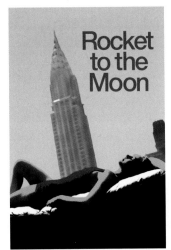

Rocket to the Moon

by Clifford Odets
Until 21 June

One Man, Two Guvnors

by Richard Bean, based on
The Servant of Two Masters
by Carlo Goldoni
From 17 May

and much more...

National Theatre

Great Theatre Exciting Actors Low Prices all on London's South Bank this Summer

020 7452 3000 Tickets £12 – £45 no bkg fee

nationaltheatre.org.uk

South Bank, London SE1 9PX ⬄ Waterloo, Embankment ⇌ Waterloo, Charing Cross

Summer 2011
AT ENO

EN
O

THE DAMNATION OF FAUST
Berlioz
Celebrated director Terry Gilliam's new
staging conducted by Edward Gardner
6 May – 7 Jun

A MIDSUMMER NIGHT'S DREAM
Britten
Christopher Alden directs a stellar cast
including Iestyn Davies and Willard White
19 May – 30 Jun

SIMON BOCCANEGRA
Verdi
Edward Gardner conducts a new production
starring Brindley Sherratt and Bruno Caproni
8 Jun – 9 Jul

TWO BOYS
Muhly
The world premiere of a new opera
by Nico Muhly directed by Bartlett Sher
24 Jun – 8 Jul

ENO LIVE AT THE
LONDON COLISEUM
www.eno.org
0871 911 0200

Tickets
from only
£17

Supported by
ARTS COUNCIL
ENGLAND

AIMING FOR FREEDOM

David Charlton introduces Weber's *Der Freischütz* and Rossini's *William Tell*, two peaks of the 19th-century 'grand opera' tradition linked by a pivotal shooting trial – the outcomes of which bring triumph over dark forces

A black-winged Caspar summons the 'Black Huntsman', Samiel, in the Wolf's Glen: Act 2 of Weber's *Der Freischütz* in David Pountney's 1999 production for English National Opera

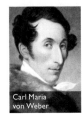

Carl Maria von Weber

Gioachino Rossini

This year's Proms festival highlights two peaks of 19th-century opera which sing of nature and nationhood, freedom and revolution. Weber's *Der Freischütz* ('The Freeshooter' or, more aptly, 'The Huntsman as Lover') and Rossini's *William Tell* were both premiered in the 1820s: after Napoleon, but before France finally ousted her Bourbon kings in the 1830 Revolution.

Der Freischütz is set in mid-17th-century Bohemia, while *William Tell* portrays the Swiss settings of Altdorf and Lake Lucerne during the last days of Austrian rule in the early 1300s. Despite their separation by over 300 years, both fables addressed the main problem of the 1820s – what kind of Europe could the world look forward to? It is not hard to see the ongoing relevance of these operas today.

In *Der Freischütz* Weber depicts the Bohemian forests and the peasants and foresters who live within them under the benevolent rulership of Prince Ottokar. The forester-hero, Max, is a fine shot, but he still has to win the Prince's traditional shooting contest before he can claim the hand of his beloved Agathe. As the big day approaches, he senses the presence of failure and is ensnared by black magic. Like Faust, but without realising the consequences, he becomes involved in a pact with the devilish Samiel, the 'Black Huntsman'. Max's fellow forester Caspar leads him to the dreaded Wolf's Glen, where they cast seven magic bullets in the presence of Samiel. It is a key moment in Romantic opera: midnight strikes, and the music paints terrifying, nightmarish visions. The dark forces are almost too much for Max

The Marau and Esther Edgerton Foundation/Palm Press, Inc./Bridgeman Art Library (main image, above); Clive Barda/ArenaPAL (p52, Der Freischütz); Lebrecht Music & Arts (p52, Weber); HIP/Topfoto/ArenaPAL (p52, Rossini)

to bear. What he doesn't know is that the seventh bullet belongs to Samiel and is destined to capture, body and soul, any victim the devil may choose. Samiel's nearness is felt through the orchestra – a sinister chord, accompanied by drum taps. He never sings, only speaks. Musical tonalities are used by Weber to underscore the struggle between dark and light.

Weber's brilliant strokes of orchestration had a strong effect on Romantic composers, and no-one more than the young Hector Berlioz, who had heard *Der Freischütz* in 1824 in Paris and was desperate to

Caspar leads Max to the dreaded Wolf's Glen, where they cast seven magic bullets … It is a key moment in Romantic opera: midnight strikes, and the music paints terrifying, nightmarish visions.

meet Weber. The German composer was briefly in Paris, *en route* to London's Covent Garden theatre to conduct his last work, *Oberon*. But the meeting was not to be. 'If you had come five minutes earlier, you would have heard him play me whole scenes from our operas – he knows them all,' teased Berlioz's teacher, Jean-François Le Sueur.

Berlioz paid homage to Weber in a famous passage of his *Treatise on Orchestration*, where he describes the big clarinet solo in the overture to *Der Freischütz*: 'Is this not the lonely virgin, the huntsman's fair bride, her eyes upturned to heaven?' She seems to battle against the shuddering

forces of nature, symbolised by tremolando strings and the blast of four horns. Her life will be spared when the seventh bullet is deflected, thanks to the intercession of God's representative: a Hermit, whom all – including Prince Ottokar – respect as the voice of nature and virtue.

Der Freischütz lies at the foundation of German Romantic opera (Richard Wagner was the self-confessed disciple who later organised the return of Weber's remains from London to Germany). But the conductor of its Proms performance this year, Sir John Eliot Gardiner, has been keen to underline the French roots of Weber's style. These roots are not the Baroque masterworks of Rameau, but rather the unconventional, early-Romantic operas of the 1790s written by Étienne Méhul, Luigi Cherubini and Le Sueur himself – works that Weber surely played to Le Sueur at the piano. One way of emphasising this connection is by reviving the French-language version, with recitatives that Berlioz composed for the Paris Opéra production of *Der Freischütz* in 1841 (for which he also orchestrated Weber's *Introduction to the Dance*, to serve as the mandatory Act 2 ballet). By then, Berlioz was the acclaimed composer of symphonies and overtures carrying themes not far removed from those of Weber's opera (think of the witches' sabbath ending the *Symphonie fantastique*; or the orgy of brigands in *Harold in Italy*).

All performances given at the Paris Opéra had to be sung in French and had to contain sung recitatives, not spoken dialogue as in *Der Freischütz*. So the management commissioned Berlioz, ▶

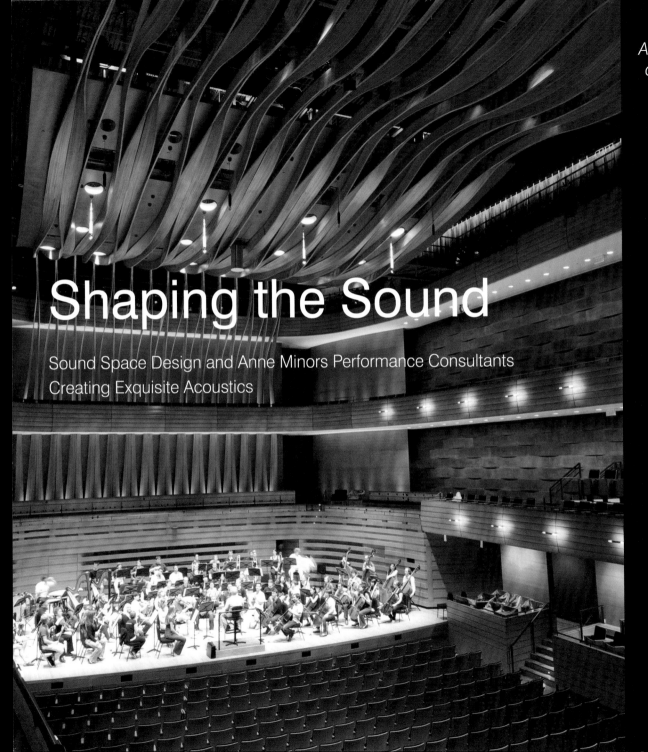

Shaping the Sound

Sound Space Design and Anne Minors Performance Consultants
Creating Exquisite Acoustics

Parting shot: William Tell's marksmanship is put to the test when the Austrian governor Gesler forces him to shoot an apple placed on his son Jemmy's head

who – although not permitted to conduct the opera – wrote a set of recitatives using Weber's own motifs. Amazingly enough, those recitatives themselves travelled round Europe for a time, being used in other productions of *Der Freischütz*. Alas, however, when Berlioz visited Covent Garden in 1851 to hear what he thought were going to be his own recitatives, he didn't recognise a note. *The Times* leaked an explanation: they had been supplanted by others, written by the conductor, Michael Costa.

It will be fascinating to hear Weber's opera given the French 'grand opera' treatment, especially since this year's Proms also features another *grand opéra*, one written by an Italian. When Gioachino Rossini took up the offer to move to Paris, it was a foregone conclusion that he would for the first time

In *William Tell*, as in *Der Freischütz*, orchestral magic brings to life the natural world of which the people form a part.

write a work specially for the French stage. After rejecting a number of ideas, the theme he chose was the classic fable of revolution, telling the story of the liberation of Switzerland from the hand of Austria. Rossini's style, in this final opera of his career, extends the glowing lyricism of earlier works in order to depict the Swiss people themselves. We see and hear them in every one of the four acts,

beginning with wedding songs and dances in Act 1. Contrasting music accompanies men from the cantons of Schwyz, Uri and Unterwalden. The people pray for Tell's safety when he ferries Leuthold over the dangerous lake; and the music depicts their full-voiced anger at the crucial moment in Act 3 when Tell is arrested: he has just successfully shot an apple, placed on his young son's head, as a terrible trial ordered by the overlord, Gesler.

Like Weber, Rossini uses the resources of the orchestra with consummate skill and imagination. As in *Der Freischütz*, orchestral magic brings to life the natural world of which the people form a part. At one moment we hear the echoing horns of Gesler's troops; then a church bell; then the muffled footsteps of men approaching through the undergrowth. Grand Opera paints both public and private worlds, and the way Rossini binds together nature, nation and freedom is by using a certain Swiss mountain-call, a *ranz des vaches*. So powerful were the effects of these melodies that they were supposed to induce uncontrollable yearning, or even death, if ever they touched the ear of a Swiss patriot abroad. No wonder, then, that as the opera closes in a magnificent C-major blaze of glory, the theme we hear resounding in the orchestra is in fact the *ranz des vaches*.

That gives us the public aspect of the revolution. For the private aspect, Rossini offers rich Italian melody requiring supreme vocal virtuosity, especially from the two lovers who are fated to exist on opposite sides of the political divide: the Swiss, Arnold (a heroic tenor part), loves the Austrian Mathilde, a Princess of the House of Habsburg. It is through these two characters that we really confront

the eternal struggles of human ties and personal sacrifice, of moral conviction which leads to armed battle. So although it is William Tell who shoots down Gesler in the end, it is the music of reluctant heroes which stays with us longer; together, that is, with the music of freedom and forest. ●

Grand Stairway of the Paris Opéra, c1875

Grand Opera at the Proms

William Tell Prom 2, 16 July
Chorus and Orchestra of the Academy of Santa Cecilia, Rome/Antonio Pappano

Der Freischütz (French version, 1841, with recitatives by Berlioz) Prom 73, 9 September
Monteverdi Choir; Orchestre Révolutionnaire et Romantique/Sir John Eliot Gardiner

akg-images (above); Gianni Dagli/Corbis (right)

Donald Runnicles
Chief Conductor

Ilan Volkov
Principal Guest
Conductor

Andrew Manze
Associate Guest
Conductor

Matthias Pintscher
Artist-in-Association

"*The biggest and arguably strongest house team of conductors in the UK*" **Michael Tumelty, The Herald**

BBC
SCOTTISH SYMPHONY
ORCHESTRA

BBC PROMS SEASON
INCLUDES

Runnicles conducts **Ravel's** *Boléro* and *Daphnis et Chloe* (3rd Aug)

Volkov conducts the World Premiere of **Thomas Larcher's** *Concerto for Violin, Cello and Orchestra* (18th Aug)

Manze conducts **Brahms** *Piano Quartet in G Minor*, orch. Schoenberg (19th Aug)

EDINBURGH INTERNATIONAL
FESTIVAL 2011

Runnicles conducts **Mahler's** *Symphony No.2*

Volkov conducts **Jonathan Harvey's** BBC SSO triptych

GLASGOW CONCERT
SEASON INCLUDES

MacMillan's *St. John Passion*, with the **London Symphony Chorus** and **BBC Singers**

Complete cycle of **Prokofiev** Piano Concertos, performed by **Denis Kozhukin**

Manze begins a cycle of **Vaughan Williams'** Symphonies

World Premieres of new works by **Matthias Pintscher** and **Detlev Glanert**

bbc.co.uk/bbcsso

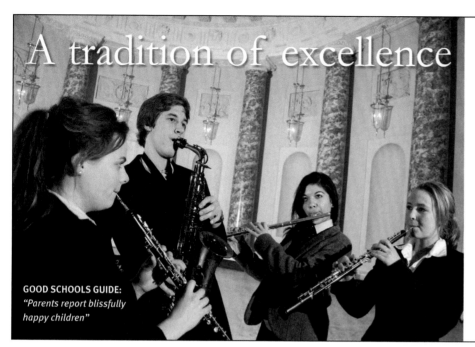

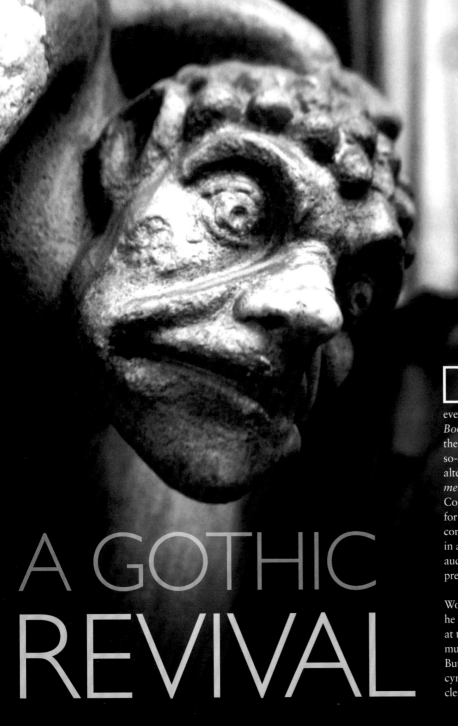

A GOTHIC REVIVAL

Only ever heard on a handful of occasions, Havergal Brian's mammoth 'The Gothic' Symphony features a staggering 10 choirs and two orchestras at its Proms premiere this year. **Calum MacDonald** delights in getting the measure of it

Dedicated to Richard Strauss – who declared it 'magnificent' – Havergal Brian's Symphony No. 1, 'The Gothic', is conceived on such an immense scale that any performance of it is a rare event that promises to be an unmissable one. Listed in *The Guinness Book of Records* (1974) within the entry for 'longest symphony', and the one requiring the largest forces, it outbulks Mahler's Eighth (the so-called 'Symphony of a Thousand') but is a work in the same world-altering spirit, along with Beethoven's Ninth and Berlioz's *Grande messe des morts*, two works which are clearly among its forebears. Completed in 1927 after eight years' labour, it had to wait until 1961 for its first (semi-professional) performance, and has only been heard complete in concert four times since – most recently last December in a blazing rendition in Brisbane, Australia, that brought a packed auditorium to its feet for a five-minute standing ovation. Its Proms premiere will be the first performance in the UK in over 30 years.

Brian had known brief success as a composer before the First World War, but had rapidly fallen from grace. He was nearing 50 when he composed 'The Gothic', in a small council house near Brighton – at the time struggling to support a growing family as a critic and music copyist, and working on his gigantic symphony mainly by night. But while many, after the War, tried to blot out the past, slipping into cynicism, satire and conscious modernity, Brian – who had served as a clerk listing the effects of soldiers killed in the trenches – felt that what

Adrian Boult using a megaphone while rehearsing 'The Gothic' Symphony for its first professional performance in 1966 (with the BBC Symphony Orchestra at the Royal Albert Hall)

was most urgent was to reconnect with the great art and aspiration of the past, to renew what had been broken and carry it forwards. In 'The Gothic' he did this on a scale so vast that it eventually called for an immensely enlarged symphony orchestra, organ, four vocal soloists, two large double choruses, children's choir and four extra brass bands.

Brian once told his friend, the composer and writer Harold Truscott, that the symphony came to him in a flash so intense that he wanted to cram the whole of it into about 20 bars. (He didn't quite manage it: the final tally runs to 2,345, though that in itself is no reliable measure of size.) This remark reveals something about Brian. He was not an extravagant or self-indulgent composer. On the contrary, he was a very concise one. In 'The Gothic' he was composing out an intense moment of vision as briefly as he knew how. One aspect of this – and it's a characteristic that persisted through all his later works – is that he hates elaborate transitions: he doesn't smooth the way between one idea and the next, and he composes *essences*, not passages of filling. The orchestra contains many unusual extras – oboe d'amore, bass oboe, basset-horn, contrabass clarinet, cornets, bass trumpet, euphoniums and so on. Brian attributed this to the suggestion made to him by Proms founder-conductor Henry Wood in 1907 that he should write a work to include the *complete* families of all the different wind instruments – all the oboe family, all the clarinets and so on. Brian uses these, not to produce a huge undifferentiated noise, but to gain an unprecedented range of subtle instrumental colour.

'The Gothic' is in two parts of three movements each – the first purely orchestral, the second an unprecedentedly elaborate setting of the *Te Deum*. In it, Brian was inspired by the ideas and especially

the architecture of the high medieval age, whose ultimate expressions are the Gothic cathedrals of Northern Europe. Into that age, and especially into the stones of those cathedrals, was etched the ultimate certainty that life is a struggle between good and evil. Brian saw Faust, as depicted by Goethe, as an archetypal Gothic-age figure in his thirst for knowledge, wherever it may lead him. Indeed, he thought at first his finale would be (as in Mahler's Eighth) a setting of parts of the final scene of Goethe's *Faust*. But, instead, he found himself drawn to the music that was sung in the cathedrals, and thus to the *Te Deum*. Not a believer in any doctrinal sense, Brian conceived his *Te Deum* as a drama of the human spirit, where the will to rejoice is threatened at every turn. Yet on the symphony's title-page, he still placed a couplet from *Faust*: 'Whoever strives with all his might/That man we can redeem', and the idea of a struggle against immense odds – with no unequivocal final victory – is central to the whole work.

'Completist' in its approach to instrumental timbre, 'The Gothic' is also a compendium of musical styles, ranging from evocations of Gregorian chant and Elizabethan church music to atonality and vibrant cluster-chords. Brian poured into it everything he knew; and one of the things he knew from his earliest years was about crack virtuoso competitive choirs that could perform the most complicated test-pieces with pinpoint accuracy. The orchestral players may be faced with some severe challenges in 'The Gothic' (movement three contains the most difficult xylophone solo ever written, for instance), but these are child's play compared with some of the choral writing, especially the intense chromatic polyphony that is one of the *Te Deum*'s hallmarks. The late Deryck Cooke once described Brian's setting as 'a dithyrambic paean of complex neo-medieval counterpoint like nothing else in music', that 'reveals the mind of a truly visionary genius'. He was right: there's no other work like this, even among Brian's own output. However infrequently, this is a symphony that demands to be heard. ●

Calum MacDonald is a writer, lecturer and broadcaster, and Editor of the new music journal *Tempo*. As Malcolm MacDonald he has written books on Brahms, John Foulds, Havergal Brian, Schoenberg and Varèse.

'The Gothic' Symphony at the Proms
Prom 4, 17 July

The imposing interior of Rouen Cathedral – an emblem of the Gothic age, whose ideas and architecture inspired Havergal Brian's colossal 'The Gothic' Symphony

GLYNDEBOURNE
ON TOUR 2011

PUCCINI
LA BOHÈME
David McVicar's acclaimed production

DONIZETTI
DON PASQUALE
New for Tour 2011

HANDEL
RINALDO
Direct from the 2011 Festival

'SIMPLY THE GREATEST
ALL-ROUND OPERA EXPERIENCE
AVAILABLE IN THIS COUNTRY'
BBC MUSIC MAGAZINE

OCTOBER – DECEMBER 2011
GLYNDEBOURNE, WOKING,
MILTON KEYNES, NORWICH, PLYMOUTH,
WIMBLEDON, STOKE-ON-TRENT

glyndebourne.com

Glyndebourne on Tour is supported by Supported by **ARTS COUNCIL ENGLAND**

Choral Sundays

Choral works have long been integral to the Proms, but this summer sees a particular focus every Sunday on peaks of the choral repertory. Gareth Malone, one of the country's most energetic choral motivators, surveys the series and celebrates the idea that many voices are better than one

Every Sunday evening throughout the Proms this summer, leading choirs from the UK and abroad gather to perform works ranging from the grand choral-society staples to the less often heard. Of course, to some degree every Sunday is a choral Sunday in churches around the UK, but Proms Choral Sundays offer us a totally different view, reflecting the passion and commitment of the many thousands of recreational singers who give up their free time to work towards the best performances they can achieve. One of the UK's leading choral directors, Stephen Layton, describes the experience of hearing large choirs as 'complete, total immersion'. Forget surround sound: this is the real thing.

Because of its size, the Royal Albert Hall is the perfect venue for large-scale pieces that other London concert halls might struggle to house. Inaugurated in 1871 at the height of the fashion for grand choral forces, the RAH boasts choir stalls that can seat around 450 singers, at least double that of other London venues. Which is just as well, because the Choral Sundays series kicks off with Havergal Brian's enormous Symphony No. 1, 'The Gothic', which in this performance features 10 massed choirs. Martyn Brabbins is in charge of unleashing these combined forces: 'It's one of those pieces that is fabled,' he explains. 'It's easily the largest work I've tackled. It could probably only ever be done by an organisation like the BBC with the resources to bring it all together. I'm looking forward to joining a very select group of conductors.' How does he plan to keep everyone together? 'A lot of tea and a megaphone.'

Because of its enormous demands and scope, Brian's symphony is hardly ever performed; the last British performance was in 1980, so this will be worth a listen for its rarity as well as its sheer audacity. After the orchestral first part, the second part features an exotic choral setting of the *Te Deum*. It promises to be an unforgettable spectacle as the 800 singers cram onto the stage and even spill over into the Stalls. David Burgess, a bass singer in the Huddersfield Choral Society, is ready for the challenge. 'I doubt anybody in the choir will have ever sung this before. I'll do my utmost to give it my very best shot, so we can reach for the highest standard

Being myself in a crowd: part of what attracts thousands around the country to choral singing

of performance. It's to do with personal pride as well as pride in the choir, which is a big part of my life.'

After just seven days' rest, the BBC National Chorus of Wales – another of the choirs involved in the 'Gothic' bonanza – is back, as one of three choral groups performing in Verdi's *Requiem* ▶

Prom 4, Sunday 17 July
Havergal Brian
Symphony No. 1, 'The Gothic'

Calling for massed choirs, soloists and an orchestra numbering almost 200 players, the mighty 'The Gothic' Symphony also features in the *Guinness Book of Records* under 'longest symphony'. This Proms premiere is only the sixth complete performance of this mammoth work.

Prom 13, Sunday 24 July
Verdi Requiem

It may have been dismissed as an 'opera in ecclesiastical garb', but Verdi's *Requiem* – conceived along 'somewhat vast proportions' – is perhaps the most potent of all 19th-century settings of the text, its music depicting consolation and the hope of redemption as vividly as it does the terrifying Day of Judgement.

Prom 22, Sunday 31 July
Rachmaninov Spring; The Bells

The sound of bells is a recurring theme in the music of Rachmaninov, not least in his 'choral symphony' *The Bells*, setting a poem by Edgar Allan Poe in which bells punctuate life's passage. The earlier cantata *Spring* centres on a Russian peasant and his unfaithful wife: the former's thoughts of revenge subside as springs arrives.

CBSO (p62); Mark Pavey (above left); Phoebe Ling/NYCGB (right); Havergal Brian Estate (Brian); BBC (Verdi); BBC (Rachmaninov)

In fine voice: the CBSO Youth Chorus joins nine other choirs to launch Proms Choral Sundays with Havergal Brian's massive 'The Gothic' Symphony

Proms Choral Sundays reflect the passion and commitment of the many thousands of recreational singers around the country who give up their free time to work towards the best performances they can achieve.

under Semyon Bychkov. In this powerful piece, spanning the terrifying Day of Judgement and a sublime depiction of 'eternal light', the Welsh voices are joined by those of the London Philharmonic Choir and of the BBC Symphony Chorus (the latter of which appears five times during the summer).

British choirs have a rest in the third week and it's just as well because singing in Russian notoriously difficult, partly due to some Russian sounds that we don't have in our language. But more importantly, its hard to replicate that particular Russian timbre, especially for the basses of the choir. For that reason I welcome the opportunity to hear an evening of Rachmaninov sung with authentic colours by the Chorus of the Mariinsky Theatre, St Petersburg.

Stephen Layton, who runs the lithe professional chamber choir Polyphony and recently took up the post of Artistic Director of the City of London Sinfonia, will then conduct these groups in Mozart's *Requiem* along with a stellar line-up of soloists

including tenor Ian Bostridge. In terms of size, Polyphony lies at the other end of the spectrum to the previous Sundays' large-scale amateur choruses, but Layton believes that his choir produces a sound that is just as exciting: 'What's intriguing when you have a smaller group, particularly professional singers, is that – because their voices are so powerful and so focused, so honed and so direct – it's still possible to create something that carries and that fills the space.' The same concert also features the world premiere of a new choral-orchestral piece by the British composer Colin Matthews, dedicated to the founder of the CLS, Richard Hickox, who died in 2008: his tireless championing of British music made him part of the country's choral fabric.

When I sang under Hickox in 1996, choral singing was beginning to make a comeback after a period of failing to appeal to the younger generations. But Stephen Layton is more confident about the current state of British choirs: 'It's at a high-water mark at the moment. There's something growing in the country.' This idea of a singing nation was one clearly held in Victorian England, where Mendelssohn's *Elijah* came second in popularity only to Handel's *Messiah*. Mendelssohn's oratorio might be seen as an unlikely work to receive the period-instrument treatment, but conductor Paul McCreesh breathes new colours into this choral favourite on Sunday 28 August with his Gabrieli Consort & Players.

Prom 32, Sunday 7 August
Mahler Das klagende Lied
(original version)

Mahler described *Das klagende Lied* as 'the first work in which I became "Mahler"'. A student work recalling a grim fairy tale, it is characteristically conceived on the largest scale and already shows the hallmarks of the master composer Mahler was to become.

Prom 41, Sunday 14 August
Britten Cantata misericordium;
Spring Symphony

Britten was the nation's leading operatic composer by 1949, the year of the *Spring Symphony* – which (as with *Peter Grimes*) was commissioned by Serge Koussevitzky. The *Cantata misericordium*, first performed for the centenary of the Red Cross, sets the parable of the Good Samaritan.

Prom 50, Sunday 21 August
Mozart, compl **Süssmayr**
Requiem in D minor

Mozart's great *Requiem*, left unfinished at his early death, was commissioned by a mysterious nobleman who wanted a work to memorialise his young wife. Mozart was said to have been convinced that he was being poisoned and that he was writing the work for his own death.

Other choral treats include Britten's upbeat *Spring Symphony* under Jiří Bělohlávek and Mahler's fairy-tale cantata *Das klagende Lied* under Edward Gardner (both pieces featuring BBC choral and orchestral forces). The last word is appropriately given to the venerable Sir Colin Davis, who rounds off the season's choral series with Beethoven's *Missa solemnis*, a notorious challenge for even the most advanced choirs. Many amateur singers might be in danger of blowing a gasket in this work, whose sheer technical difficulty and expressive intensity are a test of true choral mettle. Davis here directs the London Symphony Orchestra and Chorus, the same forces which, in a 2006 performance of the work, prompted music critic Paul Driver to write in *The Sunday Times*: 'It wasn't just that the music had a monumental power – the monuments seemed flung through the air.'

And that is the joy of choirs – they positively hurl the music at you, filling spaces with explosive and uplifting sound. Yet at the same time there is an intensely personal and immediate connection between audience and singers – recordings never quite do justice to the real thing. Choral Sundays at the Proms this summer offer a unique chance to experience choirs at their most flamboyant and expressive best. ●

Gareth Malone is a choral animateur, singer and TV presenter, best known for the BAFTA-winning *The Choir* (now recording its fourth series), *Extraordinary School for Boys* and *Gareth Malone Goes to Glyndebourne*.

CBSO (p64); Chris Christodoulou/BBC (right); akg-images (Mahler, Beethoven); BBC (Mozart, Mendelssohn); Sheila Burnett/ArenaPAL (right)

Packed to the rafters: the Royal Albert Hall can accommodate choral forces on the grandest scale

That is the joy of choirs – they positively hurl the music at you, filling spaces with explosive and uplifting sound. Yet at the same time there is an intensely personal and immediate relationship between audience and singers.

Prom 58, Sunday 28 August
Mendelssohn Elijah

Mendelssohn did much to revive the music of Bach and to import to Germany the thriving English tradition of Handelian oratorio. *Elijah* was composed for the Birmingham Festival in 1846, with the 'Swedish nightingale' Jenny Lind intended as the soprano soloist; in the event she sang in it only after Mendelssohn's early death.

Prom 67, Sunday 4 September
Beethoven Missa solemnis

The *Missa solemnis* was conceived for the elevation of Beethoven's friend and patron, Archduke Rudolph, to the post of Archbishop – but in the event it was delivered five years late. Nevertheless, it is the work Beethoven considered his finest, a magnificent fusion of music, liturgy and drama.

PROMS PLUS SING EVENTS ON CHORAL SUNDAYS

Each Choral Sunday Prom is preceded by an afternoon **Proms Plus Sing** participatory event, in which a leading choir-master introduces and rehearses part of the featured work. This is followed by a late-afternoon **Proms Intro**, in which a musical expert introduces the work, with the help of musical illustrations. (See pages 92–99 for more details)

SHELL CLASSIC INTERNATIONAL 2011/12

Great orchestras from around the world
Royal Festival Hall

BOULEZ & ENSEMBLE INTERCONTEMPORAIN

Boulez presents his masterpiece
Pli selon pli

Sunday 2 October 2011

Pierre Boulez *conductor*
Barbara Hannigan *soprano*

ABBADO & LUCERNE FESTIVAL ORCHESTRA

A world-class partnership rarely
heard outside Lucerne

Monday 10* & Tuesday 11 October 2011

Claudio Abbado *conductor*
Hélène Grimaud *paino**

TOGNETTI & AUSTRALIAN CHAMBER ORCHESTRA

Vigorous with 'the vibe of a rock band'

Tuesday 29 November 2011

Richard Tognetti *artistic director
and lead violin*
Simon Trpčeski *piano*
Tine Thing Helseth *trumpet*

FISCHER & BUDAPEST FESTIVAL ORCHESTRA

Celebrated for its fiery intensity

Sunday 4 March 2012

Iván Fischer *conductor*
Renaud Capuçon *violin*

BARENBOIM & STAATSKAPELLE BERLIN THE BRUCKNER PROJECT

Bruckner's last three symphonies

Monday 16, Tuesday 17 & Friday 20 April 2012

Daniel Barenboim *piano, conductor*

SPIRA MIRABILIS THE BEETHOVEN ENCOUNTER

Europe's finest young players return
following five-star reviews

Friday 25 & Saturday 26 May 2012

DUDAMEL & SIMÓN BOLÍVAR SYMPHONY ORCHESTRA OF VENEZUELA

A sensation wherever they play

Saturday 23 & Tuesday 26 June 2012

Gustavo Dudamel *conductor*

'A miracle of music-making.'
(*The Times*)

'The most astonishingly gifted conductor.'
(Sir Simon Rattle)

Media partner
THE TIMES

Supported by
ARTS COUNCIL ENGLAND

SOUTHBANK CENTRE

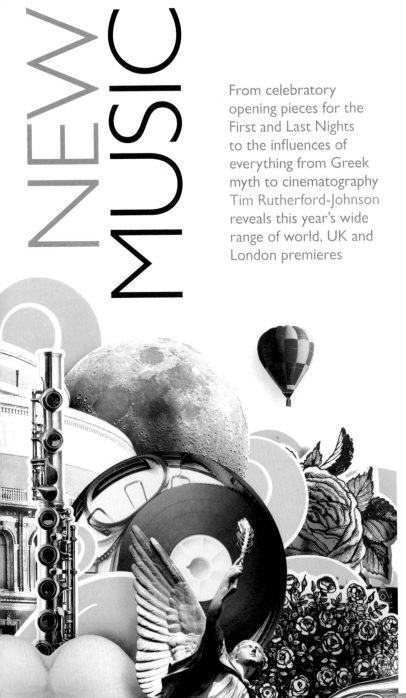

NEW MUSIC

From celebratory opening pieces for the First and Last Nights to the influences of everything from Greek myth to cinematography Tim Rutherford-Johnson reveals this year's wide range of world, UK and London premieres

Georges Aperghis (born 1945)

Champ–Contrechamp (2010)
BBC commission: world premiere

Proms Saturday Matinee 2 20 August

The works of Greek-born French composer Georges Aperghis frequently have as much to do with theatre and language as they do with music. Even his purely instrumental works are often abstract, sometimes absurd acoustic dramas that draw on the patterns of speech and dialogue. In *Babil* (1996) for clarinet and ensemble, for example, a 'conversation' between soloist and 15 instruments appears to escalate into a quarrel, eventually resolved peacefully.

Champ–Contrechamp refers to the cinematic convention of an alternating shot/ reverse shot between two characters facing each other in conversation. This concerto for piano and chamber orchestra follows Aperghis's 2008 pieces *Teeter-Totter* and *See-Saw* in dramatising a back-and-forth motion between soloist and group. The composer describes the relationship between the two points of view as 'a game of passive resistance and active resistance. The piano is "speaking" as in a recitative, the ensemble seems to respond and all of a sudden misinterpretations between them create a tension.' *Champ–Contrechamp* was written for pianist Nicolas Hodges, who gives the Proms world premiere and with whom Aperghis has often worked. 'While I was writing, I had his sounds in mind,' the composer says, but Aperghis has also introduced new elements. 'For the first time, I wished to emphasise the contrast between a Minimalism of great fragility and a booming "maximalism". It is another *champ–contrechamp*'.

Sally Beamish (born 1956)

Reed Stanzas (String Quartet No. 3) (2011)
BBC commission: world premiere

Proms Chamber Music 2 25 July

Sally Beamish's Third String Quartet, 'Reed Stanzas', takes the form of a series of variations – or 'stanzas' – on a Celtic-inspired melody. Unusually, Beamish gives the role of introducing this theme to the second violin. Her inspiration for this skewed take on the traditional balance of the string quartet lies with Donald Grant, the second violinist of the Elias Quartet, the group which gives the Proms world premiere.

Grant is a well-known traditional Scottish fiddle player. 'He has an infectious raw energy, and I decided to incorporate this skill into a quartet work,' Beamish explains. There is a technical reason too: the second violin tends to play in a lower, throatier range than the first, placing it closer to that of the traditional fiddle.

As so often in Sally Beamish's works, the sound of traditional Scots music permeates throughout. The skirling ornamentation of Highland bagpipe music is a continuing fascination for the composer – one which, she says, 'translates well to strings'. The keening 'outdoor' sound of the pipes is one source for the reeds of the title but Beamish also draws on the accursed reed, or stick, upon which vinegar was raised for Jesus to drink at the cross, and the metaphor of Mary as the Reed of God, as well as Sufi descriptions of the reed flute as a symbol of longing, producing a heartbreaking lament.

Michael Berkeley
(born 1948)

Organ Concerto (1987)
London premiere

Prom 65 3 September

Although it was composed in 1987 and has received many performances, Michael Berkeley's Organ Concerto has had to wait until now for its London premiere – not least because in recent years the organs of both the Royal Albert and Royal Festival halls have been out of commission for extensive rebuilding (the latter is still under refurbishment). However, the time has come and the composer is excited by the dramatic possibilities of a Proms performance on the RAH's massive 'Father' Willis organ.

In fact, although the work was composed with cathedral performances in mind, Berkeley describes this venue as 'ideal'. The piece has a strong ritual element: it begins with three trumpets that process onto the stage, playing chant melodies related to the plainsong Berkeley absorbed as a child, a theatrical effect that the composer hopes will take full advantage of the expansive layout of the hall.

In addition to its ritual aspect, a central theme of the concerto is that of fire, as a force that cleanses, illuminates and destroys. This, in particular, demands an organ of immense power to create 'a feeling of being engulfed' by music that is 'almost deliberately overwhelming'. It is a role that the nearly 10,000 pipes of the Albert Hall's grand instrument – restored to its full glory in 2004 – should be thrillingly capable of fulfilling.

Judith Bingham
(born 1952)

The Everlasting Crown (2010–11)
world premiere

Prom 3 17 July

The 'Everlasting Crown' is an invention of Bingham's imagination, a fantastical headpiece comprising seven of the world's most famous and dazzling gemstones – including the Orlov diamond, the pearl La Peregrina and the Incan Atahualpa emerald. Each stone represents good and bad aspects of royalty, such as divinity, ambition, isolation and spectacle.

'The stones are a witness to history and to the deeds of the powerful,' says the composer. 'In this way they seemed to me to represent the best and the worst of the human race.' The piece begins with a coronation overture, followed by a sequence of seven dances, each inspired by one of the stones. While reading about Russian gemstones in the course of researching the piece, Bingham was reminded constantly of Tchaikovsky, a composer she greatly admires, and the 'barely suppressed hysteria' that often inhabits his music finds its way into this melodramatic and visceral piece.

Bingham has contributed much to contemporary organ repertoire, including a concerto, *Jacob's Ladder* (2008). It's an instrument that brings a unique set of considerations, she says. 'The interesting thing about writing for organ is that you cannot finally control what the piece will sound like, and there is a strong element of the organist finishing the composing process for you. I cannot think of any other instrument where you have that same dilemma or satisfaction!'

Sir Harrison Birtwistle
(born 1934)

Angel Fighter (2010)
UK premiere

Proms Saturday Matinee 2 20 August

With *Angel Fighter*, Sir Harrison Birtwistle goes back to the beginning: the story of Jacob wrestling with God in the form of an angel in Genesis, Chapter 32. By surviving the night in combat, Jacob wins God's blessing and is renamed Israel.

This is not the first time that Birtwistle, known for his attachment to Greek and folk mythology, has turned to a scenario from the Bible (most obviously one recalls his opera *The Last Supper*), but his approach to sacred and secular myth is the same. 'This has been in my head like a lot of stories from childhood – like the Minotaur. They're stories that bubble up and become part of you.'

Stephen Plaice's libretto (some of which is written in the 'angelical language' Enochian, recorded by the 16th-century occultist John Dee) contains distinct but as yet unrealised theatrical possibilities – not least a wrestling match between a man and an angel. And, although the score calls for some basic stage directions, the composer insists that 'they're no big deal, they're an emphasis of some things that are in the piece'. The format is in fact closer to the tableaux of Baroque oratorio than to opera. Once more, the choral unit is important, as in the crowds of the Bach Passions. The dramatic focus is on the tenor and counter-tenor soloists, underpinned by a typically gritty, gutsy orchestral accompaniment.

Sir Harrison Birtwistle
(born 1934)

Concerto for Violin and Orchestra (2009–10)
UK premiere

Prom 70 7 September

'It's an oxymoron. A violin concerto that isn't one,' says Sir Harrison Birtwistle with a laugh. This is the 76-year-old's first attempt at a 'pure' concerto but it's anything but typical in its design. Unlike the Classical format, in which the soloist and orchestra are often at odds with one another, here the two partners – the soloist being Christian Tetzlaff, who gave the concerto's premiere earlier this year – are discussing the same things, holding the same conversation together. 'I could never do the other thing anyway,' says the composer.

Working along the lines of ideas familiar from his theatrical works, the orchestra functions as a chorus in relation to the soloist, and at certain points different instruments – secondary soloists – come forward like individual viewpoints within a crowd of voices. In fact, there is a continuous interchange between violin and orchestra, an attempt by the composer to divert musical attention away from overt melody and towards other areas such as rhythm.

This anti-Classical design is connected to Birtwistle's long-standing predilection for wind instruments over strings. 'You write a line for the violin and it sounds like the 19th century,' he explains. 'They're very human in the way that they're played. Wind instruments are more specified. There's more in the technique of playing a wind instrument that stops it sounding 19th-century. That challenge was one of the reasons I wanted to write this piece.'

Johannes Brahms (1833–97), arr. Dejan Lazić (born 1977)

'Piano Concerto No. 3' in D major (after Violin Concerto) (arr. 2004–9) *UK premiere*
Prom 37 11 August

Brahms's Violin Concerto was viewed as unplayable in its time and famously declared by the conductor Hans von Bülow to be 'written against the violin'. Some have wondered whether that difficulty arose because of Brahms's preference for the piano, and perhaps the choice of violin solo was due as much to his friendship with Joseph Joachim as to an attraction to the instrument itself.

With this transcription – a 'Third Brahms Piano Concerto' – Croatian pianist Dejan Lazić speculates on what might have happened if Joachim had been a pianist instead. The orchestral parts are unchanged but the solo has been enriched in line with the fuller possibilities afforded by the piano.

Robert Spano, Music Director of the Atlanta Symphony Orchestra, who conducted the work's first performance in October 2009, describes it as 'almost a recomposition, which provides a quite wonderful new perspective on the piece'.

Lazić sees transcriptions as a noble tradition and found his inspiration in the piano versions made by Bach and Beethoven of their own violin concertos. 'Maybe I am behaving here more as a composer than a performer – the line that divides production and reproduction is obviously an extremely thin one,' he admits. 'I sought to construct anew the violin part, recomposing the voice in a thoroughly Brahmsian style and adding my own cadenza. Throughout the piece that was my thought: to imagine what Brahms would do.'

Benjamin Britten (1913–76)

Piano Variations on a Theme of Frank Bridge (1932) *London premiere*
Proms Chamber Music 5 15 August

A Britten premiere, in 2011? Yes, thanks to the untiring efforts of the Britten–Pears Foundation, who are currently appraising and publishing the best of Britten's juvenilia. This set of six piano variations was written in 1932, while Britten was a student at the Royal College of Music, and uses the same theme that would later form the basis of his first major success, the *Variations on a Theme by Frank Bridge* for strings of 1937 (Prom 50, 21 August)

It is an entirely different piece, however, although it already bears some of the hallmarks of Britten's mature style. Britten wrote little for solo piano but these variations show he had an interesting and imaginative approach to writing for the instrument, even from an early age. According to the composer Joseph Phibbs, who prepared the performing edition of the piece, even in this teenage composition there is something unmistakable about the clarity of expression and the lightness and economy of materials.

The draw towards variations, too, is characteristic, and this set can be seen as an early essay in a form that would recur in many of Britten's landmark works. The sixth variation is a curiosity. Phibbs regards it as one of the better ones but Britten himself – and we cannot be sure why – struck a line through it. It will, however, be included in this Proms performance.

Elliott Carter (born 1908)

Flute Concerto (2008) *UK premiere*
Prom 18 28 July

Whether thanks to the mood of celebration that surrounded the composer's centenary in 2008 or simply the fact that decades of practice have forged a complete facility of technique, Elliott Carter's recent music has gained an almost Bernstein-like swagger.

Despite years of requests, he had put off writing a Flute Concerto because he felt the instrument was not capable of producing the sharp, rhythmical attacks that typically characterise his music. 'But the idea of the beautiful qualities of the different registers of the instrument and the extraordinary agility attracted me more and more,' he says, and in 2008 he finally relented at the request of Elena Bashkirova, director of the Jerusalem International Chamber Music Festival and wife of the composer's good friend Daniel Barenboim.

The floodgates opened and Carter relates that, once he started writing, 'ideas and notes for it fascinated me without relief'. The result is a single-movement showpiece that revels in the flute's lyricism, juxtaposing it against an exuberantly percussive orchestra: Carter has reduced the number of strings for the sake of balance but found room for a piano, harp and three percussionists. One critic has described the work as 'a real crowd-pleaser' – and the dramatic contrast between point and line, punch and grace is the source of its dazzling appeal.

Marc-André Dalbavie (born 1961)

Flute Concerto (2006) *London premiere*
Prom 18 28 July

Before writing his Piano Concerto, first performed at the 2005 Proms by Leif Ove Andsnes, Marc-André Dalbavie extensively researched the most famous piano concertos of the past. In contrast, his Flute Concerto (2006) came to him much more quickly.

'I had no preparation. Every moment arrived with clarity,' he says. 'I did no research because the repertoire of the flute concerto doesn't have the history of the one for piano. I don't really remember if I had something in particular in my mind when I started composing – the only thing is that I wanted to write a homage to Debussy and I wanted to write for my friend Emmanuel Pahud.'

A former researcher at Paris's state-of-the-art electronic music institute IRCAM who has worked in computer-assisted composition, Dalbavie has a daunting CV. But his music – glittering, vivid, dramatic – is anything but, and this particularly approachable concerto is fast establishing itself in the repertory. The connection to Debussy, and particularly to the *Prélude à L'après-midi d'un faune*, becomes apparent in the work's still centre but those luminous harmonies seem a long way away when the piece explodes at the start in a tumultuous stream of activity. The transformation of timbre between soloist and orchestra is a theme and Dalbavie the studio technician coaxes some sumptuous sounds from his players.

BBC (Brahms, Britten); Jeff Herman (Carter); Alix Laveau (Dalbavie); Eamonn McCabe (Davies); Collège de France/Éditions Salabert (Dusapin)

Sir Peter Maxwell Davies
(born 1934)

Musica benevolens (2011)
Musicians Benevolent Fund commission: world premiere

Prom 74 10 September

Whereas this year's First Night will be launched with a choral fanfare composed by Judith Weir (*see later panel*), so the Last Night's festivities will begin with this new work by Sir Peter Maxwell Davies. It will be the 51st work by Davies to be heard at the Proms, continuing an association that spans almost 50 years and has included all eight of his symphonies.

As Master of the Queen's Music, Davies is no stranger to occasional pieces and his list of works already includes several fanfares and other works for festive events. Then, of course, there is *A Little Birthday Music*, a setting of words by the then Poet Laureate Andrew Motion written for the 80th birthday of the Queen and first performed at the 2006 Proms.

This new opener for the Last Night encapsulates something of what the Proms is about, drawing together musical celebration and the creation of new work. Davies has written a piece that will involve not only the massed forces of the BBC Symphony Orchestra and BBC Symphony Chorus, but also – and as yet mysteriously – possibly the audience itself. The piece (whose title means 'benevolent music') has been written as a thank you from the Musicians Benevolent Fund to the volunteers of the Promenaders' musical charities who, through decades of shaking buckets outside the Royal Albert Hall, have raised hundreds of thousands of pounds to support musicians in times of need.

"The orchestra and string quartet seem to struggle ... to coexist. As one takes a certain direction, so the other goes a different way."

Pascal Dusapin on his String Quartet No. 6 for string quartet and orchestra

Pascal Dusapin
(born 1955)

Morning in Long Island (Concert No. 1 for large orchestra) (2010)
BBC co-commision with Radio France: UK premiere

Prom 5 18 July

'The title refers to a very old memory which has followed me since 1988, a particular morning in Long Island in the USA,' explains French composer Pascal Dusapin, enigmatically. 'But music cannot directly express or reflect the slightest memory,' he adds. 'Everything is a story of association or cultural reflex.'

Dusapin's prolific output has been composed from within such a stream of associations and references to earlier works. 'Writing is like a journey,' he says. 'Sometimes I have the urge to go back along the same road.' But this piece also owes a debt to other composers. 'I am enthralled by Mahler and, during the composition of *Morning in Long Island*, I scrupulously examined his symphonies,' he says. 'Also, I love the music of Sibelius, on which I never cease to meditate.'

These and other connections come together in *Morning in Long Island* – to be premiered in Paris this June – a piece that is likely to give birth to its own further musical associations: it is the first part of a projected three-work cycle that together may form something like a complete symphony – 'but a symphony,' emphasises the composer, 'which, even if it dares not carry that name, tries to tackle this ancient and eternal question: how to create a music which regenerates continuously and intrudes upon us to excess.'

Pascal Dusapin
(born 1955)

String Quartet No. 6, 'Hinterland' ('Hapax' for string quartet and orchestra (2008–9) *UK premiere*

Prom 16 27 July

A 'hapax' is a word that occurs only once in a given text or body of literature. Pascal Dusapin uses the term here to refer to what he calls the 'impossible form' of this piece – not a concerto for quartet and orchestra but a quartet extended by an orchestra. In this way it firmly belongs within the sequence of seven string quartets he has written so far.

'The thought of this piece is centred upon the quartet, on its numerous possible expansions,' says Dusapin, drawing a parallel with Schoenberg's Second String Quartet, which features a soprano soloist in its last two movements. Nevertheless, the orchestra here provides more than mere decoration or accompaniment. Although Dusapin does not place the two ensembles in opposition, they have such strong historical identities that they unsettle each other. 'The orchestra and string quartet seem to struggle to right themselves, to coexist,' he says. 'As one takes a certain direction, so the other goes a different way, and this provides a clue to the work's title.

'Each of the protagonists of this small musical adventure becomes in a certain way the other's "hinterland".' As themes and ideas are transferred between the ensembles, they are transformed and dispersed, like a refracted beam of light. 'Each party sets the other in motion – as if one was the dream of the other.'

Thierry Escaich (born 1965)

Evocation III (2008)
London premiere

Prom 66 4 September

Thierry Escaich follows in a distinguished line of great French organist-composers (he holds Maurice Duruflé's former post at the church of St-Étienne-du-Mont in Paris), yet the subtitle of his organ solo *Evocation III* – 'Paraphrase on *Nun komm, der Heiden Heiland*' – immediately suggests the German Baroque tradition of Buxtehude and Bach (in fact the piece was composed for an Austrian organ competition titled 'Bach and the Modern').

The reference is to the Lutheran chorale 'Come now, saviour of the Gentiles', on which Bach based two of his church cantatas, both of them for the first Sunday in Advent. But any musical similarity soon ends. 'This is not a variation in the Classical meaning of this word,' says the composer – who this year makes his Proms debuts both as composer and organist – 'but rather a play of echoes on the different phrases of the chorale melody, a work of sound spatialisation.'

As befits a competition showpiece, and perhaps drawing on that colourful French tradition, the organ's full range is employed: the available stops and registers – from high keyboard to low pedals – are cleverly employed to create a great sense of musical space. The symbolic idea of waiting, carried by this Advent chorale, was important to Escaich in its selection, but so was the melody's shape – 'it is flexible and at the same time seems to turn round in circles, which was ideal for giving the impression of twirl,' he explains.

Graham Fitkin (born 1963)

Cello Concerto (2010–11)
BBC commission: world premiere

Prom 61 31 August

'I didn't want to produce a piece that just demonstrates how brilliant the soloist is,' says Graham Fitkin of his new cello concerto. The piece is indeed a shop window for some of Yo-Yo Ma's strongest qualities – which Fitkin got to know well having written *L* for him in 2005 (see next panel) – but this is virtuosity without the obvious pyrotechnics. 'Yo-Yo's tone quality and the control of his bow arm are second to none,' says Fitkin.

Composer and cellist have worked closely together in the creation of the concerto, investigating the many nuances to be found in a single note. As a result, the work is full of long, sustained lines, with an attention to colour that is quite a way from the rhythmically driven music for which Fitkin is perhaps better known. 'It's quite bare, quite intimate. Much more sombre,' he says.

Fitkin describes the soloist as an individual fighting against a mass of other worlds in the orchestra. Gradually these encroach upon it and try to impress themselves, nudging the individual into more uncomfortable spaces. That sounds as though the piece has a political dimension – a Kafka-like confrontation with faceless bureaucracy – and Fitkin confirms that he and Ma talked a lot of politics during their meetings, so it is in the piece's background at least – 'but it's not what's in my head when I sit down to write,' he adds.

Graham Fitkin (born 1963)

L (2005)
London premiere

Proms Chamber Music 7 29 August

Graham Fitkin had worked once before with Yo-Yo Ma, composing this short piece for cello and piano. It was written in 2005 as a 50th-birthday present for Ma, who later toured it around North and South America with the pianist Kathryn Stott, with whom he brings it to this year's Proms Chamber Music series.

Fitkin often gives his pieces short, punchy titles – and *L* outshortens even *PK*, Fitkin's orchestral piece commissioned for last year's Proms, which combined professional and amateur players from London and Cornwall (the composer's home county).

Those enigmatic titles are often doorways into a labyrinth of inspirations behind the work: *PK* reflects the telegraphic code for Porthcurno, the Cornish village which in 1870 became the world's largest cable station. *L* is the Latin numeral for 50, but the composer points out that it also stands for 'line, for lust, life and longing'.

The piece deals in contrasts of jagged agitation and more stable plateaux; Fitkin describes it as 'occasionally kitsch, often brutal and sometimes a little sensual', and a lot of the music is indeed rhythmic and hard-edged. At times, however, the cello breaks free, leaving the piano in charge of the energetic material while it launches itself on one of those calm melodic strands that Fitkin finds so suited to Ma's playing and that perform such a strong role in the cello concerto. 'Lust, life and longing' give rise, through the liberating force of line and melody, to individuality and expression.

> "The piece deals in contrasts of jagged agitation and more stable plateaux; Fitkin describes it as 'occasionally kitsch, often brutal and sometimes a little sensual.'"
>
> Graham Fitkins's *L*

Anders Hillborg
(born 1954)

Cold Heat (2010)
UK premiere

Prom 57 27 August

'I work in a very concrete way,' Anders Hillborg says. 'My inspirations come from other music – I don't think much about extramusical things.'

His output is therefore full of interconnections between pieces and very often a section or idea from one will provide the starting point for another. This is the case in *Cold Heat*, which has its origins in a section of an earlier orchestral work, *Exquisite Corpse* (given its UK premiere at the Proms in 2004), which the composer 'sculpted' to fit into this new context. The piece also features a powerful percussion section at its centre, an idea that was derived from 1998's *Dreaming River*. And so on …

'Composing is an ongoing process,' Hillborg explains, 'so some material pops up in several places.' If this sounds like an introspective way to go about writing, Hillborg's poetic, paradoxical titles tell us more about his vivid and sensual music. Those titles often come after the piece is completed – as was the case with *Cold Heat*. The composer may not have external impulses in mind when writing but, he admits, 'once the piece is finished I can see that sometimes there are inspirations from nature, for example'. Looking back in similar fashion, it's easy to hear *Cold Heat* not as an intertextual abstraction but a geological drama of ice and boiling steam.

Robin Holloway
(born 1943)

Fifth Concerto for Orchestra (2009–10)
BBC commission: world premiere

Prom 27 4 August

Following his Schumann-inspired Proms commission of last year comes Robin Holloway's Fifth Concerto for Orchestra – a very different animal to his Fourth (2006–7). That was a work of epic proportions whose first performance was abridged. (The complete work spans 75 minutes.)

The Fifth Concerto was commissioned at a much smaller scale, something which Holloway admits does not come naturally to him – 'length is my natural way of being as a composer,' he says. One model to which he turned for guidance was Schoenberg's Five Orchestral Pieces, 'a large piece in a short duration', whose intense language became a useful example; a series of requests for miniatures in the year after composing the Fourth Concerto was also instructive.

A new density of textures emerged. In part this derived from Holloway's experience of revisiting his younger self as he set about the task of recopying his First Concerto for Orchestra (1966–9), a youthful piece of great concentration.

The first movement of the Fifth contains some of the composer's most opaque counterpoint (he describes it as 'black'), whereas the second has a volatile transparency. The remaining three movements attempt to reconcile these extremes of mood. Scale remains but, as Holloway describes it, it is the scale of a Manhattan – when sprawl is impossible, you must build upwards instead.

Simon Holt
(born 1958)

Centauromachy (2010)
London premiere

Prom 34 9 August

Since writing his violin concerto *witness to a snow miracle* (2005), Simon Holt claims to have become 'particularly interested in freeing up players much more'. In that earlier piece, the violinist breaks free from the orchestra in just one of the seven short movements. In *Centauromachy*, for clarinet, flugelhorn and orchestra, the two soloists not only break free from the orchestra but also from each other, a whirling loss of control that mirrors, perhaps, the dual nature of the mythical centaur, whose part-horse part-man form combines impulsive lustfulness and civilised wisdom.

The work's five movements not only depict scenes from Centaur mythology – Chiron, the most intelligent and noble of Centaurs, is shown dreaming and is memorialised in a closing elegy; the fourth movement tells of a battle between the Centaurs and the Lapiths (the 'Centauromachy' of the title), triggered by the centaurs' debauchery at a Lapith wedding – but also reflect upon the Centaurs' tortured duality.

'The idea of the concerto allows you this possibility, almost demands it of you: the individual or individuals pitted against the mass of the orchestra and coming awry,' Holt says with regard to the musical possibilities of freedom and constraint, and it is possible to hear this double concerto as a meditation on the struggle and consequences of maintaining such opposing forces within one body.

Thomas Larcher
(born 1963)

Concerto for Violin, Cello and Orchestra (2010–11)
BBC commission: world premiere

Prom 45 18 August

Already highly regarded as a pianist and festival director, Thomas Larcher has only allowed his compositional work to step into the limelight over the past decade. In that short time the concerto has become an important form for him: this will be his sixth.

It's his first double concerto, however, and Larcher has devised an innovative approach to the particular challenges this presents. Placed between the two soloists (violinist Viktoria Mullova and cellist Matthew Barley) and the orchestra will be a 'concertino' ensemble of accordion, drummer, electric zither and Larcher himself on prepared piano. The predominant music is, he says, 'solemn, sacred, very rhythmical … like many voices chattering'. The concertino's role is to introduce a range of colours against this orchestral background – not in a confrontational way but as foreground highlights. The piece will also be notable for its use of improvisation.

The instigation here was the mercurial cellist Barley, who encouraged an initially reluctant Larcher to incorporate free elements for the first time in his music. The concertino players as well as the soloists will have improvisational passages and the intention is to extend this into the orchestra. Nevertheless, Larcher insists that his instincts are Classically grounded. 'Composing is going into my musical roots – Mozart, Bach, Beethoven – and finding something there. I can find new things when I go into the old things.'

Colin Matthews
(born 1946)

No Man's Land (2011)
world premiere

Prom 50 21 August

No Man's Land arose from what Colin Matthews describes as an obsession with the First World War. His grandfather was killed on the Somme in 1916 and Matthews's 1993 piece *Memorial* was inspired by the cemetery at Thiepval where he is buried. However, the composer was keen to create something that, despite the presence of a solo tenor and baritone (Ian Bostridge and Roderick Williams in this world premiere performance), was not in the shadow of Britten's *War Requiem*.

'I had long conversations with the poet Christopher Reid to see how we might make something work that had no reference to any of the well-known war poetry,' he says. In the end Reid devised a scenario from his *Airs and Ditties of No Man's Land* involving two soldiers whose corpses hang on barbed wire in no-man's-land. As they do so, scraps of song, memories and reflections pass through their minds.

The work is also dedicated to the late conductor Richard Hickox, who called Matthews in November 2008 'with his usual infectious enthusiam' to request a piece to mark the 40th anniversary of his founding of the City of London Sinfonia. Matthews was happy to oblige and *No Man's Land* is the result. Sadly, that phone call was Hickox's only involvement with the piece: he died just three days later.

Henry Purcell (1659–95)
arr. **Joby Talbot** (born 1971)

Chacony in G minor (2011)
BBC commission: world premiere

Prom 41 14 August

In his 50th-birthday year, Benjamin Britten compiled a Proms programme that included his own arrangement of Purcell's famous Chacony in G minor. That programme is being recreated for this year's Proms but this time the task of arranging Purcell falls to Joby Talbot – himself 40 this year.

Talbot, also known for his film and TV scores and his arrangements for pop bands such as The Divine Comedy, has a long-standing fondness for Purcell. 'Some of my earliest formative musical memories are of singing Purcell's music with my school choir. I clearly remember being struck by the complexity of the counterpoint and the strangely sinuous beauty of the harmony.'

Purcell's Chacony is one of only two complete surviving works he wrote for four strings and is written in the composer's typically precise, poignantly understated style. Britten's 1963 arrangement opened the work up to full string orchestra but changed little of the original except in terms of dynamics and occasional rhythms. In contrast, Talbot will be taking a freer hand: 'All Purcell's notes are there but presented in a very different way to the familiar versions for strings. Enveloping and growing out from the original material are newly composed elements which form a parallel, complementary musical narrative that I hope will allow us to hear this masterpiece in a new light,' he says.

John Tavener
(born 1944)

Popule meus (2009)
UK premiere

Proms Saturday Matinee 4 3 September

'O my people, what have I done to you?' Christ's words from the Cross are among the most resonant in Christian scripture but John Tavener finds in them a universal message that transcends theological boundaries.

Although Greek Orthodoxy has long been an essential inspiration for Tavener, in recent years teachings from other faiths have become just as important. In *Popule meus*, he takes Christianity's defining moment of crisis – Christ's plea to a people who have abandoned him – and seeks its resolution within the Hindu concept of the unity of the Self with the Absolute. That is, that man's spirit is part of the Universal Divinity; no matter how much man rejects God, he cannot escape this fact. Like an ikon, mantra or koan, Tavener's music speaks both enigmatically and directly – it is an object for contemplation rather than analysis, intended for the spirit, not the mind.

In *Popule meus* Tavener returns for the first time since *The Protecting Veil* (1988) to writing for solo cello and strings but adds a part for solo timpani as well. The cello represents the all-compassionate God, while the timpani represent man's attempts at rejection. Over four repetitions of the musical material the timpani become increasingly violent and overpowering, while the cello and strings remain serene. In the end, Tavener says, 'even in winning, the Darkness loses, and even in losing, the Light wins'.

Kevin Volans
(born 1949)

Piano Concerto No. 3 (2011)
BBC co-commission with RTÉ: world premiere

Prom 51 22 August

Kevin Volans would prefer not to reveal anything about his pieces. 'I think anything said about them limits the way in which people listen to them,' he says.

For 30 years the South African-Irish composer has increasingly sought to capture musical moments as naturalistically and as clearly as possible, without any need for argument or development – he calls it a 'non-conceptual' or 'existential' approach. Rather like Japanese art, Volans's music simply presents a moment or an object, without a view to its origins or future potential. 'When I begin to write, I have little or no idea what I will write, what the material will be or where it will lead me,' he says. Instead, he devises 'strategies', or abstract principles that will determine the creative direction of a piece.

In his Piano Concerto No. 3 this takes the form of an alternation of static and forward-moving music. Each interrupts the other, 'rather like layers being stripped away and revealing another beneath, and then another'. There are two homages, one explicit, the other hidden. The piece was written to mark the bicentenary of Liszt, three bars of whose Second Piano Concerto are quoted in modified form; in the differing degrees of rhythmic order and disorder Volans also hears an implied homage to his late teacher, Karlheinz Stockhausen, on whose birthday the concerto will be given its premiere.

Judith Weir
(born 1954)

Stars, Night, Music and Light (2011)
BBC commission: world premiere
Prom 1 15 July

Proms Director Roger Wright has described contemporary music as the 'centre of gravity' of the Proms, so it's apt that the first music heard at this year's festival will be brand-new.

This short choral fanfare by leading British composer Judith Weir was commissioned with the idea not only of demonstrating the Proms' commitment to new music but also of forming a bridge between the First Night and the Last, which will begin with its own fanfare, by Sir Peter Maxwell Davies *(see earlier panel)*.

It will also start things off with a flourish: Weir is especially renowned for her theatrical and vocal music – her most recent opera, *Miss Fortune (Achterbahn)*, for the Bregenz Festival, was being completed at the same time as she was writing this fanfare – and this piece will surely start this year's festivities in fitting style.

Stars, Night, Music and Light will make full use of the combined forces of the BBC Symphony Orchestra and Chorus. Weir has long been fond of retelling folk tales, from a wide variety of traditons, but the text for the present work is simply the four words of the title, which have been extracted from lines written by the 17th-century poet and Anglican priest George Herbert, whose work Weir has set before in her *Two Human Hymns* (1995) and in *Vertue* (2005): 'The starres have us to bed / Night draws the curtain, which the sunne withdraws / Musick and light attend our head'.

Stevie Wishart

Out of This World (2011)
BBC commission: world premiere

Proms Saturday Matinee 3 27 August

Composer and performer Stevie Wishart is equally at home playing the medieval hurdy-gurdy and researching new interfaces for controlling computers with musical gestures. Although her initial studies were in electronic and contemporary composition, she was subsequently drawn to medieval music, and as a composer she often works with both ancient and modern musical traditions.

'In early music one finds contemporaneity and freshness,' she says, 'especially with regard to how music and text are combined to create song.' The four songs which comprise *Out of this World* are settings of texts by the 12th-century abbess and visionary Hildegard of Bingen, something Wishart has wanted to do for some time.

Some of the texts separate male and female voices and the composer says that utilising highly contrasting voices was one of her initial inspirations for the piece. The individual personalities of the BBC Singers are a start but, by also using singers from her own early music ensemble Sinfonye, she hopes to find 'even greater, and somewhat precarious, vocal contrasts'.

Wishart describes *Out of this World* as a sonic tapestry that has gradually materialised; the music is made up of 'frayed threads from hundreds of years ago, woven into a new pattern, design, form and timbre – but always a bit eroded at the edges, so that it can freely unravel as the songs are heard'.

Proms Plus Portraits

This year's Proms Plus Portraits at the Royal College of Music offer the chance to hear chamber music by Pascal Dusapin, Graham Fitkin, Thomas Larcher and Kevin Volans prior to premieres of their works at the Royal Albert Hall later the same evening. In each event the composer talks about his music, in conversation with a Radio 3 presenter.

Pascal Dusapin 27 July, 5.15pm
Trio Rombach
Musicians from the Guildhall School of Music & Drama
Presented by Andrew McGregor

Graham Fitkin 31 August, 5.45pm
Sciosophy; Hurl; Sinew
Musicians from the London Sinfonietta Academy Ensemble
Presented by Tom Service

Thomas Larcher 18 August, 5.15pm
Cello Sonata – final mvmt; Kraken – mvmts 3 & 4; Antennen-Requiem für H.
Musicians from the Royal Northern College of Music
Presented by Andrew McGregor

Kevin Volans 22 August, 5.45pm
Programme to include:
1,000 Bars; Asanga
Musicians from the Royal Academy of Music
Presented by Tom Service

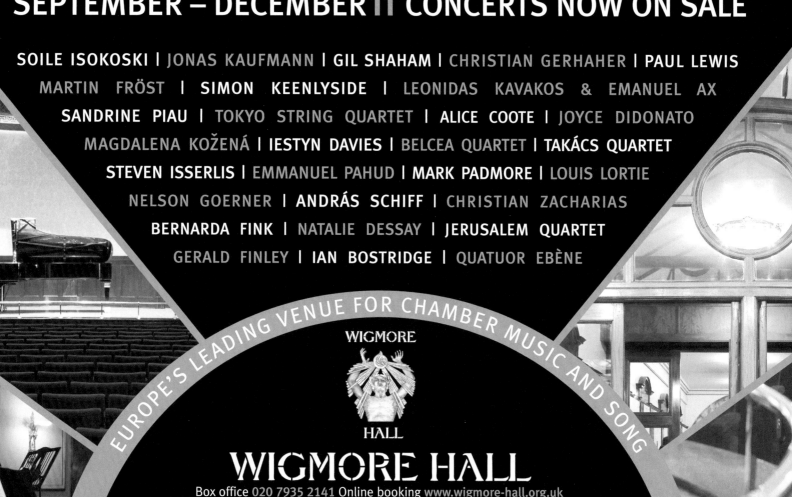

Featured Artists

As well as tracing a wider view of a composer's output, the Proms also allows a deeper engagement with a number of multi-faceted artists. Jessica Duchen shines a light on their return appearances.

I t's a familiar sensation. You hear a soloist whose performance stuns you for the short time they're on stage. A fine Chopin piano concerto can leave you wondering how the same pianist would play Prokofiev; a Romantic violin concerto could make you curious to hear the fiddler in chamber music or something contemporary. Instead, they disappear after a single piece and you end up surfing listings websites for signs of a return visit sooner than three years away.

In recent years, though, the Proms has been dealing with this problem by inviting a small number of artists to appear not just once, but twice or perhaps three times each. It's a chance to get to know their work better through a wider range of repertory and performing contexts.

The first of this year's returning artists is also the youngest: the British pianist Benjamin Grosvenor, who turns 19 this summer. An unassuming young man from Southend-on-Sea, he has been hailed as one of the most important new talents to emerge anywhere in the world in recent years. Piano finalist of the BBC Young Musician of the Year when he was only 11, he was soon the subject of a programme in BBC TV's *Imagine* series and is now participating in BBC Radio 3's New Generation Artists scheme. He takes centre stage for the First Night, playing Liszt's Piano Concerto No. 2, launching at the same time the season's bicentenary celebrations of the composer.

It's Grosvenor's first ever Prom – which, he admits, is both a daunting prospect and a thrilling one. 'I played once at the Royal Albert Hall when I was 13,' he says, 'and I found that, when you rehearse in the hall while it's empty, it seems huge; but amazingly it feels quite intimate when you're on the stage and the audience is there. And an event

Georgia Bertazzi (Tetzlaff); Shutterstock.com; J. Henry Fair (Ax); Anne-Marie Le Blé (Bullock); Michael Tammaro/Virgin Classics (G. Capuçon); Simon Fowler/Virgin Classics (R. Capuçon); Peter Warren (Connolly)

Emanuel Ax   Susan Bullock   Gautier Capuçon   Renaud Capuçon   Sarah Connolly

like the First Night of the Proms … well!' He is certainly excited about the concerto: 'It's a wonderful piece, very expansive and lyrical. It'll be fun to play.' Later he is back to perform Britten's Piano Concerto with the National Youth Orchestra.

But it's not the last of Liszt: both his piano concertos (as well as the shorter *Totentanz* for piano and orchestra) will appear this summer, with No. 1 in the capable hands of the Chinese superstar Lang Lang – who, on the Last Night, will also perform Chopin's *Grande Polonaise brillante*, having hotfooted it over to the Royal Albert Hall after performing earlier the same evening at Hyde Park's Proms in the Park event.

The German violinist Christian Tetzlaff features in three different Proms: performing Brahms's Violin Concerto, the UK premiere of a new concerto by Sir Harrison Birtwistle and a lunchtime recital of Mozart and Bartók at Cadogan Hall with his long-standing duo partner Lars Vogt. Tetzlaff's full-blooded, eloquent tone is channelled not through a famous instrument made by Stradivarius or a member of the Guarneri family, but a very modern violin by the German luthier Stefan-Peter Greiner – as suitable for up-to-the-minute music as for Classical-period repertory.

'It's a piece of wood, like all the others,' Tetzlaff says with gentle irony. 'The old instruments are fantastic and have survived all their adaptations into modern violin set-ups. But there's no reason why a maker with an incredible ear can't build good instruments today. Some people enjoy the mystique around the cost and the age of those great violins, but for me the music is mysterious enough in itself.'

There's an unusual reason, too, for his love of playing at the Proms: 'What I like is that the hall is always warm,' he declares. 'I love playing when it's warm! I always think that, emotionally, one is rather more open when one is on the warm side. If you have to put a scarf around your throat, you don't let go so much. Letting go can happen very easily at the Proms, for players and audience alike.'

Tetzlaff's first appearance is in a work in which he can let go more than most: Brahms's Violin Concerto. 'For me it's the most beautiful concerto of all, the most fascinating piece, and I'm happy whenever I have the chance to play it. The seemingly serene and beautiful quality of the opening soon moves on to violent depths: it's a work of huge scope. That, to me, makes it very close to real life.'

But he has also been busy getting to grips with the brand-new Birtwistle concerto, which will no doubt showcase a very different side of him. 'So far, I know what my own part sounds like and I can see the shape of the piece,' he says. 'It seems very communicative and I am really enthusiastic about it.'

Viktoria Mullova is the other violinist making a return visit, together with her cellist husband, Matthew Barley. Their two concerts are on the same night. Russian-born Mullova is an exceptionally versatile performer, her range extending from full-blown Romantic concertos to an equal expertise on period instruments; she also enjoys playing chamber music with her own ensemble. Barley is widely admired for his groundbreaking work in educational initiatives, improvisation and contemporary music. The pair will play a double concerto written for them by the Austrian composer Thomas Larcher; and after a scant break to catch their breath, they are back for the Late Night Prom, combining Hungarian music with the folk and jazz worlds.

Among the singers being featured across the season is the much-loved British mezzo-soprano Sarah Connolly, who is a soloist in both Beethoven's *Missa solemnis* and Mendelssohn's *Elijah*. She describes the Proms as 'the most inclusive, diverse and eclectic celebration of music in the world. There are always wonderful surprises to be heard and seen. The Proms audience is also the best in the world and I feel honoured to sing before them.'

More voices to relish include the mezzo-soprano Christine Rice, who appears in Havergal Brian's gigantic 'The Gothic' Symphony and Britten's *Spring Symphony*; bass Matthew Rose, who is in Rossini's *William Tell* and joins Connolly in the Beethoven *Missa solemnis*; and last but not least, the dramatic soprano Susan Bullock, who will assume two very different guises – starring in the first ever Comedy Prom and then, at the Last Night, in the heroic Immolation Scene from Wagner's *Götterdämmerung*.

The spotlight also falls on one of today's top flautists. Emmanuel Pahud has been visiting the Proms for some 20 years as principal flautist of the Berlin Philharmonic, but with his soloist's hat on he ▶

David Goode   Benjamin Grosvenor   Marc-André Hamelin   Lang Lang

Matthew Barley

Malcolm Crowthers (Goode); Laurie Lewis (Grosvenor); Fran Kaufman (Hamelin); Philip Glaser (Lang); Nick White (Barley)

has transformed for a new century both his instrument's image and its repertory. Many leading composers have written for him, secure in the knowledge that his technique and colouristic range will allow them to reach for the musical sky. Pahud is bringing two recent concertos – by Marc-André Dalbavie and Elliott Carter (now 102 and still composing). He also has a Cadogan Hall lunchtime Prom with the pianist Eric Le Sage.

Carter's concerto seems to mirror the way that different individuals or cultures contribute to society, Pahud suggests: 'Everybody brings a new colour, a new note,' he says. 'The flute throws out a note; that note is taken over and held by an instrument in the orchestra. Gradually by adding all these notes a melody emerges on the flute and a certain harmony from the orchestra.' By contrast, Dalbavie's work is 'a really French concerto, taking ingredients from French culture and all that it has achieved for flute and orchestra in the 20th century and building up from there. Dalbavie starts where Ibert's concerto – which closes with a dazzling third movement – leaves off, stunning the audience with a virtuosic beginning. Dalbavie's own ending is a kind of battle between the flute and the orchestra.'

And the winner of the battle is … ? 'You'll see!' Pahud laughs. Still, the real winner from these featured artists' return visits is surely the audience itself. ●

Jessica Duchen writes about music for *The Independent* and is also the author of four novels, two biographies and several stage works.

Featured Artists at the Proms

Emanuel Ax *piano*
Brahms Piano Concerto No. 1 Prom 47, 19 August
Brahms Piano Concerto No. 2 Prom 49, 20 August

Susan Bullock *soprano*
Comedy Prom Prom 40, 13 August
Wagner Götterdämmerung – Immolation Scene
(Act 3); **Arne** Rule, Britannia! Prom 74, 10 September

Renaud Capuçon *violin* & **Gautier Capuçon** *cello*
Beethoven Triple Concerto
(with Martha Argerich *piano*) Prom 5, 18 July
Brahms Double Concerto Prom 6, 19 July

Sarah Connolly *mezzo-soprano*
Mendelssohn Elijah Prom 58, 28 August
Beethoven Missa solemnis Prom 67, 4 September

David Goode *organ*
Janáček Glagolitic Mass Prom 1, 15 July
Brian Symphony No. 1, 'The Gothic' Prom 4, 17 July
Michael Berkeley Organ Concerto
London premiere Prom 65, 3 September

Benjamin Grosvenor *piano*
Liszt Piano Concerto No. 2 Prom 1, 15 July
Britten Piano Concerto Prom 30, 6 August

Marc-André Hamelin *piano*
Liszt recital Prom 54, 24 August
Rachmaninov Rhapsody on a Theme of Paganini
Prom 65, 3 September

Lang Lang *piano*
Liszt Piano Concerto No. 1; **Chopin** Grande
Polonaise brillante Prom 74, 10 September
Proms in the Park (Hyde Park), 10 September

Dejan Lazić *piano*
Brahms, arr. Lazić 'Piano Concerto No. 3'
(after Violin Concerto) Prom 37, 11 August
Liszt Totentanz Prom 63, 2 September

Viktoria Mullova *violin* & **Matthew Barley** *cello*
Thomas Larcher Double Concerto Prom 45, 18 August
Hungarian, folk and jazz music Prom 46, 18 August

Emmanuel Pahud *flute*
Marc-André Dalbavie Flute Concerto *London premiere*
Elliott Carter Flute Concerto *UK premiere*
Prom 18, 28 July
Works by **Henri Dutilleux**, **Martinů** and **Prokofiev**
(with Eric Le Sage *piano*) Proms Chamber Music 6,
22 August

Christine Rice *mezzo-soprano*
Brian Symphony No. 1, 'The Gothic' Prom 4, 17 July
Britten Spring Symphony Prom 41, 14 August

Matthew Rose *bass*
Rossini William Tell Prom 2, 16 July
Beethoven Missa solemnis Prom 67, 4 September

Christian Tetzlaff *violin*
Brahms Violin Concerto Prom 32, 7 August
Works by **Bartók** and **Mozart** (with Lars Vogt *piano*)
Proms Chamber Music 8, 5 September
Sir Harrison Birtwistle Concerto for Violin
and Orchestra *UK premiere* Prom 70, 7 September

Dejan Lazić Viktoria Mullova Emmanuel Pahud Christine Rice Matthew Rose Christian Tetzlaff

Susan Bullock … will assume two very different guises – starring in the first ever Comedy Prom and then, at the Last Night, in the heroic Immolation Scene from Wagner's *Götterdämmerung*.

Radio 3 producer Roger Short introduces the Human Planet Prom, celebrating BBC One's recent landmark *Human Planet* series, and Radio 3's ambitious complementary world music exploration, *Music Planet*

SOUNDS FROM THE
HUMAN PLANET

I hadn't actually planned to share a twin room with Radio 3 presenter Andy Kershaw – people might talk – but at our wooden-hut guesthouse in Tembin, Papua New Guinea, there was really no choice. There's not much of anything from the modern world in Tembin – no running water, no electricity, no road except for a dirt track – just some of the most gorgeous, lush coastal scenery to be found anywhere in the world, and some pretty wonderful music. At dawn we were gently awoken by some serene vocal harmonies floating across from the hut opposite. We just had to have this particular song for the Radio 3 *Music Planet* programme we were making, so we rushed over to find out more. What had inspired such heavenly sounds, we wondered? 'Killing,' said the one singer who could manage some words of English. Killing what – fish,

jungle animals? 'People,' he replied, 'killing people.' It turns out that headhunting finally died out in Papua New Guinea only in the 1950s, and this song was a reminder of that recently vanished tradition.

It was two years ago that BBC TV Executive Producer Dale Templar approached Radio 3's *World Routes* team suggesting we do a companion series to their planned blockbuster, *Human Planet* – the first time the BBC Natural History Unit had made a series about people. It was to focus on some of the extraordinary ways in which humans have adapted to their environment, and exploring the music of the cultures featured in the series seemed a natural step – hence Radio 3's *Music Planet*.

One of the first ideas for the TV series was to feature the shark-callers of Tembin. The fishermen of this shark-fishing community sing above water to

Music Planet presenter Andy Kershaw (*far right*) and engineer James Birtwistle (*second from left*), with the shark-callers of Tembin, Papua New Guinea

lure their prey to the surface. It took the TV crew a full six weeks of patient waiting before the sharks finally performed for the cameras – and during their long nights in the wooden hut, the crew was serenaded by Tembin's local musicians, performing a whole repertory of songs devoted to slaughtering sharks. This is what Andy and I had crossed half the world for, and we weren't disappointed. And now we're thrilled that we'll be meeting the musicians again in this summer's Human Planet Prom, as the Bibilang Shark-Calling Group make their first ever trip outside Papua New Guinea.

For this celebration of music from the TV and radio series, Charles Hazlewood conducts the BBC Concert Orchestra in highlights from Nitin Sawhney's evocative score for the TV programmes, complete with big-screen projections of some of *Human Planet*'s most breathtaking scenes, and live narration on stage from actor John Hurt. Radio 3's *Music Planet* is represented by five artists from the series. Our shark-calling friends from Papua New Guinea featured in the opening 'Oceans' programme. From the 'Arctic' episode comes Ayarkhaan, a

female trio hailing from the coldest city on earth – Yakutsk in Russia's Sakha Republic – who will be making their UK debut armed only with their voices and their Jew's harps. Their music, they say, mirrors the extremes of their Arctic climate. Also from the Arctic programme, we welcome Rasmus Lyberth, Greenland's greatest singer, who insists that a massive voice is required to communicate across the frozen expanses of his homeland. Africa is represented by Enock Mbongwe, a Tonga river-dweller from Zambia who sings bluesy songs to the accompaniment of his musical bow. And from the grasslands of Mongolia we have Khusugtun, a group Radio 3 presenter Lucy Duran and my producer colleague James Parkin discovered in Ulan Bator: virtuoso throat-singers who deserve an international reputation. And, as a bonus in this Human Planet Prom, we also hear the premiere of a Scrapheap Symphony – a foretaste of the forthcoming BBC TV series in which the BBC Concert Orchestra gets to grips with instruments created from junk objects found in the unlikeliest of places.

As a warm-up to the Prom, there's a special Human Planet in the Park afternoon *(see right)* – free family events in Kensington Gardens, providing a taster of some of the *Music Planet* artists appearing in the Prom, as well as showcasing special projects from the BBC Singers and BBC Concert Orchestra. There's also a chance to get hands-on with the Scrapheap Symphony instruments.

So right now, in preparation for the Prom, the Bibilang Shark-Calling Group will be busy arranging their first passports, applying for their visas, fumigating their log drum and buying their first ever suitcases for their epic journey halfway across the world. For them, as well as for us, the Human Planet Prom promises to be a unique and memorable experience. ●

Roger Short is a Senior Producer for BBC Radio 3, working extensively on world music programmes, including *World on 3* and the recent *Music Planet* series.

Ayarkhaan, the Jew's harp-playing trio from the Russian Republic of Sakha

© Tim Allen/BBC (p.84, main image & inset); Marvin Ware/BBC (bottom left); Roger Short/BBC (top right)

Human Planet at the Proms
Saturday 23 & Sunday 24 July

Human Planet in the Park
23 July, 1.00pm–5.00pm, Kensington Gardens, *admission free*

Human Planet Park Stage Experience live performances by artists ranging from international musicians featured in the Human Planet Prom to the BBC Proms Family Orchestra and Chorus. Bring a picnic and enjoy the afternoon with the whole family!

Human Planet Workshops (various times)
From learning new dance moves to writing your own poetry, from creating your own percussion instruments to folk-singing – a range of workshops for all the family (recommended age 7+), inspired by music traditions from around the world. See bbc.co.uk/proms for more details. *Please note: workshop places are unticketed, but limited by capacity; queues may be likely for entrance into popular sessions.*

Prom Plus Intro
23 July, 5.45pm–6.30pm, Royal College of Music *admission free*
Music Planet producer James Parkin discusses his journeys across six continents in making the radio series, in conversation with *Human Planet* series producer Dale Templar. Presented by Louise Fryer.

Human Planet Prom
23 July, 7.30pm & 24 July, 11.00am, Royal Albert Hall
Music from the *Human Planet* and *Music Planet* series

The London Women's Clinic

Proud sponsors of

The Choir of
St John's College, Cambridge
Quincentenary Concert
Royal Festival Hall
15 December 2011

www.sjcchoir.co.uk

IVF and fertility clinics
London, Darlington, Swansea and Cardiff

www.londonwomensclinic.com

As soon as the movies learnt to talk they also learnt to sing and dance. Following his sensational MGM and Rodgers & Hammerstein Proms tributes of the past two seasons, John Wilson returns for 'more of not quite the same', as he explains to **David Benedict**

Hooray for Hollywood

U nscrupulous managements attempting to energise sluggish sales have been known to brandish the phrase 'back by popular demand' a shade deceitfully. But applying that catchphrase to John Wilson and his orchestra is the unvarnished truth.

His 2009 Proms salute to the music of MGM film musicals wasn't just a concert, it was a sensation. The audience in the hall that night simply roared its appreciation for his scintillating players letting rip with such rhapsodic music.

Wilson laughs on recalling the occasion. 'The atmosphere on stage was electrifying – even at the dress rehearsal all the musicians were talking about it. Sir Thomas Allen, one of our soloists, said that in 40 years of music-making he'd never known anything like it. We'd been building up to that particular concert for years. We knew it would be such fun.'

What Wilson didn't know was quite how much fun audiences worldwide were having by listening on radio and watching on TV – not to mention the repeat broadcasts, catching up via the BBC iPlayer, and the inevitable DVD release. But he wasn't slow to find out.

'Ten minutes after the concert I turned on my phone and there were 138 text messages. Over the next two days I received nigh on 1,000 e-mails. Within a couple of weeks we had received literally tens of thousands. The BBC was still receiving phone calls and enquiries on Christmas Eve.'

Poster for George and Ira Gershwin's *Shall We Dance*, one of the 10 films in which Astaire and Rogers appeared together

Small wonder, then, that after last year's return with a concert devoted to the film musicals of Rodgers and Hammerstein, he's back for what he describes as 'more of not quite the same'.

'Hooray for Hollywood' is Wilson's personal celebration of the movie musical, from its inception at the end of the 1920s through its so-called Golden Age in the 1940s and 1950s, to its last blast at the end of the 1960s. Having previously drawn on scores written for the MGM studios, his new selection comes predominantly from elsewhere, including Warner Bros., where it all began with the birth of the 'talkie' and where the 'backstage' film was perfected, the genre depicting the tribulations of putting on a show as epitomised by *42nd Street*.

That film's title song is being played – as are two others, from the series created at RKO, the

The Hollywood studios were home to the best composers, lyricists and orchestrators, all writing for the cream of America's performers.

studio that in 1933 teamed up Frederick 'Fritz' Austerlitz and Virginia Katherine McMath. Who? Step forward Fred Astaire and Ginger Rogers. The title numbers of George and Ira Gershwin's *Shall We Dance* and Irving Berlin's *Top Hat* are two of five of their effervescent dance duets that Wilson will conduct.

Another Astaire number is on the bill. 'This Heart of Mine', an extravagant duet with Lucille Bremer from *Ziegfeld Follies* (1945), is heard in

Conrad Salinger's glorious arrangement, replete with multiple climaxes. But it's not just numbers written for stars that have governed Wilson's choices. He's also been juggling treasures from 40 years' worth of famous titles, illustrious composers and, most especially, Hollywood's unsung heroes, the arrangers – masterssuch as Max Steiner, Robert Russell Bennett and Ray Heindorf, who polished musical riffs into shimmering routines and turned songs into music dramas.

'I want this concert to be a faithful and authentic presentation of these miniature works of art,' says Wilson. 'They're beautifully crafted, incredibly finely honed pieces and they're the result of what I can only describe as a kind of conveyor belt of expertise.' That's an understatement. The Hollywood studios were home to the best composers, lyricists and orchestrators, all writing for the cream of America's performers. And that included the orchestral players, who had to be exceptionally versatile, capable of playing everything from *Ben-Hur* to syncopated dance routines and *Tom and Jerry* cartoons.

'For three decades almost nobody left those orchestras,' Wilson explains. 'They became like repertory companies of virtuoso players devoted to undreamt-of levels of excellence and refinement.'

To match that standard, Wilson cherry-picks the players for his John Wilson Orchestra, creating a marriage between a full symphony orchestra and a jazz big band with, for example, the woodwinds

Hooray for Hollywood

Music from the Golden Age of the movie musical, including excerpts from *42nd Street*, *Top Hat*, *Strike Up the Band*, *Swing Time* and *Shall We Dance*

Prom 59, 29 August

all doubling as saxophonists. 'You also need players right through the string section with a jazz sensibility, but who could also play a late-Romantic solo concerto at the drop of a hat – the sound needs that sort of ardour.' That would explain why, for the 2009 MGM Prom, a staggering 17 of the violinists were *leaders* (not so-called rank-and-file players) of international orchestras.

'This music makes them sound like a million dollars, because it shows everybody off, but it's a pig to play! Those Hollywood orchestras were so great, featuring such virtuoso players, that the music was often written to the extremities of playing capabilities. Anything was possible. We're trying to get somewhere near that in one concert. It's a tall order!' ●

David Benedict is the chief London critic for *Variety*.

John Wilson conducting at the MGM film musicals Prom in 2009

RKO Radio Pictures Inc./akg-images (p88, 'Swing Time,' 1936); RKO Radio Pictures Inc./Photofest/Lebrecht Music & Arts (above); Chris Christodoulou/BBC (below right)

Talented Dancer or Musician?
Then your future is **made**

Yes, TALENT is ALL you need for a place at a MADE school.

All our schools are dedicated to encouraging talented young people from all financial and cultural backgrounds... we can offer up to 100% Government funding for places.

MADE schools are committed to the highest teaching standards in Music and Dance, as well as an excellent academic education.

If you are interested in one of the MADE schools just visit our website for contact details.

www.made-schools.org.uk

There are nine MADE schools throughout the UK

- Chetham's School of Music, Manchester
- Elmhurst School for Dance, Birmingham
- St Mary's Music School, Edinburgh
- The Hammond, Chester
- The Purcell School for Young Musicians, Herts
- The Royal Ballet School, London
- Tring Park School for the Performing Arts, Herts
- Wells Cathedral School, Somerset
- Yehudi Menuhin School, Surrey

THE 9 SCHOOLS OF
**MUSIC AND DANCE
EXCELLENCE** **made**

Proms

Whether you want to listen to lively expert introductions, explore literary connections, or bring along the family to sing, play or scrape, Nick Kimberley is your genial guide to the myriad ways of getting closer to the music during this summer's Proms

I t could be a children's story: the music festival that grew and grew and grew. As if filling the Royal Albert Hall for two months was not enough, in its recent history the BBC Proms has expanded in all directions, not only into nearby Cadogan Hall, but also into public parks up and down the country. Yet the most explosive growth has been in the series of ancillary events gathered together under the capacious umbrella of Proms Plus.

And what a huge number of pluses there are this year: opportunities to hear musicians talking about their favourite literature, an encounter in Kensington Gardens with music and performers from all over the planet, even a session on junkyard instruments. You can join the Proms Family Orchestra and Chorus or take part in music-

Plus

inspired poetry workshops. Or why not drop into the Royal College of Music, just across the road from the Royal Albert Hall Box Office, and, as part of RCM Sparks 2011, take part in a day of creative music-making? Then again, if you are aged 12 to 18, you might want to take advantage of the Inspire Young Composers' Competition for the opportunity to hone your compositional skills, with a little helpful advice from the professionals.

It's a veritable festival within a festival, and the aim is to offer something for people of every age to enjoy, whether actively making music or simply enjoying the act of listening. Some will be long-standing Prom-goers, others might be moved to go to a Prom for the first time; all are welcome, everyone can find something to make their own. In some respects it's all a long way from Sir Henry Wood's original concept of the Proms, but in other ways it isn't at all. If Wood had been a politician, his Proms slogan might have been 'Access, access, access'. That is precisely what Proms Plus offers.

Pre-concert talks are nothing new at the Proms; there have been similar events since the 1970s. Only in recent years, though, has the programme become so far-reaching, embracing family occasions, composer portraits, workshops, singalongs and such innovations as Proms Out+About, a free concert in which the BBC Symphony Orchestra joins local choirs and schoolchildren at Westfield shopping centre in West London to give a surprise preview of the coming season: 2011 will be third year in which shoppers have been serenaded in this delightful way.

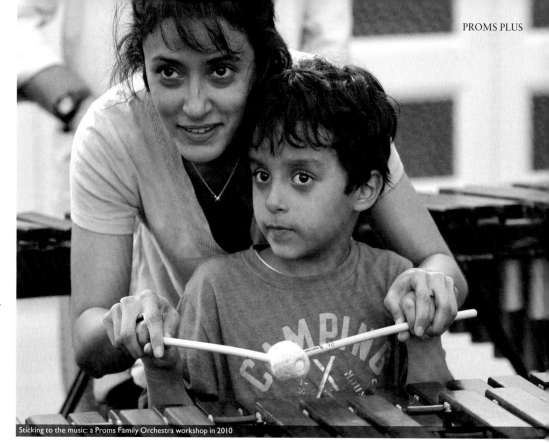

Sticking to the music: a Proms Family Orchestra workshop in 2010

PROMS PLUS INTROS

The music played at the Proms must, first and foremost, be capable of standing on its own but it does no harm to have an expert on hand to guide you through its twists and turns. Have you ever wondered why an Italian composer, Rossini, brought his operatic career to a close with a French grand opera about a Swiss freedom-fighter? Let the Proms Plus Intro make everything clear before the Academy of Santa Cecilia's complete performance of *Guillaume Tell* (16 July, prior to Prom 2). Have you ever been thrilled by the heaven-storming music of Verdi's *Requiem*? Semyon Bychkov conducts the BBC Symphony Orchestra in a starry performance (24 July, Prom 13); Proms Plus Intro sets the scene. Does the idea of Mahler excite you, but you've never found a way into his music? Let musicians from the

Stuttgart Radio Symphony Orchestra lead the way with some well-chosen examples before they deliver the composer's Ninth Symphony in all its magnificence (25 July, Prom 14). Going further back into musical history, you may perhaps have wondered what's so serious about *opera seria*; the Proms Plus Intro to Handel's *Rinaldo* (25 August, Prom 55) will shed a little light.

Proms Plus Intros, which take place in the Royal College of Music, are deliberately free of jargon but they are also put together in such a way that novices and aficionados alike will enjoy them. Many offer musical examples played or sung by performers from the evening's concert; others benefit from the lightly worn expertise of musicians, authors, academics and fans. It was back in the 1970s that the Proms came up with the idea of ▶

String theory: a young cellist receives advice at a Proms Family Orchestra workshop in 2010

providing audiences with points of access (that word again) to the music they're about to hear. The Proms Plus series is now as much a part of the festival as the Royal Albert Hall organ or Henry Wood's bust; while the Royal College of Music, imposing and welcoming like the hall itself, has become an honorary annexe, at least for the duration of the Proms season.

PROMS PLUS LATES

If you're not quite ready to leave when the last note of the concert has faded into silence, then the new series of eight Proms Plus Lates offers a kind of decompression chamber. Adjourn to the Royal Albert Hall's Elgar Room for a leisurely drink, some lively conversation and a little bit of poetry and music with up-and-coming young artists – the perfect way to end your evening (15, 22, 30 July; 5, 13, 20, 27 August and 3 September). Free tickets are available to ticket-holders of the evening Prom from Door 6 in the interval of the concert (except 5 August, available 30 minutes before the concert).

PROMS PLUS LITERARY

Since the earliest notes were sounded and the earliest words written, music and literature have enjoyed a healthy symbiosis. Too often, though, they are kept apart, as if each must exist in not-so-splendid isolation. Proms Plus Literary reunites them in a myriad different ways. The part that the cello has played in literary history remains largely unsung, but Peggy Reynolds provides chapter and verse in advance of Jean-Guihen Queyras's performance of Dvořák's Cello Concerto (20 July, Prom 8). Where would musical history be without its numberless retellings of the Faust myth? And what price would you put on your mortal soul? Playwright Mark Ravenhill and novelist Ali Smith strike a Faustian pact to raise the curtain on the London Philharmonic Orchestra's account of Liszt's *A Faust Symphony* (26 July, Prom 15). And, like a thread running through the whole season, a starry line-up of musicians will lay bare their literary enthusiasms: pianist Stephen Hough (30 July, Prom 21), conductor Andrew Litton (20 August, Prom 49), cellist Matthew Barley (27 August, Prom 57) and violinist Tasmin Little (3 September, Prom 65).

In advance of the Proms themselves, the Proms Poetry Competition will be launched in May, inviting contributions from across the age spectrum (age categories are: 7–11, 12–18 and over-18s; and there will be a winner in each category). Entrants will take their inspiration from a piece of music to be performed during the 2011 Proms season. Ian McMillan, poet and presenter of Radio 3's *The Verb*, will be joined by fellow judge and former Children's Laureate Michael Rosen to announce the competition winners at a Proms Plus event at the Royal College of Music on 5 September.

Peggy Reynolds   Mark Ravenhill   Ian McMillan

Proms Poetry Competition

Ian McMillan, presenter of Radio 3's *The Verb*, launches a Proms first in May: a competition for adults and children to write a poem inspired music from this year's Proms season. Former Children's Laureate Michael Rosen will join Ian to announce the winning poems in a Proms Plus Literary event on 5 September for broadcast on Radio 3. *For more information, visit bbc.co.uk/proms.*

Indian Voices in the Park: 2009's park event in Kensington Gardens

Chris Christodoulou/BBC (p94, top left); Ross Marriott (p94, Reynolds); Simon Annand (p94, McMillan); Des Willie (p94, Ravenhill); Chris Christodoulou/BBC (above left)

PROMS PLUS FAMILY

Families come in all shapes and sizes, and Proms Plus Family offers them all a chance to take part. The series of family-friendly introductions probes the stories behind the music, as when musicians from the BBC Scottish Symphony Orchestra precede their all-French concert (3 August, Prom 26) by delving into Debussy's *Prélude à L'après-midi d'un faune* and Ravel's *Daphnis and Chloë*, or when members of the Gustav Mahler Jugendorchester lead you through the pieces they will be playing later that evening (24 August, Prom 53). Each of these Intros presents the opportunity to bring along your own instrument and take part.

If you have a taste for participation, the other strand of Proms Plus Family offers even greater scope to get involved. In a series of two-hour sessions at the Royal College of Music, the Proms Family Orchestra and Chorus takes shape, and then takes wing: the ability to read music is not necessary, enthusiasm is – as is an instrument, which may be just your voice, or one of the array of percussion instruments provided. Professional musicians will be on hand to offer guidance and you can choose which session (or sessions) you want to join: World Music (23 July), Horrible Histories (linked to the CBBC series, 30 July); Mozart and Beethoven (27 August) or Hollywood (29 August).

By the end of each session, as the players and singers grow in confidence, they will take on the task of creating and then performing a new group composition derived from what they have played; the 'world music' orchestra will also have the opportunity to play on the Human Planet stage in Kensington Gardens. If your preference is to explore words on music, you can sign up for one of the two Poetry Workshops. Poet and former Children's Laureate Michael Rosen and Ian McMillan, presenter of Radio 3's *The Verb*, will help the whole family write a poem about a piece of music in this ▶

Proms Plus Family
Proms Plus events for all the family

Proms Plus Family Intro †
Royal College of Music,
Prince Consort Road, London SW7 2BS
An interactive introduction to the music of the Proms
19 July, 5.00pm–6.00pm
3 August, 5.30pm–6.30pm
11 August, 5.30pm–6.30pm
15 August, 5.30pm–6.30pm
24 August, 5.00pm–6.00pm

Proms Plus Family Orchestra & Chorus ‡
Royal College of Music
Creative sessions for all the family
World Music: 23 July, 10.00am–1.30pm
(including a Human Planet in the Park performance
in Kensington Gardens)
Horrible Histories: 30 July, 2.00pm–4.00pm
Mozart and Beethoven: 27 August, 1.00pm–3.00pm
Hollywood: 29 August, 1.00pm–3.00pm

Human Planet in the Park †
Kensington Gardens, London
An afternoon of performances, workshops and other events, showcasing music and arts from around the world, prior to the evening's Human Planet Prom
23 July, 1.00pm–5.00pm (see page 85 for details)

Poetry Workshops
Kensington Gardens (23 July †) and
Elgar Room, Royal Albert Hall (30 July ‡)
Your chance to write a poem inspired by music, in workshops led by former Children's Laureate Michael Rosen (23 July) and Radio 3 'The Verb' presenter Ian McMillan (30 July).
23 July, 1.00pm–5.00pm (various times, see bbc.co.uk)
30 July, 2.00pm–2.45pm & 3.00pm–3.45pm

All events are free and aimed at family members aged 7 upwards
† Turn up early to secure your place
‡ Places must be booked in advance: visit bbc.co.uk/proms, or call 020 7765 0557

A participatory Proms Plus singing event, 2010

Proms Plus Sing

In line with our Choral Sundays series (see pages 62–65) this is a chance for adults (aged 16-plus) to join a free two-hour session at the Royal College of Music (except 28 August, Royal Albert Hall), where you will explore and sing some of the music from the evening Prom with professional singing leaders and members of the BBC Singers. All voice types and skill-levels welcome! To sign up, visit www.bbc.co.uk/proms

17 July, 1.00pm–3.00pm
Brian Symphony No. 1, 'The Gothic'

24 July, 1.00pm–3.00pm
Verdi Requiem

31 July, 1.00pm–3.00pm
Rachmaninov Spring; The Bells

7 August, 1.00pm–3.00pm
Mahler Das klagende Lied

14 August, 1.00pm–3.00pm
Britten Cantata misericordium; Spring Symphony

21 August, 1.00pm–3.00pm
Mozart Requiem

28 August, 2.00pm–4.00pm
Mendelssohn Elijah

4 September, 1.00pm–3.00pm
Beethoven Missa solemnis

year's Proms. Budding young writers as well as enthusiasts are all welcome to join their Family Poetry Workshops. The first of them, led by Michael Rosen, will take place in Kensington Gardens as part of the Human Planet festivities (see pages 84–85). The second, in the Royal Albert Hall's Elgar Room, will be led by Ian McMillan (30 July).

PROMS PLUS SING

Ladies and gentlemen, please raise your voices. All the Sunday-evening Proms in the 2011 season include music that demands a significant contribution from a chorus. Complementing these Choral Sundays performances is a series of afternoon participatory workshops, in which vocalists of every voice-type and ability can join animateur Mary King and others to discover the joys of singing together. Music from the evening's concert will be sung and members of the BBC Singers will be on hand to lend

> "It has been such fun to play in the same orchestra as my daughter. So often as a parent you are instructing, encouraging practice ... but this time we were both in it together, 'equal partners' on the journey."

Proms Family Orchestra participant, 2010

support and a little vocal oomph. Each workshop focuses on a different composer whose work will feature in the following Prom, from Havergal Brian (17 July, Prom 4) to Benjamin Britten (14 August, Prom 41), from Mahler (7 August, Prom 32) to Mendelssohn (28 August, Prom 58). These sessions might pay dividends when it comes to the two mass singalong items of the Last Night of the Proms, when lusty participation (in the hall, in the parks or at home) is positively encouraged.

Out+About

21 June, Westfield London, Ariel Way, London W12 7GF
time to be confirmed, visit bbc.co.uk/proms
The BBC Symphony Orchestra returns to Westfield London to provide shoppers with a full-scale Prom as a sneak preview of what's to come in the 2011 season. Bring a picnic and come and sing along.

Out+About in Westfield London, 2010

This year's Proms Plus Portraits feature *(clockwise from top left)* Pascal Dusapin, Graham Fitkin, Kevin Volans and Thomas Larcher

PROMS PLUS PORTRAITS

Contemporary music has long been one of the cornerstones of the Proms; this year is no exception. The range of work on offer is dazzling, covering just about every musical style available to the 21st-century composer. To help listeners through this cornucopia of contemporary delights, a series of four pre-concert composer portraits serves to unveil the new piece to be performed at that evening's Prom. In each portrait, the composer talks us through their new work and introduces performances of their chamber music, a rare opportunity to get close to the creative process behind some of the most original music being written today *(see page 75)*.

INSPIRE – for young composers

Who knows, it may well happen that, in some future season, the Proms Plus Portraits will include a composer who has benefited from the BBC Proms Inspire scheme. This is aimed at young composers aged 12 to 18, who are given the chance to take part in BBC Proms Composer Labs before setting off on the difficult path that leads them to a finished composition. They may also enter the BBC Proms Inspire Young Composers' Competition; winning pieces will be broadcast on BBC Radio 3, following a live performance by the Aurora Orchestra at Inspire Day, a day of workshops and events for all Inspire participants. Surely incentive enough for any budding composer to get to work. ▶

Inspire

Do you know a budding young composer aged 12 to 18 who should be entering the BBC Proms Inspire Young Composers' Competition? Whatever their style of music or experience, this is a chance for them to be inspired and could lead to having their music performed at the BBC Proms and heard on BBC Radio 3. The deadline for entries is Friday 27 May. For more details, visit www.bbc.co.uk/proms.

The BBC Proms Inspire Day 2011, including the Inspire Young Composers' Concert at the Royal College of Music (5.00pm–6.00pm) will be held on 6 August. *Please note capacity for the concert is very limited. For more information about the competition, visit www.bbc.co.uk/proms or email promslearning@bbc.co.uk*

"Fill your world with culture"

...and open up new opportunities in your life and career

The Open University

If you've got a passion for arts and culture then why not explore our exciting array of courses at every level from beginner to postgraduate? Be inspired by Shakespeare's prose, develop a talent for philosophy or even try learning a language. Whatever intrigues or fascinates you, we'll use our talent for delivering learning to help you develop valuable, transferable skills such as generating ideas, creative thinking, working to deadlines and self-evaluation. Skills that can go towards gaining careers in many different areas.

"When you've completed this course, you might review films differently, analyse art instead of 'looking' at it and automatically interpret written sources. I cannot recommend the course highly enough; it has given me great confidence to join in and discuss topics"

John Charlesworth, *The arts past and present* (AA100) student

Courses to fuel your imagination

Art History	History	Philosophy
Classical Studies	Languages	Religious Studies
English Language and Literature	Music	Social Sciences

Our most popular courses include:

The arts past and present (AA100)

Voices and texts (A150)

Start writing fiction (A174)

Making sense of the arts (Y180)

Introducing the social sciences (DD101)

Beginners' Chinese (L197)

Vivace: intermediate Italian (L150)

Discover new horizons

▶ openuniversity.co.uk/culture

▶ 0845 300 8845   Quote: FAMABU

INSPIRING LEARNING

RCM Sparks Summer Music 2011

The Learning and Participation Department at the Royal College of Music has developed a complementary programme of events this summer. When visiting the Proms, why not pop across the road to the Royal College of Music? Whether it's playing, composing or uncovering treasures from the Museum or Library, RCM Sparks is providing opportunities for everyone to engage in Proms-related musical activities.

Summer Music Workshops – for ages 6 to 9 and 10 to 12
27 July; 3, 11 & 15 August

Play and sing, compose and create, bang and shake! These fun, hands-on workshops offer both beginners and more experienced players the opportunity to take part in a day of live music-making while learning more about music featured in the Proms. Come and meet our young and energetic team of talented RCM musicians and be inspired by our enthusiastic workshop leaders. Join the participants at the end of the day for performances of their work and the special opportunity to attend a BBC Proms Plus Family event. Why not continue into the evening and hear amazing live performances at the Prom concert and benefit from a special introductory ticket offer?

Summer Springboard – for ages 13 to 18
Composition Course, 5–9 August

Take part in some incredible music-making this summer. With the support of professional workshop leaders and a team of young RCM musicians, improvise, jam, compose, create and perform a new piece inspired by music from the Proms. This is for all abilities and musical styles, so come along and share your ideas. During the course you will take part in the BBC Inspire scheme, where you will join other young composers from all over the country for a day of music-making and experimentation. You can then watch performances of award-winning compositions before attending the evening Prom at the Royal Albert Hall.

Discovery Sessions
Throughout the summer, 3.30pm–4.30pm*

Join us at the RCM to explore some of the College's hidden treasures from our famed Museum and Library, including original manuscript scores and letters, ancient instruments and music-related portraits. Discovery Sessions link closely to Proms, adding an extra dimension to your concert experience.

* Visit www.rcm.ac.uk/summermusic for full listings

Tickets for RCM Sparks events must be booked and paid for in advance (Summer Music Workshops, £10.00 per day; Summer Springboard, £75.00 for the course; Discovery Sessions, free). Please contact the RCM Box Office on 020 7591 4314 to book tickets. RCM Sparks offers subsidised tickets: for more information, please call 020 7591 4300 and ask for a member of the RCM Sparks team. For more information on all RCM Sparks events, please visit www.rcm.ac.uk/summermusic

Chris Christodoulou/BBC

A young violinist under guidance at a Proms Family Orchestra workshop in 2010

RCM SPARKS and the HORRIBLE HISTORIES PROM

The Royal College of Music is home to Proms Plus as it also is to RCM Sparks Summer Music 2011. This consists of a series of music workshops for 6- to 12-year-olds, a composition course for those aged 13 to 18 and discovery sessions, open to all, which reveal the delights (manuscripts, scores, letters, instruments and much else besides) to be found in the RCM's venerable museum and library.

Many histories come together in the Royal College's museum, but some are not to be found there, including the Horrible Histories, gleefully celebrated in the CBBC series of that name. Here, Boudicca becomes a rap queen and Charles II is the King of Bling. That streak of joyous irreverence will resurface in this year's free children's Prom (30 July, Prom 20), in which music will provide a kind of *Do-re-mi* of what Vikings and Romans, kings and queens and serfs and lords really got up to: everything historical that children aged 7 to 12 really need to know, in fact.

The Aurora Orchestra is the ensemble charged with making musical sense of proceedings and among those who will join them is a choir of young people put together by Kids Company. This London-based charity, founded in 1996 by Camila Batmanghelidjh, offers practical and emotional help to the most vulnerable inner-city children. Kids Company has not worked with the Proms before; this promises to be an auspicious debut, and it serves to reinforce the fact that the Proms are, as Henry Wood always intended, for everyone. ●

Nick Kimberley is a freelance writer and editor. He reviews classical music and opera for the London *Evening Standard*

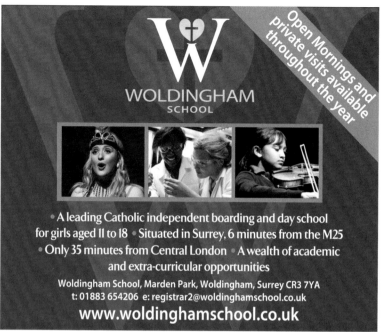

The Haberdashers' Aske's Boys' School
Nurturing Excellence

An outstanding independent day school for boys aged between 5 and 18.

Open Day Saturday 1st October 2011, 1–4pm
(no appointment necessary)

Headmaster Peter B Hamilton MA
Butterfly Lane, Elstree, Hertfordshire WD6 3AF
Tel: 020 8266 1700 office@habsboys.org.uk
www.habsboys.org.uk
registered charity no: 313996

Haberdashers' Aske's School for Girls

Outstanding academic achievement: imagination and creativity

Open Day
1st October 2011
Juniors 10am-12.30pm
Seniors 2pm-5pm

Music Scholarships available at 11+

Independent Day School for Girls from 4-18

Aldenham Road, Elstree, Herts, WD6 3BT
e: admissions@habsgirls.org.uk
t: 020 8266 2338
www.habsgirls.org.uk
Registered Charity No. 313996

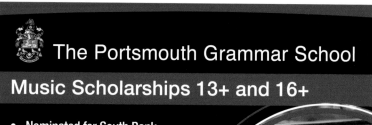

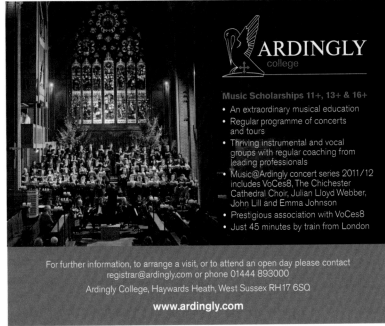

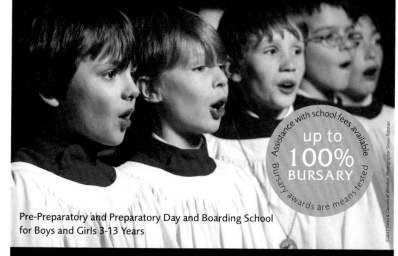

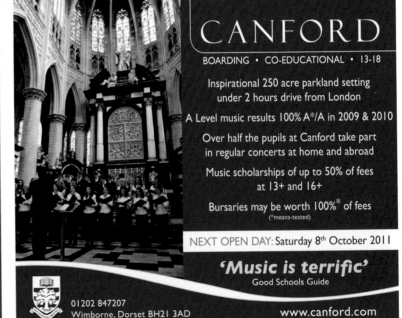

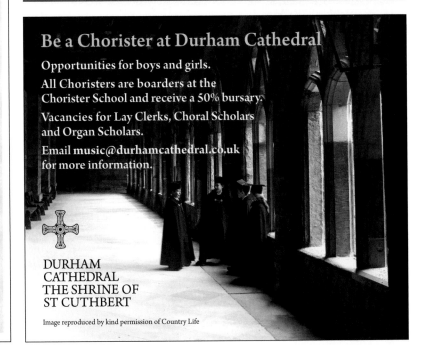

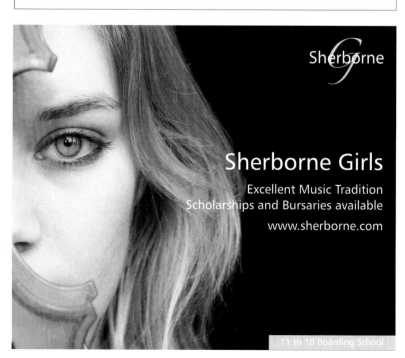

PIERINO
PASTA PIZZA RESTAURANT
37 THURLOE PLACE, LONDON SW7 2HP

Telephone 020 7581 3770

Monday to Friday 12–3.00pm, 5.30–11.30pm

Saturday & Sunday 12 noon–11.30pm

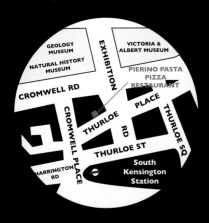

Prompt service guaranteed for you to be in time for the performance.

We are within walking distance of the Royal Albert Hall, near South Kensington tube station.

You are welcome before and after the performance.

36 YEARS

EXPERIENCE OF SERVING GENUINE ITALIAN FOOD AND FOR HOME-MADE PASTA AND THE BEST PIZZA IN LONDON

Concert Listings

BOOKING

Tickets will go on sale at 9.00am on Saturday 7 May – online, by telephone and in person. Tickets may also be requested by post.

Plan your Proms concert-going online, before tickets go on sale, by using the new Proms Planner at bbc.co.uk/proms from 12 noon on Thursday 14 April until midnight on Friday 6 May.

Online bbc.co.uk/proms
Telephone 0845 401 5040∗

For full booking information, see pages 156–165

The BBC: bringing the Proms to you – in concert, on radio, television and online

PRICE CODES

A **▼** **G** Each concert at the Royal Albert Hall falls into one of seven price bands, colour-coded for ease of reference. For a full list of prices, see page 161. For special offers, see page 158.

Please note: *concert start-times vary across the season – check before you book*

All concert details were correct at the time of going to press. The BBC reserves the right to alter artist or programme details as necessary.

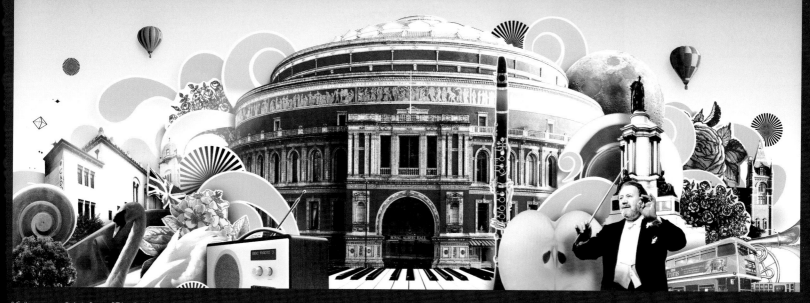

∗*Calls cost up to 5p/min from a BT landline (min connection fee of 11.8p may apply). Calls from mobiles and other networks may cost considerably more. All calls will be recorded and may be monitored for training and quality-control purposes.*

115

WEEKEND PROMMING PASS • BEAT THE QUEUES AND SAVE MONEY *(SEE PAGE 158)*

FRIDAY 15 JULY

Proms Plus 5.00pm, Royal College of Music
Sean Rafferty and Petroc Trelawny present a special Proms edition of BBC Radio 3's *In Tune*, featuring artists and music from the season as well as highlights of the Proms Plus series.
Broadcast live on BBC Radio 3

Proms Plus Late Elgar Room, Royal Albert Hall
Informal post-Prom music and poetry. For details see bbc.co.uk/proms

---

7.30pm–c9.40pm

Judith Weir
Stars, Night, Music and Light   c4'
BBC commission: world premiere

Brahms
Academic Festival Overture   11'

Liszt
Piano Concerto No. 2 in A major   20'

INTERVAL

Janáček
Glagolitic Mass   45'

Benjamin Grosvenor *piano*
Hibla Gerzmava *soprano*
Dagmar Pecková *mezzo-soprano*
Stefan Vinke *tenor*
Jan Martiník *bass*
David Goode *organ*

BBC Singers
BBC Symphony Chorus
BBC Symphony Orchestra
Jiří Bělohlávek *conductor*

Jiří Bělohlávek

New British music, Brahms, Liszt and a lavish choral work blaze a trail for some of 2011's Proms musical strands. Benjamin Grosvenor makes his Proms debut, and there's Janáček's extraordinary celebration of Slavic culture, the *Glagolitic Mass*. See 'A Lust for Liszt', pages 24–27; 'Back to Brahms', pages 30–33; 'New Music', pages 68–75; 'Featured Artists', pages 78–81

Broadcast
RADIO Live on Radio 3
ONLINE Live and 'listen again' options at bbc.co.uk/proms
TV Live on BBC Two

SATURDAY 16 JULY

Proms Plus Intro 4.45pm, Royal College of Music
Opera historian Benjamin Walton and Royal Opera House programme contributor Sarah Lenton join Petroc Trelawny to explore Rossini's final opera, *William Tell*, and the influence it had on the grand tradition of French opera.
Edited version broadcast on BBC Radio 3 during tonight's interval

---

6.30pm–c10.55pm

Rossini
William Tell   180'
(concert performance; sung in French)

Michele Pertusi *William Tell*
John Osborn *Arnold Melchthal*
Matthew Rose *Walter Furst*
Frédéric Caton *Melchthal*
Elena Xanthoudakis *Jemmy*
Nicolas Courjal *Gesler*
Carlo Bosi *Rodolphe*
Celso Albelo *Ruodi*
Mark Stone *Leuthold*
Malin Byström *Mathilde*
Patricia Bardon *Hedwige*
Davide Malvestio *Huntsman*

Orchestra and Chorus of the Academy of Santa Cecilia, Rome
Antonio Pappano *conductor*

Antonio Pappano returns with his Italian forces for a rare revival of Rossini's magnum opus about the legendary founding fathers of Switzerland and the hero who shoots an apple from his son's head. The galloping climax of the overture is familiar, yet barely anything else from this grandest of operas has been heard at the Proms. Raising the roof with large-scale choral ensembles that look forward to Verdi and Wagner, the composer also makes extreme demands on his soloists. Tenor John Osborn, one of several members of tonight's line-up who participated in the sensational Rome performances with which Pappano launched the orchestra's 2010–11 season, will tackle the challenging role of Arnold, with its fabled high Cs. See 'Aiming for Freedom', pages 52–55; 'Featured Artists', pages 78–81

There will be two intervals of 30 minutes

PROM 2
Spotlight on … Antonio Pappano

'You can hear the Swiss mountains in *William Tell*,' says Antonio Pappano, 'and the vision of "liberté" in the finale.' Indeed, nature and freedom are the overarching themes of Rossini's final stage work before his early retirement from opera aged only 37.

But he left at the top, with a spectacle that became an early classic of the French grand opera tradition – eschewing mythological figures in favour of Romantic subjects and featuring dramatic accompanied recitatives as well as rousing choral and ensemble scenes.

'It is written with great panache,' Pappano says. 'All of Rossini's operas have a sense of drive. This one is unusual in that it manages to keep that incredible momentum, and across a big scale, but there's also time to smell the roses along the way. Rossini was so successful in creating visual images in the music that this opera lends itself to the imagination, so you don't miss the staging in a concert version.'

In *William Tell*'s depiction of the Swiss and the Austrians, there's no doubt as to which side is the oppressor. 'The music for the Austrian villain Gesler can be quite foursquare, even comical. And the famously impossible tenor writing for the Swiss Arnold is clearly heroic.'

Broadcast
RADIO Live on Radio 3
ONLINE Live and 'listen again' options at bbc.co.uk/proms

SUNDAY 17 JULY

Proms Plus Sing
1.00pm–3.00pm, Royal College of Music
Whether you're a trained singer, a member of a community choir or just sing in the shower, come and tackle excerpts from Havergal Brian's monumental 'The Gothic' Symphony alongside professional singers. Ideal for enthusiastic amateur singers aged 16-plus. See pages 92–99 for details of how to sign up.

4.00pm–c5.00pm

Alain
Litanies · 5'

Liszt, arr. Winterberger
Prelude 'Weinen, Klagen, Sorgen, Zagen' · 8'

J. S. Bach
Chorale Prelude 'Erbarm dich mein, o Herre Gott', BWV 721 · 5'

Judith Bingham
The Everlasting Crown · c35'
world premiere

Stephen Farr *organ*

Stephen Farr

Stephen Farr puts the Royal Albert Hall's titanic instrument through its paces in the first of this year's two organ recitals (see also Prom 66). Among the most adaptable virtuosos of his generation, he takes in music by J. S. Bach and two of this year's anniversary composers, Jehan Alain and Liszt. There's also the world premiere of a large-scale solo piece composed for Farr: expect something direct and communicative from Judith Bingham, a past member of the BBC Singers. See 'A Lust for Liszt', pages 24–27; 'French Connections', pages 36–39; 'New Music', pages 68–75

There will be no interval

Broadcast
RADIO Live on Radio 3
ONLINE Live and 'listen again' options at bbc.co.uk/proms

SUNDAY 17 JULY

Proms Plus Intro 5.15pm, Royal College of Music
The first in the series of introductions to the music performed in Proms Choral Sundays. Sarah Walker explores Havergal Brian's 'The Gothic' Symphony with recorded extracts and with live music examples from members of the BBC National Orchestra of Wales. Ideal for anyone wanting to explore classical music.
Broadcast live on BBC Radio 3

7.00pm–c9.00pm

Brian
Symphony No. 1 in D minor, 'The Gothic' · 110'

Susan Gritton *soprano*
Christine Rice *mezzo-soprano*
Peter Auty *tenor*
Alastair Miles *bass*

CBSO Youth Chorus
Eltham College Boys' Choir
Southend Boys'
and Girls' Choirs
Bach Choir
BBC National Chorus of Wales
Brighton Festival Chorus
Côr Caerdydd
Huddersfield Choral Society
London Symphony Chorus
BBC Concert Orchestra
BBC National Orchestra of Wales
Martyn Brabbins *conductor*

Christine Rice

This season's sequence of Choral Sundays kicks off with arguably the grandest statement in British music, Havergal Brian's 'The Gothic', a gargantuan work that earned an entry in the *Guinness Book of Records* under 'Longest Symphony'. Completed in the 1920s but unplayed until 1961, its most famous outing came in 1966, when Sir Adrian Boult presided over a BBC-sponsored rendition at the Royal Albert Hall. Its Proms debut features not one but two orchestras and a raft of choirs. Even Mahler never contemplated a work on quite this scale, although he too found inspiration in Goethe's Faust. See 'A Gothic Revival', pages 58–59; 'Choral Sundays', pages 62–65; 'Featured Artists', pages 78–81

SAME-DAY SAVER
Book for both Proms 3 and 4 and save (see page 158)

There will be no interval

PROM 4
Spotlight on ... Martyn Brabbins

Martyn Brabbins is under no illusions about the challenges involved in putting on a performance of Havergal Brian's mighty 'The Gothic' Symphony. 'It's an absolutely incredible piece, with extraordinary demands, size and forces,' he says. 'Our performance features roughly 600 adult singers, about 200 children and around 200 musicians in the orchestra. I've never worked with so many people before: I think it will be like driving a juggernaut, or a supertanker.'

'The Gothic' is considered Brian's crowning achievement. 'Despite its size, a lot of the piece is actually very delicate,' explains Brabbins. 'The first three movements are for orchestra alone and feature some beautiful instrumental solos in a very chamber music-like orchestration. There are also some very grand moments with wonderful *tuttis* but it's by no means a big, loud, bombastic experience from start to finish.'

The title was apparently inspired by the façade of Lichfield Cathedral, 'so it's Gothic in the sense of architecture and detail and grandeur and mystery,' says Brabbins. 'I imagine this performance will be one of the biggest classical undertakings ever mounted – it's going to be a fantastic sonic spectacle!'

Broadcast
RADIO Live on Radio 3
ONLINE Live and 'listen again' options at bbc.co.uk/proms

MONDAY 18 JULY

1.00pm–c2.00pm

Proms Chamber Music at Cadogan Hall

J. S. Bach

'Goldberg' Variations   55'

Mahan Esfahani *harpsichord*

The Proms Chamber Music series begins at the top with one of the unassailable peaks of the repertoire. The first edition of the 'Goldberg' Variations declared it as having been 'composed for music-lovers to refresh their spirits' – an apt motto for the whole PCM season. Acclaimed former BBC Radio 3 New Generation Artist Mahan Esfahani was the first harpsichordist to join the scheme, in 2008.

There will be no interval

Mahan Esfahani

MONDAY 18 JULY

> **Proms Plus Literary** 5.45pm, Royal College of Music
> From the romance of Proust to the existentialism of Camus, Kate Mosse, author of the best-selling *Labyrinth* trilogy set in France, and prize-winning writer and artist Edmund de Waal, author of *The Hare with Amber Eyes*, discuss the great French literary classics.
> Edited version broadcast on BBC Radio 3 during tonight's interval

7.30pm–c9.30pm

Messiaen

Les offrandes oubliées   11'

Pascal Dusapin

Morning in Long Island
(Concert No. 1 for large orchestra)   33'
BBC co-commission with Radio France: UK premiere

INTERVAL

Beethoven

Concerto in C major for Violin, Cello and Piano (Triple Concerto)   33'

Martha Argerich *piano*
Renaud Capuçon *violin*
Gautier Capuçon *cello*

Orchestre Philharmonique de Radio France
Myung-Whun Chung *conductor*

Introducing the French strand in this year's season, Myung-Whun Chung and his Paris-based orchestra preface an exciting new commission from a prominent contemporary voice with the first orchestral work of a great man briefly his teacher. Shaping the raw power of massed orchestral forces comes naturally to the eclectic and prolific Pascal Dusapin, who combines stylistic experimentation – earlier works have featured archaic-sounding scales and microtones – with emotional directness. After the interval a Beethovenian rarity, one of several concertos for two or more instruments being presented in 2011. The inimitable Martha Argerich is joined by her frequent musical partners, the brothers Capuçon, who, like Dusapin, are Proms first-timers. See *'French Connections', pages 36–39; 'New Music', pages 68–75; 'Featured Artists', pages 78–81*

Gautier Capuçon   Renaud Capuçon

PROMS 5 & 6

Spotlight on ... Gautier & Renaud Capuçon

It's hard to believe it's taken this long for Gautier and Renaud Capuçon to come to the Proms as soloists for the first time. But, as compensation, they're playing not one but two major 19th-century multi-instrument concertos: Beethoven's Triple (Prom 5) and Brahms's Double (Prom 6). They're in good company too: both concerts are conducted by Myung-Whun Chung, with whom the brothers recorded the Brahms in 2007, while in the Beethoven they're joined by none other than Martha Argerich.

Sibling synchrony is a powerful part of their appeal as musicians, as they both acknowledge. 'The communication between the artists is so important in these pieces,' says Gautier. 'If you put two soloists together and there is no kind of connection between them, then it is difficult.'

'Obviously, we know each other so well,' agrees Renaud, 'but at the same time we're so very different. There is this link between us, which is great for this repertoire.' And working again with Argerich and Chung? 'It's a wonderful way to be spending two days together.' His brother concurs. 'It's a luxury to play music you like with people you also like – it's like having a great meal with friends. Music is so intimate and so important that you need to share it with people with whom you're ready to share it.'

TUESDAY 19 JULY

Proms Plus Family 5.00pm, Royal College of Music
Join Matthew Rowe and musicians from the Orchestre Philharmonique de Radio France for an interactive introduction to tonight's music. Ideal for all the family – bring along your instrument and join in!

7.00pm–c9.00pm

Weber
Oberon – overture   9'

Brahms
Concerto in A minor for Violin and Cello
(Double Concerto)   32'

INTERVAL

Stravinsky
The Rite of Spring   33'

Renaud Capuçon *violin*
Gautier Capuçon *cello*

Orchestre Philharmonique de Radio France
Myung-Whun Chung *conductor*

In the first half of his second Prom Myung-Whun Chung pairs works by German Romantics from opposite ends of the 19th century, including the meltingly beautiful Brahms Double Concerto with Renaud and Gautier Capuçon. After the interval comes a piece with French connections which swept away that old order. A sensational *succès de scandale* in 1913

Myung-Whun Chung

for Diaghilev and his Ballets Russes, *The Rite of Spring* not only prompted the most famous riot in musical history but sounds sensational still, rediscovering rhythm as music's primal driving force. See 'Back to Brahms', pages 30–33

SAME-DAY SAVER Book for both Proms 6 and 7 and save (see page 158)

Broadcast
RADIO Live on Radio 3
ONLINE Live and 'listen again' options at bbc.co.uk/proms
TV Recorded for broadcast on BBC Two on 23 July

TUESDAY 19 JULY

10.00pm–c11.00pm

Schubert
String Quintet in C major, D956   47'

Belcea Quartet
Valentin Erben *cello*

Belcea Quartet

Dating from the last months of Schubert's life, the String Quintet operates on the loftiest plane yet goes straight to the heart. It is a piece the Belcea Quartet has toured and recorded to great acclaim alongside Valentin Erben, longtime cellist with the Alban Berg Quartet. Corina Belcea-Fisher, first violinist of the Belcea, comments: 'It is a great challenge to capture all the varied emotions of the piece, emotions that can switch from one second to the next. It has been a great privilege for us to explore this work with Valentin, to be able to draw from his resources and his knowledge.' The ethereal elements of the famous slow movement should chime especially well with the relaxed but raptly attentive atmosphere of a Late Night Prom.

There will be no interval

Broadcast
RADIO Live on Radio 3
ONLINE Live and 'listen again' options at bbc.co.uk/proms

WEDNESDAY 20 JULY

Proms Plus Literary 5.45pm, Royal College of Music
How well do the great works of fiction portray instruments in their pages? Music critic and Professor of English Peggy Reynolds is joined by a cellist from the BBC Symphony Orchestra to explore the cello's literary life across the ages – and to perform its fictional incarnations.
Edited version broadcast on BBC Radio 3 during tonight's interval

7.30pm–c10.00pm

Dvořák
Cello Concerto in B minor   40'

INTERVAL

Smetana
Má vlast   72'

Jean-Guihen Queyras *cello*

BBC Symphony Orchestra
Jiří Bělohlávek *conductor*

Dvořák's Cello Concerto is full of melody and heartfelt sentiment, to which French cellist Jean-Guihen Queyras will bring both youthful urgency and intimacy, if his recording with tonight's conductor is anything to go by. The work is widely regarded as the finest concerto ever written for the instrument. Nostalgia turns to nationalism in the second half, moving from a Proms staple to a Proms premiere. This is the first time the six symphonic poems of *Má vlast* have been given complete and in sequence at the Proms. Together they constitute a glorious musical touchstone for 'the resurrection of the Czech nation, its future happiness and glory'.

Jean-Guihen Queyras

Broadcast
RADIO Live on Radio 3
ONLINE Live and 'listen again' options at bbc.co.uk/proms

WEEKEND PROMMING PASS • BEAT THE QUEUES AND SAVE MONEY (*SEE PAGE 158*)

THURSDAY 21 JULY

Proms Plus Intro 5.45pm, Royal College of Music
Musicologist and author Malcolm Gillies joins Hungarian poet and translator George Szirtes to explore the life and works of one of the most important composers of the 20th century, Béla Bartók. Presented by Louise Fryer.
Edited version broadcast on BBC Radio 3 during tonight's interval

7.30pm–c9.45pm

Sibelius
Scènes historiques – Suite No. 2   19'
Symphony No. 7 in C major   23'

INTERVAL

Bartók
Piano Concerto No. 3   24'

Janáček
Sinfonietta   24'

András Schiff *piano*

Hallé
Sir Mark Elder *conductor*

Sir Mark Elder

Sir Mark Elder and the Hallé contextualise the lofty preoccupations of Sibelius's last surviving symphony with a rarity, a suite revealing the composer's lighter side. Bartók's last completed concerto was written in exile and is generally mellow, even nostalgic in tone. It is championed tonight by András Schiff, appearing at the Proms for the first time since his 2006 solo recital. And, to close, a joyous sequence of sonic snapshots: Janáček's Sinfonietta is his typically bold evocation of a beloved city, the Moravian regional capital, Brno. *See 'Bartók Piano Concertos', pages 42–45*

Broadcast
RADIO Live on Radio 3
ONLINE Live and 'listen again' options at bbc.co.uk/proms
TV Live on BBC Four

FRIDAY 22 JULY

Proms Plus Intro 5.30pm, Royal College of Music
Stephen Johnson explores the inner workings of the colourful world of Debussy's Images with the Royal College of Music Symphony Orchestra conducted by Sian Edwards.
Recorded for future broadcast in BBC Radio 3's *Discovering Music*

Proms Plus Late Elgar Room, Royal Albert Hall
Informal post-Prom music and poetry. For details see bbc.co.uk/proms

7.30pm–c9.50pm

Debussy
Images – Gigues   7'
Ravel
Rapsodie espagnole   15'
Debussy
Images – Rondes de printemps   9'

INTERVAL

Ravel
Alborada del gracioso   8'
Falla
Nights in the Gardens of Spain   24'
Debussy
Images – Ibéria   20'

Steven Osborne *piano*

BBC Philharmonic
Juanjo Mena *conductor*

Basque-born Juanjo Mena, recently named Chief Conductor of the BBC Philharmonic, makes his Proms debut with this dazzling Franco-Spanish evening. Debussy's three orchestral *Images* are interspersed with evocations of an idealised South filled with the rhythms of Gypsy dancing and the scent of jasmine. The brilliant showpieces of Ravel are complemented by Falla's Impressionistic Andalusian concerto, in which the orchestra is joined by pianist Steven Osborne. *See 'French Connections', pages 36–39*

Broadcast
RADIO Live on Radio 3
ONLINE Live and 'listen again' options at bbc.co.uk/proms
TV Live on BBC Four

SATURDAY 23 JULY

Proms Plus Family Orchestra and Chorus
10.00am–1.30pm, Royal College of Music
Would you like to create a brand-new piece in two hours, influenced by the music featured in the Human Planet Prom, and then perform it on the stage in Kensington Gardens? If so, come and join the Family Orchestra and Chorus. See pages 92–99 for details of how to sign up.

Proms Plus Family 1.00pm–5.00pm,
Human Planet in the Park, Kensington Gardens
An afternoon showcasing music and musicians from around the world, plus workshops and other events. See page 85 for details.

Proms Plus Intro 5.45pm, Royal College of Music
Music Planet producer James Parkin gives an insider's view of the journeys he made through six continents to gather material for the radio programme, in conversation with *Human Planet* series producer Dale Templar. Presented by Louise Fryer.

7.30pm–c9.45pm

Human Planet Prom

Music composed by **Nitin Sawhney** for the *Human Planet* television series, and performances by artists including:

Ayarkhaan (Sakha Republic)
Bibilang Shark-Calling Group
(Papua New Guinea)
Khusugtun (Mongolia)
Rasmus Lyberth (Greenland)
Enock Mbongwe (Zambia)
John Hurt *narrator*

BBC Concert Orchestra
Charles Hazlewood *conductor*

Nitin Sawhney

Big-screen video projections and excerpts from Nitin Sawhney's score for the acclaimed landmark BBC One series *Human Planet*, alongside artists heard in BBC Radio 3's accompanying *Music Planet* series. *See 'Sounds from the Human Planet', pages 84–85*

There will be one interval

Broadcast
TV Recorded for broadcast on BBC Four on 5 August

WEEKEND PROMMING PASS • BEAT THE QUEUES AND SAVE MONEY (SEE PAGE 158)

SUNDAY 24 JULY

11.00am–c1.15pm

Human Planet Prom

Music composed by **Nitin Sawhney** for the *Human Planet* television series, and performances by artists including:

Ayarkhaan (Sakha Republic)
Bibilang Shark-Calling Group (Papua New Guinea)
Khusugtun (Mongolia)
Rasmus Lyberth (Greenland)
Enock Mbongwe (Zambia)
John Hurt *narrator*

BBC Concert Orchestra
Charles Hazlewood *conductor*

There will be one interval

For programme details, see Prom 11

Bibilang Shark-Calling Group

SAME-DAY SAVER Book for both Proms 12 and 13 and save (see page 158)

Broadcast
RADIO Live on Radio 3
ONLINE Live and 'listen again' options at bbc.co.uk/proms

SUNDAY 24 JULY

Proms Plus Sing 1.00pm–3.00pm, Royal College of Music
As the performers warm up for their performance this evening of Verdi's *Requiem*, come and sing your own version alongside professional singers. Ideal for enthusiastic amateur singers aged 16-plus. See pages 92–99 for details of how to sign up.

Proms Plus Intro 5.15pm, Royal College of Music
The second in the series of introductions to the music performed in Proms Choral Sundays. Matthew Rowe explores Verdi's *Requiem* with recorded extracts and with live music examples from members of the BBC Symphony Orchestra. Ideal for anyone wanting to explore classical music.
Broadcast live on BBC Radio 3

7.00pm–c8.40pm

Verdi
Requiem   86'

Marina Poplavskaya *soprano*
Sonia Ganassi *mezzo-soprano*
Joseph Calleja *tenor*
Ferruccio Furlanetto *bass*

BBC Symphony Chorus
BBC National Chorus of Wales
London Philharmonic Choir
BBC Symphony Orchestra
Semyon Bychkov *conductor*

The ultimate in dramatic intensity, this extraordinary work speaks of heaven and hell, fire and earth, darkness and light in music that is as much theatrical as devotional. The *Requiem* is always a special event – the more so when we have on the podium a Verdi specialist whose recent Cologne recording, which also featured Ferruccio Furlanetto, has been much acclaimed. Tonight's stellar line-up also includes Marina Poplavskaya and Joseph Calleja, who both sang alongside Furlanetto in last year's *Simon Boccanegra*. See 'Choral Sundays', pages 62–65

Joseph Calleja

There will be no interval

PROM 13
Spotlight on … Marina Poplavskaya

Soprano Marina Poplavskaya is no stranger to London's opera-goers. As a Jette Parker Young Artist at Covent Garden, she sang in roles that grew from Third Norn (*Götterdämmerung*) to Rachel (*La Juive*) and Donna Anna (*Don Giovanni*), and she made her Proms debut last year as Amelia in *Simon Boccanegra*.

This season she returns in Verdi's *Requiem*, that most dramatic of sacred works. The mezzo may take on the lion's share of the solo work in the electrifying 'Dies irae' sequence at the core of the *Requiem*, but it's the soprano who has the last word, in the extended 'Libera me'. 'Verdi put this unresolved chord on "Libera me",' says Poplavskaya. 'He's saying you cry for God's help and instead of liberation comes "Dies irae" every time. After the consolation of "Lux aeterna", Verdi brings us back to earth with this desperate cry of "Libera me", with the question of whether he will give us "requiem" or not, if he will give our souls peace.'

Performances of the *Requiem* at the Proms always seem to inspire something extra, something undefinable from its musicians. 'That's Verdi!' laughs Poplavskaya. 'That's what moves you beyond human possibilities to create something special.'

Broadcast
RADIO Live on Radio 3
ONLINE Live and 'listen again' options at bbc.co.uk/proms
TV Recorded for broadcast on BBC Four on 21 August

MONDAY 25 JULY

1.00pm–c2.00pm

Proms Chamber Music at Cadogan Hall

Purcell

Fantasia No. 6 in F major   3'

Fantasia No. 7 in C minor   4'

Sally Beamish

Reed Stanzas (String Quartet No. 3)   c12'

BBC commission: world premiere

Brahms

Clarinet Quintet in B minor   39'

Julian Bliss clarinet
Elias Quartet

Elias Quartet

A potent mix of old and new in which the youthful members of the Elias Quartet, current BBC Radio 3 New Generation Artists, are joined by a young clarinettist who is already a Proms veteran. Before Julian Bliss brings his flair to Brahms's autumnal masterpiece, there's the world premiere of a new work by Sally Beamish, based on a Celtic-inspired melody. See 'Back to Brahms', pages 30–33; 'New Music', pages 68–75

There will be no interval

Broadcast
RADIO Live on Radio 3
ONLINE Live and 'listen again' options at bbc.co.uk/proms

MONDAY 25 JULY

Proms Plus Intro 5.45pm, Royal College of Music
Rachel Leach and musicians from the Stuttgart Radio Symphony Orchestra offer an illustrated guide to Mahler's Symphony No. 9 with recorded and live musical examples. Ideal for anyone wanting to explore classical music.

7.30pm–c8.50pm

Mahler

Symphony No. 9   73'

Stuttgart Radio Symphony Orchestra (SWR)

Sir Roger Norrington conductor

Sir Roger Norrington has chosen Mahler's last completed symphony for his final concerts as Principal Conductor of the Stuttgart Radio Symphony Orchestra, a post he has held since 1998. Written at a time of personal crisis, the Ninth begins with what some have heard as the irregular rhythm of Mahler's own failing heartbeat and it ends with a long fade to eternal nothingness. In between comes perhaps the greatest, certainly the most cathartic, of all late-Romantic symphonies. Sadly, the composer did not live to hear it. Tonight's performance promises to be both a moving occasion and a revealing one, taking up the faster pacing and purer orchestral sonorities of the composer's own time.

There will be no interval

Sir Roger Norrington

Broadcast
RADIO Live on Radio 3
ONLINE Live and 'listen again' options at bbc.co.uk/proms
TV Recorded for broadcast on BBC Four on 28 July

TUESDAY 26 JULY

Proms Plus Literary 5.45pm, Royal College of Music
What would persuade a man to sell his soul? Since the 16th century, the myth of Faust has fascinated writers. Playwright Mark Ravenhill, author of *Faust is Dead*, and novelist Ali Smith discuss why it continues to speak to us today.
Edited version broadcast on BBC Radio 3 during tonight's interval

7.30pm–c9.55pm

Kodály

Dances of Galánta   16'

Bartók

Piano Concerto No. 1   24'

INTERVAL

Liszt

A Faust Symphony   62'

Jean-Efflam Bavouzet piano
Christopher Ventris tenor

London Philharmonic Choir (men's voices)
London Symphony Chorus (men's voices)
London Philharmonic Orchestra
Vladimir Jurowski conductor

Jean-Efflam Bavouzet

Vladimir Jurowski's Hungarian Prom kicks off with Kodály's effervescent *Dances of Galánta*. Bartók's more acerbically ebullient First Piano Concerto will give pianist Jean-Efflam Bavouzet a chance to use both hands: his previous Proms appearances, in 2008 and 2010, both involved pieces conceived for the left hand alone! In tonight's second half, an influential masterwork from one of this year's featured composers, born 200 years ago. Liszt's *A Faust Symphony* 'in three character portraits, after Goethe' will be played in the version that concludes with a grandiose setting of the 'Chorus mysticus' unheard at the Proms since 1967. See 'A Lust for Liszt', pages 24–27; 'Bartók Piano Concertos', pages 42–45

Broadcast
RADIO Live on Radio 3
ONLINE Live and 'listen again' options at bbc.co.uk/proms
TV Recorded for broadcast on BBC Four on 29 July

WEDNESDAY 27 JULY

Proms Plus Portrait 5.15pm, Royal College of Music
Pascal Dusapin discusses his String Quartet No. 6, 'Hinterland', with Andrew McGregor, and introduces a performance of his chamber work *Trio Rombach* by musicians from the Guildhall School of Music & Drama.
Edited version broadcast on BBC Radio 3 after tonight's first Prom

7.00pm–c9.05pm

Berlioz
Overture 'Le corsaire'   9'

Fauré
Pavane   7'

Pascal Dusapin
String Quartet No. 6, 'Hinterland' ('Hapax' for string quartet and orchestra)   23'
UK premiere

INTERVAL

Stravinsky
The Firebird   46'

Arditti Quartet

BBC National Orchestra of Wales
Thierry Fischer *conductor*

Contrasting French favourites herald the season's second UK premiere of a recent work by Pascal Dusapin, this one owing its existence to the persistence of tonight's soloists. According to the composer, 'Irvine Arditti asked me for many years to compose a quartet with orchestra. I refused as politely as possible … Irvine went on trying, again and again.' The result is a discourse in which, he says, 'each party sets the other one into motion, as if one were the dream of the other'. Acclaimed for their recent live and recorded Stravinsky, Thierry Fischer and the BBC NOW revisit *The Firebird*, the iridescent ballet that effectively launched the composer's international career and remains among his best-loved scores. *See 'French Connections', pages 36–39; 'New Music', pages 68–75*

Broadcast
RADIO Live on Radio 3
ONLINE Live and 'listen again' options at bbc.co.uk/proms

WEDNESDAY 27 JULY

10.00pm–c11.15pm

BBC Radio 3
World Routes Academy

Aruna Sairam *vocalist*
Hari Sivanesan *veena*

Patri Satish Kumar *mridangam*
Bangalore RN Prakash *ghatam*
Jyotsna Srikanth *violin*
Pirashanna Thevarajah *percussion*

Following the success of last year's World Routes Academy Late Night Prom, the focus shifts this year from Iraq to India. Aruna Sairam, widely regarded as the leading South Indian female vocalist of her generation, has long sought to create a larger following for Carnatic music, seducing Indian audiences with her unusual deep vocal timbre and defying boundaries in her collaborations with internationally renowned artists from Europe and Africa. Recently she has been mentoring the young veena virtuoso Hari Sivanesan, the latest recipient of the BBC Radio 3 scheme founded to support outstanding young artists working in world music. London-born to Sri Lankan parents, Sivanesan believes that 'it's time for Carnatic music – India's music of the South – to shine in the West, and I'm looking forward to diving into the roots of our music further!' The veena is one of India's oldest and most beautiful instruments, dating back 3,000 years and said to be the predecessor of the sitar. Sivanesan too has quite some musical past. First invited to perform with Ravi Shankar as a young teenager, he played and sang on his *Chants of India* album produced by Beatle George Harrison.

There will be no interval

SAME-DAY SAVER
Book for both Proms 16 and 17 and save (see page 158)

Hari Sivanesan   Aruna Sairam

PROM 17
Spotlight on … Hari Sivanesan & Aruna Sairam

This year Radio 3's World Routes Academy crosses the Arabian Sea to focus on music from South India. Born in London to Sri Lankan parents, Hari Sivanesan, 28, is this year's protégé, an exponent of the veena – a lute-like instrument prefiguring the sitar.

'The artists, places and opportunities that the Academy will expose me to means that there will be so many new sounds, new genres and new emotions to experience,' says Sivanesan. 'They say that music is an ocean, so it's all just about constantly trying to learn more, feel more, play more and grow, because there's no end to that.'

The young player is thrilled to be mentored by Aruna Sairam, one of the leading vocalists of South Indian music. 'She has a unique ability to capture an audience. She lives and breathes each note, word and phrase, making sure that whatever she is feeling is felt by the audience too. It's really quite moving.'

For Sairam's part, she hopes to help Sivanesan bring 'an authentic flavour' to his playing by introducing him to 'some great maestros in their eighties and nineties – wonderful human beings and artists who are keen to share their knowledge with a young student'.

Broadcast
RADIO Live on Radio 3
ONLINE Live and 'listen again' options at bbc.co.uk/proms

WEEKEND PROMMING PASS (SEE PAGE 158)

THURSDAY 28 JULY

Proms Plus Intro 5.15pm, Royal College of Music
Sarah Walker and musicians from the BBC National Orchestra
of Wales offer an illustrated guide to the works in tonight's
programme with live and recorded musical examples. Ideal
for anyone wanting to explore classical music.

7.00pm–c9.25pm

Beethoven
Symphony No. 1 in C major   27'

Marc-André Dalbavie
Flute Concerto   18'
London premiere

INTERVAL

Elliott Carter
Flute Concerto   13'
UK premiere

Beethoven
Symphony No. 7 in A major   40'

Emmanuel Pahud *flute*

BBC National Orchestra of Wales
Thierry Fischer *conductor*

Thierry Fischer

Two Beethoven symphonies
of dancing athleticism, the
Seventh being the last
work directed by Proms
founder-conductor
Sir Henry Wood before
his death, frame a pair of
what he would have called
'novelties'. Emmanuel Pahud
has sought to compensate
for the dearth of celebrated
flute concertos by
championing new ones. Marc-André Dalbavie's recent
piece is opulent, tender and squarely in the French
tradition, Elliott Carter's dazzler an engaging product
of his remarkable Indian summer – it was completed
early in 2008, when the composer was 99 years old.
See 'French Connections', pages 36–39; 'New Music',
pages 68–75; 'Featured Artists', pages 78–81

PROM 18
Spotlight on ... Emmanuel Pahud

What challenges remain for a musician
appointed to a Principal position with the Berlin
Philharmonic at the age of 22? Alongside his
orchestral work, Swiss-born flautist Emmanuel
Pahud, now 41, has managed to sustain parallel
careers as a soloist and chamber musician.
Then there are recordings and jazz performances.
And there's also the creation of important new
work for the instrument. For this season's Proms,
Pahud gives the UK and London premieres
respectively of concertos by Elliott Carter and
Marc-André Dalbavie, as well as a chamber
recital (see PCM 6).

'The two concertos are very different,' the
flautist explains. 'Dalbavie's concerto is eminently
French in the way that he takes over where Ibert's
Flute Concerto left off, in terms of virtuoso
challenge. But in the middle you can recognise the
legacy of Ravel and Debussy or even of Messiaen
and Boulez. It's easy to identify with, as it refers
to musical genres heard in other pieces. In Carter's
concerto, it is more as if the music is organising
itself; you hear flute notes leaving an imprint on
the orchestra; they start to build chords and the
flute notes develop into melodies. In the Dalbavie,
it is as if the past is being assimilated, while the
Carter seems to reflect the history of America,
to which it brings its own contribution.'

Broadcast
RADIO Live on Radio 3
ONLINE Live and 'listen again' options at bbc.co.uk/proms

FRIDAY 29 JULY

Proms Plus Intro 5.45pm, Royal College of Music
Rachel Leach and musicians from the BBC Symphony Orchestra
offer an illustrated guide to the works in tonight's programme
with recorded and live musical examples. Ideal for anyone
wanting to explore classical music.

7.30pm–c9.45pm

Honegger
Pacific 231   7'
Pastorale d'été   8'

Bridge
There is a Willow Grows Aslant a Brook   11'

Berg
Der Wein   15'

INTERVAL

Castiglioni
Inverno in-ver   22'

Debussy
La mer   24'

Claire Booth *soprano*

BBC Symphony Orchestra
Oliver Knussen *conductor*

Oliver Knussen

A typically thought-provoking programme from
Oliver Knussen, the BBC SO's Artist in Association,
showcasing pieces rarely heard in the concert hall
alongside established 20th-century classics. Arthur
Honegger's depiction of a train and pastoral idyll
are followed by Frank Bridge's quietly anguished
Shakespearean scene of death by drowning and the
splintered, wintry fluidity of Italian composer Niccolò
Castiglioni. Soprano Claire Booth (who made her
professional debut in the music of Knussen) sings Berg's
heady paean to the restorative powers of fermented
grape juice. And the concert closes with Debussy's
astonishing, inspirational evocation of shifting seas.
See 'French Connections', pages 36–39; 'Out of the
Shadows', pages 48–49; 'New Music', pages 68–75

Broadcast
RADIO Live on Radio 3
ONLINE Live and 'listen again' options at bbc.co.uk/proms

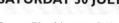

SATURDAY 30 JULY

Proms Plus **Family Orchestra and Chorus**
2.00pm–4.00pm, Royal College of Music
Join the Family Orchestra to create your own musical journey through time and space, just like the musicians performing in the Horrible Histories Prom. See pages 92–99 for details of how to sign up.

Proms Plus **Family** 2.00pm–2.45pm and 3.00pm–3.45pm, Elgar Room, Royal Albert Hall
Family Poetry Workshops: Ian McMillan, poet and presenter of BBC Radio 3's *The Verb*, hosts afternoon workshops for parents and children to write a poem inspired by a piece of music in this year's Proms. See pages 92–99 for details of how to sign up.

11.00am–c1.00pm

Horrible Histories
Free Family Prom

Louise Fryer *presenter*
Horrible Histories cast
Choirs from The Music Centre
Kids Company Choir
Aurora Orchestra
Nicholas Collon *conductor*

Anyone who has split their sides laughing at CBBC's hit television series *Horrible Histories* now has the chance to see and hear the cast perform some of the most popular songs from the show, ranging from the Savage Stone Age and the Vicious Vikings to the Gorgeous Georgians and the Vile Victorians. Backed by children's choirs and the Aurora Orchestra, the songs will be interspersed with some great music by composers such as King Henry VIII, Lully, Mozart and the prolific 'Anon'.

Horrible Histories, based on the best-selling books by Terry Deary with illustrations by Martin Brown, has proved a massive success. Children love the series, and the songs (music by Richie Webb) have proved among the most memorable elements of the show. Come to see the stars and sing along!

 Following the success of the first-ever signed Prom last year, Dr Paul Whittaker, Artistic Director of Music and the Deaf, returns to guide you through this free Prom.

FREE TICKETS *available from 8 July*

Broadcast
RADIO Live on Radio 3
ONLINE Live and 'listen again' options at bbc.co.uk/proms

SATURDAY 30 JULY

7.30pm–c9.55pm

R. Strauss
Don Juan — 17'

Walton
Violin Concerto — 32'

INTERVAL

Prokofiev
Alexander Nevsky – cantata — 40'

R. Strauss
Salome – Dance of the Seven Veils — 12'

Midori

Midori *violin*
Nadezhda Serdiuk *mezzo-soprano*

CBSO Chorus
City of Birmingham Symphony Orchestra
Andris Nelsons *conductor*

Strauss at his most passionate (and lascivious!) bookends a concert full of spectacle and panache. At its heart is the patriotic cantata Prokofiev drew from his music for Eisenstein's epic film about a medieval Russian hero's defeat of the Teutonic invader. That score had quite an impact on Walton's own wartime work for the cinema but it is the subtler brio of his Violin Concerto that is heard before the interval. Midori is one of relatively few international superstars to have taken up a piece whose formidable technical challenges were actively encouraged by Jascha Heifetz, its original soloist, but whose lyricism is all-pervasive too.

Broadcast
RADIO Live on Radio 3
ONLINE Live and 'listen again' options at bbc.co.uk/proms
TV Live on BBC Two

WEEKEND PROMMING PASS (SEE PAGE 158)

SUNDAY 31 JULY

7.00pm–c9.05pm

Rachmaninov

Spring	17'
Aleko – Women's and Men's Dances	9'
Three Russian Songs	14'

INTERVAL

Rachmaninov

Vocalise	7'
The Bells	38'

Svetla Vassileva soprano
Misha Didyk tenor
Alexei Tanovitsky baritone

Chorus of the Mariinsky Theatre
BBC Philharmonic
Gianandrea Noseda conductor

Much of Rachmaninov's best music has been slow to enter the repertoire. His evocative choral symphony *The Bells*, unheard at the Proms until 1973, is based on an adaptation by the Russian Symbolist poet Konstantin Balmont of verses by Edgar Allan Poe. Never previously given complete at the Proms, the Three Russian Songs are poignant, gem-like time capsules of a Russia now irretrievably lost.
See 'Choral Sundays', pages 62–65

Broadcast
RADIO Live on Radio 3
ONLINE Live and 'listen again' options at bbc.co.uk/proms

MONDAY 1 AUGUST

1.00pm–c2.00pm

Proms Chamber Music at Cadogan Hall

Lully
Les amours déguisés – 'Ah Rinaldo, e dovè sei?'   7'

F. Couperin
Les nations – La Piemontaise   19'

Montéclair
Cantata 'Morte di Lucretia'   14'

Rameau
Pièces de clavecin en concerts – Premier Concert   12'

Eugénie Warnier soprano

Les Talens Lyriques
Christophe Rousset harpsichord/director

Christophe Rousset

Christophe Rousset's supremely elegant ensemble, which has been breathing new life into the rich legacy of the French Baroque for more than 20 years, presents a programme squarely in the Gallic tradition but with influences from across the Alps. The programme includes a selection from Couperin's colourful *Les nations* and Rameau's delicately poised *Pièces en concerts*. Less familiar may be the eloquent cantata by Michel Pignolet de Montéclair, an important musical figure in the period between Lully and Rameau, who counted Couperin's daughters among his pupils. The story of Lucretia and her suicide is taken up by a young soprano who has been making quite a name for herself since abandoning a career in medicine for the healing balm of music. See 'French Connections', pages 36–39

There will be no interval

Broadcast
RADIO Live on Radio 3
ONLINE Live and 'listen again' options at bbc.co.uk/proms

MONDAY 1 AUGUST

7.30pm–c9.50pm

Beethoven
Symphony No. 4 in B flat major   34'

Saint-Saëns
Piano Concerto No. 5 in F major, 'Egyptian'   27'

INTERVAL

Liszt
Dante Symphony   41'

Stephen Hough piano
Julia Doyle soprano

CBSO Chorus (women's voices)
BBC Philharmonic
Gianandrea Noseda conductor

First the sunny surfaces and barely contained energy of Beethoven's Fourth Symphony. Next, a favourite Proms performer in the last of five discreetly glittering, very French piano concertos he has done so much to champion in recent years. After the interval, a major peak of Romanticism as conceived by one of this year's anniversary composers, Liszt, whom the young Saint-Saëns knew and greatly admired. Written back to back with the *Faust Symphony* heard earlier in the season, Liszt's *Dante Symphony* should leave listeners looking to the heights of Heaven. See 'A Lust for Liszt', pages 24–27

Stephen Hough

Broadcast
RADIO Live on Radio 3
ONLINE Live and 'listen again' options at bbc.co.uk/proms

TUESDAY 2 AUGUST

7.00pm–c9.15pm

Elgar

| There is sweet music | 4' |
| Violin Concerto | 50' |

INTERVAL

Sir Andrew Davis

Grainger

| Irish Tune from County Derry | 4' |
| Suite 'In a Nutshell' | 20' |

R. Strauss

| Till Eulenspiegels lustige Streiche | 15' |

Tasmin Little violin

BBC Singers
BBC Symphony Orchestra
Sir Andrew Davis conductor

Tasmin Little

Tasmin Little and Sir Andrew Davis tackle a favourite
concerto which the violinist has only recently felt ready
to commit to disc. It is preceded by one of Elgar's most
radical part-songs, notated in two keys simultaneously
in a manner which might be said to parallel the
incorrigible experiments of Percy Grainger. To mark
the 50th anniversary of that composer's death,
his *In a Nutshell* suite receives a first outing at the
Proms, reaching its popular march finale by way
of some unpredictable and darkly complex
invention. Once considered dangerously
radical itself, Strauss's perky symphonic
poem documents the adventures of
a purely mythical rascal.

SAME-DAY SAVER Book for both Proms 24 and 25 and save (see page 158)

TUESDAY 2 AUGUST

10.15pm–c11.30pm

Grainger

Green Bushes	9'
Molly on the Shore	5'
Shepherd's Hey – medley	12'
Early One Morning	5'
Shallow Brown	8'
Scotch Strathspey and Reel	9'

*Interspersed with traditional and contemporary
folk music, including material which formed the
basis for Grainger's arrangements*

June Tabor folk singer
Wilson Family
BBC Singers (men's voices)
Kathryn Tickell Band
Northern Sinfonia
John Harle conductor

Grainger is celebrated in a special Late Night sequence
as star Northumbrian smallpiper Kathryn Tickell and
friends take a fresh look at the prodigious activities of
this wild colonial boy. A pioneering collector of folk
music from around the globe and arguably the world's
first crossover artist, Grainger explored new worlds
and invented new sounds, by turns touching, funny and
provocative. Special guests, including the distinguished
English folk singer June Tabor, place his achievement
in its folk-music context.

There will be no interval

PROM 25
Spotlight on … Kathryn Tickell

'The thing about Grainger,' says Kathryn Tickell,
'is the exhilaration you get listening to his
arrangements. The way he treats folk music is
never twee.' The Northumbrian smallpipes player
and the guiding force behind this celebration of
the Australian's folk-music explorations could
be forgiven for her opinion that some composers
used the traditional music of these islands to
present a 'chocolate-box' view of the peasantry.

'There's a tendency to treat traditional
melodies in a rather worthy and slightly
patronising way. Grainger absolutely did not
have that attitude. He would choose tunes that
maybe weren't the most beautiful but use them as
vehicles for his creativity. The way he orchestrates
and arranges this music makes me listen to it with
absolute awe and admiration – and jubilation.'

Since beginning to research Grainger, Tickell
says she has found his approach to folk music
'quirky and outrageous and very unconventional,'
which suits his material well. 'His music can have
quite a bit of aggression about it, of fierceness,
but at the same time a lot of humour.' And it's
addictive, too: 'The only problem is that there's
so much material I was desperate to include.
I could do a whole week of Percy Grainger and
his folk music!'

WEDNESDAY 3 AUGUST

Proms Plus Family 5.30pm, Royal College of Music
Rachel Leach and musicians from the BBC Scottish Symphony Orchestra bring tonight's concert to life by uncovering the stories behind the pieces. Live musical examples and jargon-free explanations make this perfect for all the family! Bring your instrument and join in.

7.30pm–c9.55pm

Debussy
Prélude à L'après-midi d'un faune   8'

Henri Dutilleux
'Tout un monde lointain …'   27'

Ravel
Boléro   15'

INTERVAL

Ravel
Daphnis and Chloë   50'

Lynn Harrell cello

Edinburgh Festival Chorus
BBC Scottish Symphony Orchestra
Donald Runnicles conductor

Returning to the Proms for the first time since 1988, cellist Lynn Harrell celebrates the 95th-birthday year of Henri Dutilleux with a performance of one of his best-loved works, nocturnal, mysterious and beautifully coloured. Debussy's languorous reverie fired up a stylistic revolution and gained notoriety when Nijinsky choreographed it for Diaghilev's Ballets Russes. The same company commissioned Ravel's sumptuous evocation of Ancient Greece, embracing the most atmospheric sunrise in all music, but before that there's room for his notionally Hispanic experiment in writing 'orchestral tissue without music' – the ever-popular Boléro. See 'French Connections', pages 36–39

PROMS 26 & 27
Spotlight on … Donald Runnicles

Donald Runnicles took up his position as Chief Conductor of the BBC Scottish Symphony Orchestra in 2009 and combines this role with his work as General Music Director of the Deutsche Oper Berlin. 'The attributes of the BBC SSO players are those you would expect from a world-class orchestra – technical mastery, great musicianship and a pride in excellent ensemble,' he says. 'There's also a passionate commitment to contemporary music.'

Runnicles precedes his largely Austro-German programme of Holloway, Strauss and Brahms (Prom 27) with French classics spanning more than 75 years, including Debussy's *Prélude à L'après-midi d'un faune*, Ravel's *Boléro* and his ballet *Daphnis and Chloë*, which, according to the conductor, features 'breathtaking orchestral textures you could almost touch'.

Just as Debussy evoked the atmosphere of Mallarmé's sultry poem in the *Prélude*, so Henri Dutilleux was inspired by Baudelaire in his cello concerto '*Tout un monde lointain …*'. Runnicles sees other connections between the two. 'There are many ravishing orchestral colours and textures in the Dutilleux which are reminiscent of Debussy, as well as of Ravel: they are all utterly, uniquely, sensuously French.'

Broadcast
RADIO Live on Radio 3
ONLINE Live and 'listen again' options at bbc.co.uk/proms
TV Recorded for broadcast on BBC Four on 7 August

THURSDAY 4 AUGUST

Proms Plus Intro 5.15pm, Royal College of Music
Matthew Rowe and musicians from the BBC Scottish Symphony Orchestra offer an illustrated guide to the music in tonight's programme with recorded and live musical examples. Ideal for anyone wanting to explore classical music.

7.00pm–c9.05pm

Robin Holloway
Fifth Concerto for Orchestra   c25'
BBC commission: world premiere

R. Strauss
Four Last Songs   22'

INTERVAL

Brahms
Symphony No. 2 in D major   40'

Hillevi Martinpelto soprano

BBC Scottish Symphony Orchestra
Donald Runnicles conductor

Hillevi Martinpelto

Donald Runnicles and his orchestra open their second Prom this season with a major world premiere, the latest in Robin Holloway's unique series of allusive and extravagantly inventive showpieces for orchestra. In his willingness to make a big Romantic splash, Holloway is sometimes likened to Richard Strauss, although that composer is at his most reflective in the *Four Last Songs*. Brahms's Second Symphony has its melancholic, contemplative aspect but ends on a note of unalloyed triumph. See 'Back to Brahms', pages 30–33; 'New Music', pages 68–75

SAME-DAY SAVER
Book for both Proms 27 and 28 and save (see page 158)

Broadcast
RADIO Live on Radio 3
ONLINE Live and 'listen again' options at bbc.co.uk/proms

THURSDAY 4 AUGUST

10.00pm–c11.15pm

Victoria

Dum complerentur	5'
Lamentations for Good Friday	15'
Officium defunctorum (Requiem)	42'

Tallis Scholars
Peter Phillips *conductor*

Who better to mark the 400th anniversary of the death of Tomás Luis de Victoria than the Tallis Scholars, long established under conductor Peter Phillips as among the world's finest interpreters of Renaissance polyphony? Celebrating a composer who featured in their very first Proms appearance in 1988, the focal point tonight is the magisterial *Office for the Dead* of which they made a much-praised recording some years ago. The Spanish master's exceptional expressive charge is achieved with a directness of musical means which sets his work apart from that of contemporaries active in England and Italy. Comparisons have been drawn with the equally intense religious paintings of Velázquez and El Greco. This promises to be a moving and evocative Late Night experience.

There will be no interval

SAME-DAY SAVER Book for both Proms 27 and 28 and save (see page 158)

Peter Phillips

Broadcast
RADIO Live on Radio 3
ONLINE Live and 'listen again' options at bbc.co.uk/proms

FRIDAY 5 AUGUST

Proms Plus Intro 5.45pm, Royal College of Music
Mahler was one of the most complex and enigmatic composers. Julian Johnson, author of *Mahler's Voices* and Professor of Music at Royal Holloway, University of London, and broadcaster and classical music enthusiast Dr Christian Jessen discuss what his music means to them and why they will always come back for more. Presented by Louise Fryer.

Proms Plus Late Elgar Room, Royal Albert Hall
Informal post-Prom music and poetry. For details see bbc.co.uk/proms

7.30pm–c9.10pm

Mahler

Symphony No. 2 in C minor, 'Resurrection'   85'

Miah Persson *soprano*
Anna Larsson *mezzo-soprano*

National Youth Choir of Great Britain
Simón Bolívar Symphony Orchestra
Gustavo Dudamel *conductor*

Now Music Director of the Los Angeles Philharmonic, Gustavo Dudamel – known by his own musicians as 'the Dude' – joins his old friends in the Simón Bolívar Symphony Orchestra and some mightily distinguished guests to tackle a colossus of the standard repertoire. Writing for vast forces including offstage brass, two solo singers and a large choir, Mahler takes listeners on a spectacular journey through the entire gamut of emotions. Beginning at the graveside, he remembers happier, busier and (spiritually) emptier times on the way to an apocalyptic revelation of the Day of Judgement. The promise of eternal life is then renewed in some of music's most uplifting pages.

There will be no interval

Gustavo Dudamel

PROM 29
Spotlight on …
Simón Bolívar Symphony Orchestra

When the Simón Bolívar Youth Orchestra of Venezuela (as it was then called) first performed at the Proms in 2007, its young players set the hall alight with their sense of joy and exuberant music-making. Led by their dynamic conductor, Gustavo Dudamel, they won over audiences and critics alike, prompting the *Daily Telegraph* to ask: 'Was this the greatest Prom of all time?'

The musicians are formed from Venezuela's El Sistema programme, an initiative that offers every child a free musical education – and one which has sparked a musical renaissance there. 'I think the reason the orchestra and all the youngsters of El Sistema generate such a positive interest is because for us this isn't a job, not even a concert; for us music is all of life,' says concertmaster Alejandro Carreño.

The orchestra performs Mahler's 'Resurrection' Symphony, 'a magnificent monument to two great truths of humanity: one being the fear of that unknown world of death, and the other the faith that drives us forward to a belief in eternal life,' explains Carreño. 'Mahler's music is so descriptive, the atmosphere it creates is like that of an opera. We hugely enjoy playing his music.'

Broadcast
RADIO Live on Radio 3
ONLINE Live and 'listen again' options at bbc.co.uk/proms
TV Recorded for broadcast on BBC Two on 6 August and on BBC Four on 28 August

WEEKEND PROMMING PASS • BEAT THE QUEUES AND SAVE MONEY *(SEE PAGE 158)*

SATURDAY 6 AUGUST

Proms Plus Inspire 4.30pm, Royal College of Music
The Aurora Orchestra, conducted by Nicholas Collon, performs the winning entries from this year's Proms Inspire Young Composers' Competition. *(Reduced seating capacity)*
Edited version broadcast on BBC Radio 3 on 12 August

6.30pm–c9.05pm

Gabriel Prokofiev
Concerto for Turntables and Orchestra   21'

Britten
Piano Concerto   35'

INTERVAL

Prokofiev
Romeo and Juliet – selection   50'

Benjamin Grosvenor *piano*
DJ Switch *turntables*

National Youth Orchestra of Great Britain
Vladimir Jurowski *conductor*

The music of Sergey Prokofiev looms large in this fascinating collaboration between Vladimir Jurowski and the National Youth Orchestra of Great Britain. First, an esoteric offering from the master's London-based grandson, a crossover artist in the best sense, determined to find new audiences and to reconfigure the classical tradition by way of Minimalist grooves, dancefloor beats, club nights and remixes. The influence of the senior Prokofiev is plain in the sizzling keyboard writing of Britten's early Piano Concerto, which gives BBC Radio 3 New Generation Artist Benjamin Grosvenor another chance to shine, following his First Night Proms debut. In the second half, Prokofiev's ballet music recounts the doomed love of Verona's most romantic couple.
See 'Featured Artists', pages 78–81

Broadcast
RADIO Live on Radio 3
ONLINE Live and 'listen again' options at bbc.co.uk/proms
TV Recorded for broadcast on BBC Two on 13 August

SATURDAY 6 AUGUST

10.00pm–c11.00pm

J. S. Bach
Solo violin works

Nigel Kennedy *violin*

When in 2008 Nigel Kennedy came back to the Proms after an absence of 21 years, his Late Night concert with his own quartet followed an early-evening performance of Elgar's Violin Concerto which he capped with a solo Bach encore. Tonight's special event confirms that JSB continues to mean a great deal to him. The man dubbed 'the people's violinist' has recorded Bach concertos with the Irish Chamber Orchestra and with members of the Berlin Philharmonic. Discovering something new every time he explores the composer's music, Kennedy points up the parallels with jazz. Bach loved the dance forms of his own day and his music benefits from being played with emotional freedom and a keen rhythmic sense.

There will be no interval

SAME-DAY SAVER
Book for both Proms 30 and 31 and save (see page 158)

Nigel Kennedy

Broadcast
RADIO Live on Radio 3
ONLINE Live and 'listen again' options at bbc.co.uk/proms
TV Recorded for broadcast on BBC Four on 9 September

SUNDAY 7 AUGUST

Proms Plus Sing
1.00pm–3.00pm, Royal College of Music
Enter the fairy-tale world of Mahler's *Das klagende Lied* by preparing your own performance alongside professional singers. Ideal for enthusiastic amateur singers aged 16-plus. See pages 92–99 for details of how to sign up.

Proms Plus Intro 5.15pm, Royal College of Music
The fourth in the series of introductions to the music performed in Proms Choral Sundays. Andrew McGregor explores Mahler's *Das klagende Lied* with recorded extracts and with live music examples from members of the BBC Symphony Orchestra and BBC Singers. Ideal for anyone wanting to explore classical music.
Broadcast live on BBC Radio 3

7.00pm–c9.25pm

Brahms
Violin Concerto in D major   40'

INTERVAL

Mahler
Das klagende Lied (original version)   68'

Christian Tetzlaff *violin*
Melanie Diener *soprano*
Ekaterina Gubanova *mezzo-soprano*
Stuart Skelton *tenor*
Christopher Purves *baritone*

BBC Singers
BBC Symphony Orchestra
Edward Gardner *conductor*

Featured artist Christian Tetzlaff has played many of the great violin concertos but this is his first Proms performance of the big-boned, technically demanding work by Brahms, all of whose concertos can be heard during this Proms season. With his early *Das klagende Lied*, Mahler hit upon his own unique style. Tonight's account includes 'Waldmärchen', the emotive first panel dealing with the quest of brother knights for a flower that will win a queen's hand but leads to sibling murder. The score resurfaced as recently as 1969.
See 'Back to Brahms', pages 30–33; 'Choral Sundays', pages 62–65; 'Featured Artists', pages 78–81

Broadcast
RADIO Live on Radio 3
ONLINE Live and 'listen again' options at bbc.co.uk/proms

MONDAY 8 AUGUST

1.00pm–c2.00pm

Proms Chamber Music at Cadogan Hall

Liszt
Piano Sonata in B minor *30'*

Liebesträume – No. 3: O Lieb, so lang du lieben kannst! *5'*

Prokofiev
Piano Sonata No. 7 in B flat major *19'*

Khatia Buniatishvili *piano*

Khatia Buniatishvili

BBC Radio 3 New Generation Artist Khatia Buniatishvili is already turning heads with her mesmerising stage presence and a unique style of pianism mixing uncanny sensitivity with old-school fireworks. In this recital she explores the different brands of virtuosity perfected by two composer-pianists. Liszt, one of this year's prominent anniversary figures, shares the bill with a more recent practitioner whose Seventh Sonata contains the most dynamic music ever devised by a composer renowned for his motoric piano style. See *'A Lust for Liszt'*, pages 24–27

There will be no interval

Broadcast
RADIO Live on Radio 3
ONLINE Live and 'listen again' options at bbc.co.uk/proms

Prom 33

MONDAY 8 AUGUST

Proms Plus Literary 5.45pm, Royal College of Music
Val McDermid and Louise Welsh, award-winning crime writers, explore the explosion in Scandinavian crime-writing, from Henning Mankell's Wallander to Stieg Larsson's *The Girl with the Dragon Tattoo* and rising star Jo Nesbø. Rana Mitter hosts.
Edited version broadcast on BBC Radio 3 during tonight's interval

7.30pm–c9.45pm

Sibelius
Symphony No. 6 in D minor *28'*

Grieg
Piano Concerto in A minor *30'*

INTERVAL

Nielsen
Symphony No. 4, 'Inextinguishable' *35'*

Alice Sara Ott *piano*

Royal Stockholm Philharmonic Orchestra
Sakari Oramo *conductor*

Absent from the Proms since 2004, the Royal Stockholm Philharmonic Orchestra is back with a new Chief Conductor, no stranger to these shores (as a former Music Director of the CBSO), and a suitably Nordic programme. Sibelius claimed to be offering the public 'pure cold water' with music like his magical Sixth Symphony – other composers were, he said, 'engaged in the manufacture of cocktails'. Nielsen's Fourth is a more extrovert piece, a celebration of the tenacity of the human spirit from the dark days of the First World War, complete with battling sets of timpani and earth-shattering climaxes. Between the two symphonies, critically acclaimed young German-Japanese pianist Alice Sara Ott makes her Proms debut in one of the most popular of all piano concertos.

Sakari Oramo

PROM 33
Spotlight on … Alice Sara Ott

This will be the first time the young German-Japanese pianist Alice Sara Ott has stepped into the Royal Albert Hall. 'I've known about the Proms since I was a child but I have never been – I was incredibly happy to be invited!'

Nerves are unlikely to deter her, however: she already has a terrific track record of jumping into the breach – and winning over audiences. Having stood in for Hélène Grimaud in a concert conducted by Daniel Harding, she was subsequently a last-minute replacement for Lang Lang with the LSO last autumn. However, perhaps the most difficult occasion was when she replaced Murray Perahia. 'The audience had no idea he wasn't coming and I could actually hear the sound of their disappointment,' she recalls. 'But it was an opportunity. They had no expectations of me, so their response was more honest. If you find a good response in a disappointed audience, then you have really achieved something.'

She recently toured Japan with Oramo and the Royal Stockholm PO, and they have a close relationship. 'It was a great experience; every hall was different, every acoustic, every concert unique and unrepeatable. It's so exciting to tour! But I did realise I also have physical limits, and I'll be spending some time at home learning repertoire before the Prom this summer.'

Broadcast
RADIO Live on Radio 3
ONLINE Live and 'listen again' options at bbc.co.uk/proms

*Calls cost up to 5p/min from a BT landline (min connection fee of 11.8p may apply). Calls from mobiles and other networks may cost considerably more. All calls will be recorded and may be monitored for training and quality-control purposes.

131

TUESDAY 9 AUGUST

Proms Plus Intro 5.15pm, Royal College of Music
Louise Fryer is joined by Dr Kate Kennedy and composer and
writer Anthony Payne to explore the life and works of English
composer Frank Bridge, and to discuss why he should be
better known.

7.00pm–c9.05pm

Bridge
Enter Spring   17'
Blow out, you bugles   5'

Simon Holt
Centauromachy   20'
BBC commission: London premiere

INTERVAL

Dupré
Cortège et litanie   6'

Saint-Saëns
Symphony No. 3 in C minor, 'Organ'   36'

Ben Johnson tenor
Robert Plane clarinet
Philippe Schartz flugelhorn
Thomas Trotter organ

BBC National Orchestra of Wales
François-Xavier Roth conductor

An Anglo-French evening launched by the greatest of
the nature tone-poems written by featured composer
Frank Bridge. Simon Holt's double concerto for clarinet
and flugelhorn takes its inspiration from the fantastical
beasts of Greek mythology. His solo instruments are
drawn from different species, two distinct natures in
one orchestral body. Marcel Dupré was a masterly
executant who himself played Saint-Saëns's much-loved
'Organ' Symphony at the Proms in 1935. See 'French
Connections', pages 36–39; 'Out of the Shadows',
pages 48–49; 'New Music', pages 68–75

Broadcast
RADIO Live on Radio 3
ONLINE Live and 'listen again' options at bbc.co.uk/proms

WEDNESDAY 10 AUGUST

Proms Plus Intro 5.15pm, Royal College of Music
Matthew Rowe and musicians from the Bournemouth Symphony
Orchestra offer an illustrated guide to the works in tonight's
programme with recorded and live musical examples. Ideal
for anyone wanting to explore classical music.

7.00pm–c9.40pm

Liszt
Mazeppa   17'

Glière
Concerto for Coloratura Soprano   14'

INTERVAL

Rachmaninov
Symphony No. 2 in E minor   62'

Ailish Tynan soprano

Bournemouth Symphony Orchestra
Kirill Karabits conductor

Ailish Tynan

Liszt's symphonic poem
(he invented the genre)
is based on Victor Hugo's
poem about the
legendary Mazeppa,
a nobleman caught in
flagrante who is tied to
a wild horse which is
then driven into the night.
Continuing this season's
exploration of non-
standard concertos,
Ailish Tynan tackles a Glière rarity unheard at the
Proms since the 1980s. By contrast, Rachmaninov's
gloriously lyrical Second Symphony has become a firm
favourite in recent years. A sense of symphonic unity is
provided by its network of thematic cross-references,
which also give rise to some of the composer's best
tunes. The Adagio is especially famous for its lovely,
long-breathed clarinet melody over softly murmuring
violins. See 'A Lust for Liszt', pages 24–27

Broadcast
RADIO Live on Radio 3
ONLINE Live and 'listen again' options at bbc.co.uk/proms

PROM 35
Spotlight on … Kirill Karabits

Kirill Karabits won't easily forget his Proms debut
in 2009 with Khachaturian's *Spartacus*, just at
the start of his tenure in Bournemouth. 'It was
a unique experience – I've never conducted such
a concert in my life. I've been to huge events, like
at the Hollywood Bowl, but what struck me at
the Proms was the energy and commitment of the
audience, the way they almost seemed to breathe
with us when we played.'

This year the Ukrainian brings a Proms rarity,
Glière's Concerto for Coloratura Soprano. 'In our
former Soviet Union this piece was very popular
but I know it will be a surprise for many of the
Prommers. It's highly original, full of beautiful
melodies, with a wordless part for the singer.
It celebrates the soprano voice.' Karabits is eagerly
anticipating Ailish Tynan's performance as soloist.
'I'm very interested in hearing a non-Russian
soprano tackle this. I'm sure it will be totally
different to the approach of a native singer.'

His choice of Liszt's *Mazeppa* is
more than a nod to the composer's
bicentenary: 'Mazeppa is an
important historical figure for us
in Ukraine. Liszt was fascinated by
Victor Hugo's poem on the subject and
this is his response – a highly virtuosic
piece and rarely played.'

SAME-DAY SAVER
Book for both
Proms 35 and 36
and save (see
page 158)

WEDNESDAY 10 AUGUST

10.15pm–c11.30pm

Reich

Clapping Music	5'
Electric Counterpoint	15'
Music for 18 Musicians	55'

Synergy Vocals
Ensemble Modern
Steve Reich

The Proms celebrates Steve Reich's 75th birthday year with a distinguished instrumental ensemble – making its first appearance since 2004 – and a clutch of seminal pieces. While this founding father of American Minimalism remains extraordinarily active, his *Music for 18 Musicians* is widely recognised as a peak in his own output and that of post-war music in general. The Ensemble Modern, no strangers to a work whose sonic architecture is founded on subtle shifts of harmonic and rhythmic direction, are sure to illuminate every instrumental strand, pointing connections with the composer's earlier process music. An amazing score that can be enjoyed on many levels, simultaneously propulsive and calming, this is the first time *Music for 18 Musicians* has been heard at the Proms.

There will be no interval

PROM 36
Spotlight on … Steve Reich

The distinctive music of American composer Steve Reich, a pioneer of Minimalism, is notable for its hypnotic use of compelling rhythms and repetitive patterns. His work incorporates a wide range of influences, from jazz to non-Western harmonies and African drumming styles.

Electric Counterpoint is one such example. 'One of the melodies in the first movement comes from central Africa, from a book of transcriptions of African horn music,' says Reich. 'It's basically a unison canon but with many different harmonisations of that melody.' Although written for electric guitar accompanied by guitar ensemble, guitarists often record their own accompaniment, multi-tracking themselves. 'The way a player uses his instrument is very idiomatic, so when you multiply that, it becomes more forceful and apparent.'

The programme opens with *Clapping Music* – 'when two people come out and show that music can be made with no more than their bodies' – and ends with *Music for 18 Musicians*, 'probably my best-known piece, which I wrote in 1976,' says Reich. 'As I get older, I find perhaps the most gratifying thing is to encounter really idiomatic, excellent performances of my music, such as I regularly do with Ensemble Modern.'

SAME-DAY SAVER
Book for both Proms 35 and 36 and save (see page 158)

Broadcast
RADIO Live on Radio 3
ONLINE Live and 'listen again' options at bbc.co.uk/proms

THURSDAY 11 AUGUST

Proms Plus Family 5.30pm, Royal College of Music
Rachel Leach and musicians from the BBC Philharmonic take you on a fast-paced ride through the works in this evening's concert. Come along with your instrument, meet the musicians and get to know the stories behind the music.

7.30pm–c9.50pm

Bridge
Overture 'Rebus'   9'

Brahms, arr. Lazić
'Piano Concerto No. 3' in D major
(after Violin Concerto)   39'
UK premiere

INTERVAL

Holst
Invocation   10'

Elgar
Enigma Variations   28'

Dejan Lazić *piano*
Julian Lloyd Webber *cello*

BBC Philharmonic
Vassily Sinaisky *conductor*

Julian Lloyd Webber

Vassily Sinaisky

The BBC Philharmonic's Chief Guest Conductor (who becomes Conductor Emeritus in September) continues his exploration of less-frequented corners of the repertoire, proceeding from an invigorating British concert-opener to an uncommon yet inescapably familiar concerto. Inspired by the fact that Bach and Beethoven arranged their own violin concertos for the keyboard, Dejan Lazić has done the same for the Brahms with engagingly idiomatic results. Julian Lloyd Webber is an ardent champion of Holst's *Invocation*. The concert ends with Elgar's affectionate sketches of 'friends pictured within' – a firm favourite that retains its own aura of mystery. *See 'Back to Brahms', pages 30–33; 'Out of the Shadows', pages 48–49; 'New Music', pages 68–75; 'Featured Artists', pages 78–81*

Broadcast
RADIO Live on Radio 3
ONLINE Live and 'listen again' options at bbc.co.uk/proms

WEEKEND PROMMING PASS • BEAT THE QUEUES AND SAVE MONEY (*SEE PAGE 158*)

FRIDAY 12 AUGUST

Proms Plus Literary 5.15pm, Royal College of Music
Sir Ronald Harwood, Oscar-winning screenwriter of *The Pianist* and *The Diving Bell and the Butterfly*, and Neil Brand, doyen of silent film pianists, discuss the role of music in film – from the Keystone Kops to indie films. Matthew Sweet presents.
Edited version broadcast on BBC Radio 3 during tonight's interval

7.00pm–*c*9.20pm

Film Music Prom

Herrmann
Music from The Man Who Knew Too Much, Citizen Kane, North by Northwest and Psycho   *18'*

Ennio Morricone
Cinema Paradiso – theme   *7'*

Walton, arr. Muir Mathieson
Henry V – suite   *21'*

INTERVAL

John Williams
Music from Star Wars, Schindler's List and Harry Potter   *14'*

Jonny Greenwood, arr. Robert Ziegler
Norwegian Wood – suite   *10'*
BBC commission: world premiere

Sir Richard Rodney Bennett
Murder on the Orient Express – suite   *8'*

Barry
Out of Africa – Love Theme   *7'*

Various
Music from the James Bond films   *10'*

Chloë Hanslip *violin*

BBC Concert Orchestra
Keith Lockhart *conductor*

Assisted by guest star Chloë Hanslip, Keith Lockhart and the BBC Concert Orchestra bring the silver-screen excitement of music associated with the cinema, from Pinewood to Hollywood, from *Psycho* to *Star Wars*, with a special tribute to the late John Barry.

PROM 38
Spotlight on … Keith Lockhart

'I'm so looking forward to conducting the Film Music Prom. This is a serious look at some truly great scores, with a focus on the great British film composers. It's an evening where we can hear an incredibly wide variety of really good music, where each work has enough of a dramatic and emotional life of its own to exist away from the film it was created for.

'Some of the most beautiful film music comes from the pens of John Williams and John Barry. They're both so brilliant at variety. It's extraordinary to think the same composer wrote the music for *Star Wars* and the score for *Schindler's List*. I'm a huge James Bond junkie, so it's great to include a tribute to the immense amount of music that's been composed for the James Bond films, especially since the sad passing of John Barry. I'm really looking forward to the Walton suite too; his music creates some of the most beautiful and stirring movie moments ever.

'It's fantastic to be working with the BBC Concert Orchestra again. I find the players incredibly quick and flexible. They're just totally committed in a really wonderful way to working at their highest individual levels, which results in a collective thing that is really great.'

SAME-DAY SAVER Book for both Proms 38 and 39 and save (see page 158)

Broadcast
RADIO Live on Radio 3
ONLINE Live and 'listen again' options at bbc.co.uk/proms
TV Broadcast on BBC Four at 7.30pm

FRIDAY 12 AUGUST

10.15pm–*c*11.30pm

Spaghetti Western Orchestra

Spaghetti Western Orchestra

The five inventive multitaskers of the Spaghetti Western Orchestra have their own way of presenting film music in concert. Fascinated by the scores of Ennio Morricone, they have devised an unclassifiable entertainment in which his epic soundtracks for film-maker Sergio Leone are recreated with extraordinary virtuosity on instruments both conventional and rather less so. 'We really embraced the absurdity of a bunch of Aussie guys trying to do what Morricone did with a cast of hundreds and so we went about listening to the music and exploring the idea that every sound is equal and giving equal importance to all sounds.' Expect a loose narrative, new uses for the asthma inhaler and the cornflake packet, and a rich harvest of post-modern laughs.

There will be no interval

Broadcast
RADIO Live on Radio 3
ONLINE Live and 'listen again' options at bbc.co.uk/proms
TV Recorded for broadcast on BBC Four on 26 August

WEEKEND PROMMING PASS • BEAT THE QUEUES AND SAVE MONEY (SEE PAGE 158)

SATURDAY 13 AUGUST

3.00pm–c4.30pm

Proms Saturday Matinee at Cadogan Hall

Sir Richard Rodney Bennett
Dream Dancing   16'

Henri Dutilleux
Les citations   14'

Maconchy
Romanza   12'

Sir Richard Rodney Bennett
Jazz Calendar   30'

Paul Silverthorne viola

London Sinfonietta
Nicholas Collon conductor

Sir Richard Rodney Bennett

Sir Richard Rodney Bennett, one of Britain's most respected and versatile musicians, turned 75 this year and the first of this season's contemporary music matinees pays tribute to his distinctive creative voice and its French connections. His sensuous, Debussy-inspired *Dream Dancing* was written for the London Sinfonietta in the mid-1980s. Dutilleux is one of the living composers he most admires, while Elizabeth Maconchy, impulsively contacted when he was still a schoolboy, would later become a friend. Her *Romanza* is quietly tough-minded, though not too tough to disturb its prevailing mood of gentle soulfulness. Starting life as a BBC commission for an extended jazz composition, *Jazz Calendar* was developed into a Frederick Ashton ballet, starrily cast and with designs by the young Derek Jarman. See 'French Connections', pages 36–39

There will be no interval

Broadcast
RADIO Live on Radio 3
ONLINE Live and 'listen again' options at bbc.co.uk/proms

SATURDAY 13 AUGUST

Proms Plus Literary 5.45pm, Royal College of Music
Since Chaucer's *Canterbury Tales* 600 years ago, writers have been making us laugh – but what makes literary comic gold? Comedians Natalie Haynes and Steve Punt join Matthew Sweet to unveil and perform their favourite humorous writing from down the ages.
Edited version broadcast on BBC Radio 3 during tonight's interval

Proms Plus Late Elgar Room, Royal Albert Hall
Informal post-Prom music and poetry. For details see bbc.co.uk/proms

7.30pm–c9.40pm

Comedy Prom

Tim Minchin
Sue Perkins
Kit and The Widow
Susan Bullock soprano
Danny Driver piano

BBC Concert Orchestra
Jules Buckley conductor

Musician, actor, comedian and rock 'n' roll superstar Tim Minchin hosts a Proms first – the Comedy Prom. Joined by guests including BBC Two *Maestro* winner Sue Perkins, musical cabaret duo Kit and The Widow, soprano Susan Bullock and rising star British pianist Danny Driver (making his Proms debut), Tim will weave his way through a spectacular evening of comedy, musical fun and surprises. Highlights will include Franz Reizenstein's *Concerto popolare*, a whistlestop tour through competing favourite piano concertos, in a programme which offers a fresh, accessible and funny take on the Proms, accompanied on a grand scale by the ever-versatile BBC Concert Orchestra. See 'Featured Artists', pages 78–81

Tim Minchin

There will be one interval

Broadcast
RADIO Live on Radio 3
ONLINE Live and 'listen again' options at bbc.co.uk/proms
TV Recorded for broadcast on BBC Two on 13 August

SUNDAY 14 AUGUST

Proms Plus Sing
1.00pm–3.00pm, Royal College of Music
Come and take up the challenge of singing Britten's choral music by joining the chorus for a session exploring some of the works from tonight's Prom. Ideal for enthusiastic amateur singers aged 16-plus. See pages 92–99 for details of how to sign up.

Proms Plus Intro 5.15pm, Royal College of Music
The fifth in the series of introductions to the music performed in Proms Choral Sundays. Sara Mohr-Pietsch explores Britten's *Spring Symphony* with recorded extracts and with live music examples from members of the BBC Symphony Orchestra and BBC Singers. Ideal for anyone wanting to explore classical music.
Broadcast live on BBC Radio 3

7.00pm–c9.15pm

Purcell, arr. Joby Talbot
Chacony in G minor   7'
BBC commission: world premiere

Britten
Cantata misericordium   20'
Sinfonia da Requiem   20'

INTERVAL

Britten
Spring Symphony   45'

Amanda Roocroft soprano
Christine Rice mezzo-soprano
John Mark Ainsley tenor
Christopher Maltman baritone

Trinity Boys Choir
BBC Singers
BBC Symphony Chorus
BBC Symphony Orchestra
Jiří Bělohlávek conductor

A recreation of an all-Britten concert conducted in 1963 by the composer, but with a contemporary twist provided by Joby Talbot. For Britten, the *Spring Symphony* represented 'the reawakening of the earth and life'. See 'Choral Sundays', pages 62–65; 'New Music', pages 68–75; 'Featured Artists', pages 78–81

Broadcast
RADIO Live on Radio 3
ONLINE Live and 'listen again' options at bbc.co.uk/proms

MONDAY 15 AUGUST

1.00pm–c2.00pm

Proms Chamber Music at Cadogan Hall

Britten
Phantasy   14'

Bridge
Three Idylls – No. 2   3'

Britten
Piano Variations on a Theme of Frank Bridge   4'
London premiere

Bridge
Piano Quintet   27'

Nicholas Daniel *oboe*
Tom Poster *piano*
Aronowitz Ensemble

The Aronowitz Ensemble, former BBC Radio 3
New Generation Artists, explore Britten's musical
relationship with his teacher, Frank Bridge. The Piano
Variations, composed while Britten was still a student,
looks forward to his celebrated *Variations on a Theme
of Frank Bridge*, that masterpiece for string orchestra
to be performed later in the season (see Prom 50).
Today's concert begins with a striking composition
from the young Britten in which the oboist is Nicholas
Daniel, past winner of the BBC Young Musician of the
Year competition. Bridge's Piano Quintet comes from
relatively early in his own career, before the events of
the First World War cast a dark shadow on his creative
outlook. See 'Out of the Shadows', pages 48–49;
'New Music', pages 68–75

There will be no interval

PCM 5
Spotlight on … Nicholas Daniel

Oboist Nicholas Daniel has a special connection
with Britten's music, having worked closely with
the composer's partner Peter Pears at the start of
his musical career. 'Pears was very helpful when
I was starting out and it was wonderful to play
Britten's music to him,' says Daniel. 'Apparently
Britten used to talk about the oboe as a vocal
instrument. He writes in a flamboyant and lyrical
way for the oboe in this wonderful *Phantasy*
quartet. It's a virtuoso piece in every respect.'

Britten uses the pentatonic scale throughout
the piece, creating a seemingly improvised,
Eastern-sounding atmosphere, says Daniel. 'It
marches, it dances and feels very English but then
suddenly turns Indian. It's a very important piece
in the repertoire, which I absolutely love playing!'

The *Phantasy* quartet plays as one continuous
movement and the central section is scored for
strings only, thanks to a request from oboist
Leon Goossens, the work's dedicatee. 'Goossens
always used to ask composers for a good bit of
time off in the middle so he could rest his lips,
and Britten made this into a really massive gesture,'
says Daniel. 'He eventually brings the oboe back
in with a very high, very beautiful improvisatory-
sounding passage, played over a repeating rhythm
in the strings, which is a beautiful effect. It's a
short piece but it really packs a punch.'

Broadcast
RADIO Live on Radio 3
ONLINE Live and 'listen again' options at bbc.co.uk/proms

MONDAY 15 AUGUST

Proms Plus Family 5.30pm, Royal College of Music
Join Rachel Leach and dancer Monica Mason for an interactive
introduction to tonight's music. Ideal for all the family – bring
along your instrument and join in!

7.30pm–c10.05pm

Tchaikovsky
Swan Lake   118'

Orchestra of the Mariinsky Theatre
Valery Gergiev *conductor*

Valery Gergiev has often come to the Proms with
music from his native land and in 2008 it was the turn
of *The Sleeping Beauty*. This year the maestro brings his
Russian-based ensemble with another of Tchaikovsky's
three great ballet scores: *Swan Lake*, whose lyricism
and full-blown drama featured in the recent Oscar-
winning *Black Swan*. The plot concerns a Prince who
is expected to choose a bride from among the guests
at a forthcoming ball. Instead he falls in love with
Odette, the Swan Queen, whose swan subjects
revert to human form between midnight and dawn.
Early spectators were puzzled by the symphonic
proportions and sheer depth of feeling Tchaikovsky
brings to the tale, qualities brought into fuller focus
when all of this glorious score is heard.

There will be one interval

Valery Gergiev

Broadcast
RADIO Live on Radio 3
ONLINE Live and 'listen again' options at bbc.co.uk/proms

Booking opens 9.00am on 7 May: online at bbc.co.uk/proms • by telephone 0845 401 5040* • in person at the Royal Albert Hall

TUESDAY 16 AUGUST

> **Proms Plus Intro** 5.15pm, Royal College of Music
> Sara Mohr-Pietsch and musicians from the Royal Philharmonic Orchestra offer an illustrated guide to the works in tonight's programme with recorded and live musical examples. Ideal for anyone wanting to explore classical music.

7.00pm–c10.35pm

Copland
Fanfare for the Common Man   *3'*

Bax
Symphony No. 2   *39'*

INTERVAL

Barber
Adagio for strings   *8'*

Bartók
Piano Concerto No. 2   *28'*

INTERVAL

Prokofiev
Symphony No. 4 in C major
(revised version, 1947)   *37'*

Yuja Wang *piano*

Royal Philharmonic Orchestra
Andrew Litton *conductor*

Yuja Wang

Tonight's composers have something, or someone, in common: Boston Symphony Orchestra conductor Serge Koussevitzky. Copland's Fanfare was later incorporated into his Third Symphony, written for the Koussevitzky Music Foundation, which also commissioned Bartók's *Concerto for Orchestra*. Bax's Second Symphony was dedicated to the conductor, who also championed Barber's music in the 1940s. The original version of Prokofiev's Fourth Symphony was commissioned for the BSO's 50th anniversary and premiered under Koussevitzky. See 'Bartók Piano Concertos', pages 42–45

Broadcast
RADIO Live on Radio 3
ONLINE Live and 'listen again' options at bbc.co.uk/proms

WEDNESDAY 17 AUGUST

> **Proms Plus Literary** 5.45pm, Royal College of Music
> Dante's *Divine Comedy* and his character Francesca da Rimini have inspired writers from Milton to T. S. Eliot and the Beats. Historical novelist Sarah Dunant and Margaret Kean, author of *Inferno*, discuss the great Italian poet with presenter Susan Hitch.
> Edited version broadcast on BBC Radio 3 during tonight's interval

7.30pm–c10.05pm

Shostakovich
The Age of Gold – suite   *16'*
Violin Concerto No. 1 in A minor   *39'*

INTERVAL

Stravinsky
Petrushka (1947 version)   *34'*

Tchaikovsky
Francesca da Rimini   *22'*

Lisa Batiashvili *violin*

Philharmonia Orchestra
Esa-Pekka Salonen *conductor*

Esa-Pekka Salonen

Former BBC Radio 3 New Generation Artist Lisa Batiashvili has a special relationship with Shostakovich's profoundly moving concerto, as she demonstrated in a recent recording with tonight's conductor. She sees the work as peculiarly emblematic of the Soviet era, whose later days she experienced at first hand – a metaphorical escape and symbol of freedom for those struggling to function within the system. Stravinsky's tragic puppet love triangle dazzles in its 1947 revision, while Tchaikovsky's Russian-sounding music animates Dante's timeless tale of forbidden love and eternal punishment.

PROM 44
Spotlight on ... Lisa Batiashvili

Georgian violinist Lisa Batiashvili is a particularly welcome presence at this year's Proms after illness prevented her from performing the Berg Concerto last year. This time she brings Shostakovich's First Violin Concerto, a work she will always associate with David Oistrakh, who gave the 1955 premiere. 'This concerto is a great pleasure to play, because Shostakovich was able to work with the greatest violinist of his time and their collaboration helped to make it an enduring masterpiece.'

Shostakovich has been an important influence on Batiashvili. 'I've always been inspired by his life, his music and example. It's a great challenge for us to delve back into that time and what it must have meant: I experienced the final 10 years of Soviet rule but in Georgia people were more optimistic and had a sense of their own identity. But I used to go to Russia and to feel the oppressive weight on everyone. My father travelled in the West and told us exactly how limited our lives were, how we had lost any sense of responsibility for our own destiny. Every artistic person had this inner fight, and the fight in Shostakovich produced miraculous things.'

Batiashvili recorded the work last year with Esa-Pekka Salonen. 'As a Finn, he really understands where this music is coming from and has an instinctive access to that darkness.'

Broadcast
RADIO Live on Radio 3
ONLINE Live and 'listen again' options at bbc.co.uk/proms

THURSDAY 18 AUGUST

Proms Plus Portrait 5.15pm, Royal College of Music
Thomas Larcher discusses his Double Concerto with Andrew McGregor, and introduces performances of his *Antennen-Requiem für H.* and extracts from his Cello Sonata and *Kraken* by musicians from the Royal Northern College of Music.
Edited version broadcast on BBC Radio 3 after tonight's concert

7.00pm–c9.15pm

Thomas Larcher
Concerto for Violin, Cello and Orchestra   c25'
BBC commission: world premiere

INTERVAL

Bruckner
Symphony No. 5 in B flat major (ed. Nowak)   75'

Viktoria Mullova *violin*
Matthew Barley *cello*

BBC Scottish Symphony Orchestra
Ilan Volkov *conductor*

Previously featured at the Proms as a pianist (a role to which he returns in this concert, playing the prepared piano), Thomas Larcher has become one of Austria's leading composers, writing for prominent artists and ensembles in a style that steers a refreshing course between the old avant-garde and the newer wave of simplicity. Tonight sees the world premiere of a double concerto written for Viktoria Mullova and Matthew Barley. Anticipate an unconventional concertante group and an element of improvisation. After the interval, a different kind of soundscape, as Ilan Volkov and the BBC Scottish Symphony Orchestra realise the vast architectural design of Bruckner's Fifth Symphony. See *'New Music', pages 68–75; 'Featured Artists', pages 78–81*

Ilan Volkov

SAME-DAY SAVER
Book for both Proms 45 and 46 and save (see page 158)

THURSDAY 18 AUGUST

10.15pm–c11.30pm

Bratsch, arr. Barley
Bi Lovengo   3'

Lewis/Bratsch, arr. Barley
Django   6'

Kodály
Duo, Op. 7   26'

Zawinul, arr. Barley
Pursuit of the Woman with the Feathered Hat   6'

Matthew Barley
Yura   4'

Zawinul, arr. Barley
The Peasant   10'

DuOud, arr. Barley
For Nedim (For Nadia)   6'

Viktoria Mullova *violin*
Matthew Barley *cello*
Julian Joseph *piano*
Paul Clarvis *percussion*
Sam Walton *percussion*

Join Viktoria Mullova, Matthew Barley and friends in a colourful Late Night entertainment of contrasted styles and unexpected player combinations. The worlds of the Gypsy and of jazz are represented alongside a Hungarian classic but the programme is also making a statement about Viktoria herself, says Matthew – 'how she relates to the world, and more importantly to the music she loves and plays. She loves simplicity, and emotional directness and power, as well as virtuosity that comes from the heart and for the heart (as opposed to showing off).' The pair hope that 'this binding factor will prove more important than any definition of genre. Music is music.' See 'Featured Artists', pages 78–81

There will be no interval

Viktoria Mullova   Matthew Barley

PROMS 45 & 46
Spotlight on ... Viktoria Mullova & Matthew Barley

Husband-and-wife team Matthew Barley and Viktoria Mullova knew composer Thomas Larcher long before the idea arose of a double concerto. Barley met him while rehearsing one of his works some years ago: 'I was blown away by his music and warmed to his quirky charm and straightforward manner.' Mullova recalls hearing one of his string quartets: 'I straight away loved the incisive rhythms and colours he found in the string writing.' For Barley it's his 'great rhythm' that makes his music distinctive, 'and his very broad palette – melodies that are comprehensible and moving, and an incredible range of colours'. Larcher, for his part, had always been a huge fan of Mullova and was excited by the idea of writing for her. 'Thomas played us the opening of the concerto on the piano,' she says. 'It was haunting and very beautiful – I can't wait to see how it gets orchestrated. It will be very atmospheric, I think.'

Mullova and Barley reappear in a Late Night Prom which draws inspiration from folk, jazz and Gypsy music. 'It's amazing how differently you listen to Kodály in this context,' says Barley. 'The Gypsy music makes you realise where his source material came from. There's quite a lot of flexibility and improvisation in our set – but it all seems to fit together. Not sure how!'

FRIDAY 19 AUGUST

7.00pm–c9.00pm

Brahms
Symphony No. 3 in F major   *38'*

INTERVAL

Brahms
Piano Concerto No. 1 in D minor   *45'*

Emanuel Ax *piano*

Chamber Orchestra of Europe
Bernard Haitink *conductor*

Bernard Haitink

The Chamber Orchestra of Europe is celebrating its 30th anniversary with two years of Brahms under Bernard Haitink, and brings a pair of concertos and a pair of symphonies to the Proms. Haitink describes the COE as 'a group of exceptionally talented musicians. As true chamber musicians, they are used to listening to each other, without being exclusively focused on the conductor. This matches exactly the idea I have of conducting an orchestra.' After Brahms's relatively mellow Third Symphony, one of the world's best-loved pianists performs a work boiling over with youthful passions. The same musicians return with more Brahms in Prom 49. See 'Back to Brahms', pages 30–33; 'Featured Artists', pages 78–81

Broadcast
RADIO Live on Radio 3
ONLINE Live and 'listen again' options at bbc.co.uk/proms
TV Broadcast on BBC Four at 7.30pm

FRIDAY 19 AUGUST

10.00pm–c11.15pm

Brahms
Three Intermezzos, Op. 117 – Nos. 1 & 2   *7'*

Schumann
Introduction and Concert Allegro, Op. 134   *13'*

Brahms, arr. Schoenberg
Piano Quartet No. 1 in G minor   *42'*

Angela Hewitt *piano*

BBC Scottish Symphony Orchestra
Andrew Manze *conductor*

Angela Hewitt picks up the Brahms thread from the early evening Prom and launches this Late Night Prom that takes in an unjustly neglected score by Brahms's mentor, Robert Schumann, before observing the composer through the prism of an admirer, Arnold Schoenberg. Andrew Manze, conducting his first Prom as Associate Guest Conductor of the BBC Scottish Symphony Orchestra, sees Brahms as a misunderstood figure, full of warmth. He will bring his own insights to an increasingly popular arrangement in which Schoenberg incorporates some surprising 20th-century effects. Don't miss the Gypsy-style finale! See 'Back to Brahms', pages 30–33

There will be no interval

SAME-DAY SAVER
Book for both Proms 47 and 48 and save (see page 158)

Angela Hewitt

PROM 48
Spotlight on … Andrew Manze

A regular performer at the Proms, Andrew Manze has turned his attention in recent years from early music to the 19th century and beyond. 'It is different repertoire,' he agrees, 'but the processes and the questions you ask about the music are just the same. It doesn't matter whether it is a piece of Bach or a piece of Brahms, so for me it has been a very natural evolution to step into later repertoire.'

Associate Guest Conductor of the BBC Scottish Symphony Orchestra, Manze brings the ensemble to perform a richly Romantic programme. 'We start in the most intimate way, with Angela Hewitt playing two of Brahms's heavenly solo piano pieces, before the orchestra joins her to play Schumann's passionate Introduction and Concert Allegro – which is dedicated to Brahms – and we finish with this huge orchestra playing Schoenberg's orchestration of one of Brahms's most romantic pieces.' It may be inauthentic but Manze adores it: 'Schoenberg creates a huge amount of energy with his wonderful orchestration and treats Brahms's work with the greatest respect. As the Americans would say, it's going to be a blast!'

Broadcast
RADIO Live on Radio 3
ONLINE Live and 'listen again' options at bbc.co.uk/proms
TV Recorded for broadcast on BBC Four on 2 September

SATURDAY 20 AUGUST

3.00pm–c4.30pm

Proms Saturday Matinee at Cadogan Hall

Sir Peter Maxwell Davies
Il rozzo martello   12'

Georges Aperghis
Champ–Contrechamp   c15'
BBC commission: world premiere

Sir Harrison Birtwistle
Angel Fighter   35'
UK premiere

Andrew Watts *counter-tenor*
Jeffrey Lloyd-Roberts *tenor*
Nicolas Hodges *piano*

BBC Singers
London Sinfonietta
David Atherton *conductor*

Nicolas Hodges

For its second Proms Saturday Matinee, the London Sinfonietta is joined by its founding conductor David Atherton. Greek-born, Paris-based Georges Aperghis is intimately involved with French musical theatre but his new piece takes its title from cinematic techniques of cutting and continuity. Sir Harrison Birtwistle reflects on more ancient traditions in *Angel Fighter*, a pocket oratorio for voices and ensemble in the tradition of his previous examinations of pivotal myths that resonate down the ages. Sir Peter Maxwell Davies's *Il rozzo martello*, a contemplation on a sonnet by Michelangelo, was composed for the BBC Singers in 1997. See 'French Connections', pages 36–39; 'New Music', pages 68–75

There will be no interval

Broadcast
RADIO Live on Radio 3
ONLINE Live and 'listen again' options at bbc.co.uk/proms

WEEKEND PROMMING PASS • BEAT THE QUEUES AND SAVE MONEY *(SEE PAGE 158)*

SATURDAY 20 AUGUST

Proms Plus Literary 5.45pm, Royal College of Music
Eminent American conductor Andrew Litton continues our new four-part series of events in which musicians from this year's Proms season introduce a personal choice of readings from their favourite fiction and poetry.
Edited version broadcast on BBC Radio 3 during tonight's interval

Proms Plus Late Elgar Room, Royal Albert Hall
Informal post-Prom music and poetry. For details see bbc.co.uk/proms

7.30pm–c9.40pm

Brahms
Piano Concerto No. 2 in B flat major   50'

INTERVAL

Brahms
Symphony No. 4 in E minor   42'

Emanuel Ax *piano*

Chamber Orchestra of Europe
Bernard Haitink *conductor*

The Chamber Orchestra of Europe's second pairing of Brahms masterworks opens with a work long central to Emanuel Ax's repertoire which he has recorded with tonight's conductor. Brahms's Second Piano Concerto is even bigger in scale than the First and just as technically demanding. After the interval, the composer's astonishing final symphony, where the balance between expressiveness and iron structural control is most perfectly maintained. It ends with an imposing set of variations, Brahms's late-Romantic take on the Baroque-style passacaglia, which uses material borrowed from J. S. Bach. See 'Back to Brahms', pages 30–33; 'Featured Artists', pages 78–81

PROM 49
Spotlight on ... Emanuel Ax

Emanuel Ax first came to public attention in 1974 when, aged 25, he won the Arthur Rubinstein International Piano Competition in Tel Aviv. Since then he has enjoyed a distinguished career across the globe, participating in a wide range of musical activities, from frequent concerto performances to solo recitals and chamber music collaborations. 'Performing with the Chamber Orchestra of Europe feels like you're part of a great chamber music endeavour,' says Ax. 'There's less weight and bulk than with a large orchestra, so there's a lot of energy. It's amazing.'

Ax's relationship with the Brahms concertos spans virtually his whole career. 'They're cornerstones of any pianist's life,' he says. 'I learnt the First when I was 21 or so and the Second when I was about 30 – and have been trying to get them right ever since! They're incredibly difficult but they're very much worth the effort. There are just so many ways to look at them – but I still love them as much as I ever did.' Ax also has a long-standing relationship in these concertos with Bernard Haitink. 'It's always incredibly exciting working together,' says Ax. 'I've certainly learnt a lot from him. It's an incredible honour to be performing with him at the Proms.'

Broadcast
RADIO Live on Radio 3
ONLINE Live and 'listen again' options at bbc.co.uk/proms
TV Broadcast on BBC Two at 9.00pm

WEEKEND PROMMING PASS (SEE PAGE 158)

SUNDAY 21 AUGUST

Proms Plus Sing
1.00pm–3.00pm, Royal College of Music
Come and join professional singers to produce a performance of parts of Mozart's *Requiem* in only two hours. Ideal for enthusiastic amateur singers aged 16-plus. See pages 92–99 for details of how to sign up.

Proms Plus Intro 5.15pm, Royal College of Music
The sixth in the series of introductions to the music performed in Proms Choral Sundays. Matthew Rowe explores this evening's works with recorded extracts and with live music examples from members of the City of London Sinfonia. Ideal for anyone wanting to explore classical music.
Broadcast live on BBC Radio 3

7.00pm–c9.15pm

Britten
Variations on a Theme of Frank Bridge   25'

Colin Matthews
No Man's Land   c20'
world premiere

INTERVAL

Mozart, compl. Süssmayr
Requiem in D minor   55'

Emma Bell *soprano*
Renata Pokupić *mezzo-soprano*
Ian Bostridge *tenor*
Roderick Williams *baritone*
James Rutherford *bass*

Polyphony
City of London Sinfonia
Stephen Layton *conductor*

Ian Bostridge

Britten's *Variations* is one of many British pieces championed by the late Richard Hickox, two of whose distinguished vocal collaborators, Ian Bostridge and Roderick Williams, are featured in Colin Matthews's new work, which Hickox commissioned. The *Requiem* was recently voted the Nation's Favourite Mozart by Radio 3 listeners. See 'Out of the Shadows', pages 48–49; 'Choral Sundays', pages 62–65; 'New Music', pages 68–75

Broadcast
RADIO Live on Radio 3
ONLINE Live and 'listen again' options at bbc.co.uk/proms

MONDAY 22 AUGUST

1.00pm–c2.00pm

Proms Chamber Music at Cadogan Hall

Martinů
Flute Sonata   18'

Henri Dutilleux
Sonatine   9'

Prokofiev
Flute Sonata   24'

Emmanuel Pahud *flute*
Eric Le Sage *piano*

Featured artist Emmanuel Pahud returns with his regular accompanist for a recital of pieces composed in the 1940s. Martinů's amiable work plumbs unexpected depths in its central core, while the Prokofiev Sonata's delightfully sunny nature makes it an ideal vehicle for the brilliant sparkle of the flute. In between comes the *Sonatine* by Dutilleux, here at his most pastoral and Debussyan, carrying the flag for the Paris Conservatoire tradition of commissioning new scores for its final examinations. See 'French Connections', pages 36–39; 'Featured Artists', pages 78–81

There will be no interval

Emmanuel Pahud   Eric Le Sage

Broadcast
RADIO Live on Radio 3
ONLINE Live and 'listen again' options at bbc.co.uk/proms

MONDAY 22 AUGUST

Proms Plus Portrait 5.45pm, Royal College of Music
Kevin Volans, in conversation with Tom Service, discusses the world premiere of his Piano Concerto No. 3 and introduces performances of his chamber works, including *1,000 Bars* and *Asanga*, by musicians from the Royal Academy of Music.
Edited version broadcast on BBC Radio 3 after tonight's concert

7.30pm–c9.50pm

Wagner
The Mastersingers of Nuremberg – overture   10'

Liszt
La notte   12'

Kevin Volans
Piano Concerto No. 3   c30'
BBC co-commission with RTÉ: world premiere

INTERVAL

Brahms
Symphony No. 1 in C minor   45'

Barry Douglas *piano*

BBC Symphony Orchestra
Jiří Bělohlávek *conductor*

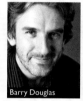
Barry Douglas

First the familiar strains of Wagner's rousing overture. Next a real rarity: Liszt's *La notte* is an extended version of a piano piece from the *Années de pèlerinage* to which the composer added a middle section recalling his Hungarian roots. A late work that he wanted played at his own funeral, it is new to the Proms. So too is Kevin Volans's concerto, hot off the press and written for tonight's soloist. Expect the unexpected from a creative figure born in South Africa but now resident in Ireland whose output resists compartmentalisation. The long shadow of Ludwig van Beethoven inhibited Brahms's early attempts at symphonic writing but he surpassed all expectations with the magnificence of his First Symphony.
See 'A Lust for Liszt', pages 24–27; 'Back to Brahms', pages 30–33; 'New Music', pages 68–75

Broadcast
RADIO Live on Radio 3
ONLINE Live and 'listen again' options at bbc.co.uk/proms

TUESDAY 23 AUGUST

Proms Plus Intro 5.45pm, Royal College of Music
Fraser Trainer and musicians from the London Symphony Orchestra offer an illustrated guide to the works in tonight's concert with recorded and live musical examples. Ideal for anyone wanting to explore classical music.

7.30pm–c9.40pm

Prokofiev
Symphony No. 1 in D major, 'Classical'   15'

Henri Dutilleux
L'arbre des songes   25'

INTERVAL

Henri Dutilleux
Slava's Fanfare   4'

Prokofiev
Symphony No. 5 in B flat major   43'

Leonidas Kavakos violin

London Symphony Orchestra
Valery Gergiev conductor

Tonight's concert features two composers central to the musical lives of their respective countries. Birthday composer Henri Dutilleux is represented by the nocturnal imaginings of the violin concerto he wrote for Isaac Stern plus there's a chance to hear his birthday tribute to one of Prokofiev's most ardent supporters, the late Mstislav Rostropovich. Flanking these are Prokofiev's entrancing 'Classical' Symphony and his Fifth, a different, grander kind of utterance reflecting the soul of war-torn Moscow and the greatness of the human spirit. See 'French Connections', pages 36–39

Leonidas Kavakos

Broadcast
RADIO Live on Radio 3
ONLINE Live and 'listen again' options at bbc.co.uk/proms

WEDNESDAY 24 AUGUST

Proms Plus Family 5.00pm, Royal College of Music
Rachel Leach and musicians from the Gustav Mahler Jugendorchester invite you to join them in a lively and interactive guide to the pieces in tonight's Prom. Bring along your instrument and get involved!

7.00pm–c9.00pm

Stravinsky
Symphony in Three Movements   20'

Ravel
Shéhérazade   17'

INTERVAL

Tchaikovsky
Symphony No. 4 in F minor   42'

Susan Graham mezzo-soprano

Gustav Mahler Jugendorchester
Sir Colin Davis conductor

Sir Colin Davis

A great youth orchestra and a distinguished and much-loved conductor. The programme begins with Stravinsky's Symphony in Three Movements, partly inspired by newsreel footage of the Second World War. A long-standing favourite of Sir Colin's, it is a work he first conducted at the Proms all of 50 years ago. The biggest piece is Tchaikovsky's Fourth Symphony, in which the composer grapples with a malign Fate and, in his coruscating finale, makes use of a well-known Russian folk song. Before the interval, Ravel's exotic, ambiguous Shéhérazade is sung by Susan Graham, a supreme interpreter of the cycle. See 'French Connections', pages 36–39

Broadcast
RADIO Live on Radio 3
ONLINE Live and 'listen again' options at bbc.co.uk/proms

PROM 53
Spotlight on … Susan Graham

Following her two appearances in 2009, Susan Graham returns to the Proms this year to perform Ravel's exotically coloured Shéhérazade. Accompanying her will be the Gustav Mahler Jugendorchester – the group with which she made her Proms debut in 2006. She can point to any number of characteristic touches in Ravel's music. 'My heart starts fluttering from that violin tremolo at the very opening, but there's the beauty of the arrival in China and the delicate hands of the princesses there; and also a barbaric side, with the smiling executioner cutting off heads with his sabre. There's misty Impressionism, suggestive harmonies – and we're still only in the first song!'

'As we all do, these young players will be hanging on Colin Davis's every word,' Graham says. 'He's so generous and quite intuitive towards singers. He has immense knowledge and great ideas, yet is somehow very accommodating.' At the end of her most recent tour with the GMJO, after Graham had witnessed 'the joy filtering to the very back desks', she felt moved to offer the players some advice. 'I said to them, "Always remember the joy you feel right now, and bring that to everything that you do".' Which is clearly what Graham, too, aims for in her own performances.

SAME-DAY SAVER Book for both Proms 53 and 54 and save (see page 158)

WEDNESDAY 24 AUGUST

10.00pm–c11.15pm

Liszt

Legend No. 2, 'St Francis of Paola
Walking on the Water'   9'

Fantasia and Fugue on B–A–C–H   12'

Bénédiction de Dieu dans la solitude   18'

Venezia e Napoli   18'

Marc-André Hamelin piano

For Liszt's bicentenary year, Marc-André Hamelin
pays late-night tribute, recalling the composer-pianist's
own jaw-dropping keyboard technique and spanning
the whole imaginative and emotional range of his
musical world. See 'Featured Artists', pages 78–81

There will be no interval

Marc-André Hamelin

Broadcast
RADIO Live on Radio 3
ONLINE Live and 'listen again' options at bbc.co.uk/proms

THURSDAY 25 AUGUST

Proms Plus Intro 5.15pm, Royal College of Music
Handel expert Ruth Smith and writer, critic and Handel
biographer Jonathan Keates join Louise Fryer to explore *Rinaldo*,
Handel's first opera for London, and place it in the context of his
extraordinary genius as a theatre composer.

7.00pm–c10.25pm

Handel

Rinaldo (semi-staged; sung in Italian)   140'

Sonia Prina Rinaldo
Varduhi Abrahamyan Goffredo
Tim Mead Eustazio
Sandrine Piau Almirena
Brenda Rae Armida
Luca Pisaroni Argante
William Towers A Christian Magician

Glyndebourne Festival Opera
Orchestra of the Age of Enlightenment
Ottavio Dantone conductor

Glyndebourne Festival Opera makes its annual Proms
visit with Robert Carsen's new production of *Rinaldo*,
the latest in the company's distinguished line of Handel
stagings, not least the sensational *Julius Caesar* also seen
at the Proms in 2005. *Rinaldo* is the work with which
Handel made his London debut (exactly 300 years
ago), an Italian opera set during the First Crusade.
Out to impress, the composer assembled a score
of great vitality and colour. Period-music specialist
Ottavio Dantone conducts a strong cast led by
Sonia Prina in the title-role of the heroic crusader
with Sandrine Piau as his beloved Almirena.

There will be two intervals of 20 minutes

PROM 55
Spotlight on … Ottavio Dantone

'*Rinaldo* fascinates me particularly for its blend
of historical, literary, magical and romantic
elements. It's an inspiring mix and allows rich
possibilities for an interpreter when exploring
its very distinct atmospheres and colours. All
Handel's operas are beautiful but this contains
some of his loveliest arias. It is no accident that
Rinaldo – although one of his first works for
the theatre – was his greatest success of all.

'Different elements coexist in this opera,
giving it its variety and richness. There are heroic
characters such as Goffredo, those torn between
warrior instinct and romantic passion such as
Rinaldo and Argante, pathetic roles such as
Almirena, or varied characters full of magic,
love, cruelty and rage such as Armida.

'Handel vivdly depicts these extremely
recognisable figures through his use of rhythm,
tonality, melody and instrumentation – none of
the characters has to strain to express their true
nature. Handel is very "modern" in his musical
structuring of the opera: he has this ability to
bring the characters to life and to make us forget
their artificiality – another element that makes
his music still so widely appreciated and
successful today.'

Broadcast
RADIO Live on Radio 3
ONLINE Live and 'listen again' options at bbc.co.uk/proms

WEEKEND PROMMING PASS (SEE PAGE 158)

FRIDAY 26 AUGUST

Proms Plus Literary 5.45pm, Royal College of Music
Prince Albert, who died 150 years ago, inspired the creation of the Royal Albert Hall, the home of the Proms. Historians A. N. Wilson and Kate Williams join Matthew Sweet to reassess the Prince Consort and his legacy, 'Albertopolis'.
Edited version broadcast on BBC Radio 3 during tonight's interval

7.30pm–c9.50pm

R. Strauss
Burleske   20'

INTERVAL

Mahler
Symphony No. 6 in A minor   85'

Kirill Gerstein *piano*

BBC Symphony Orchestra
Semyon Bychkov *conductor*

For his second Prom this season, Semyon Bychkov conducts one of Mahler's most perfectly realised works, 'the only sixth, despite the "Pastoral"', in the words of Alban Berg. This is music of exceptional range and power, whose fateful hammer-blows seem to

Semyon Bychkov

portend the crises in Mahler's own life and the wider world. The curtain-raiser is a mini-concerto with echoes of Brahms and Liszt, especially in its treatment of the piano. Kirill Gerstein, an exceptional artist with roots in jazz as well as the classics, makes his first Proms appearance in the main hall.

Broadcast
RADIO Live on Radio 3
ONLINE Live and 'listen again' options at bbc.co.uk/proms

SATURDAY 27 AUGUST

3.00pm–c4.30pm

Proms Saturday Matinee at Cadogan Hall

Hildegard of Bingen
Symphonia armonie celestium revelationum – selection   10'

Britten
Sacred and Profane   14'

Sir Harrison Birtwistle
Narration: A Description of the Passing of a Year   10'

Stevie Wishart
Out of This World   25'
BBC commission: world premiere

BBC Singers
Sinfonye
Robert Hollingworth *conductor*
Stevie Wishart *conductor*

A concert performed jointly by the BBC Singers and Stevie Wishart's Sinfonye, a group which applies new learning on period performance to the improvisatory freedom associated with traditional music. The exploration of material sung, inspired or composed by women is another aim and this concert not only pays tribute to the music of Hildegard of Bingen but ends with four new songs based on her texts. 'For Hildegard, it seems music was a way for mortals to experience something of heavenly or spiritual ecstasy,' says Stevie Wishart, 'and it is perhaps this desire which we can most clearly empathise with today. Hers is a creative spirit which soars high, as much in our time as in her own.' As a centrepiece, two British settings of medieval texts express visionary fervour through the sound-worlds of the second half of the 20th century.

There will be no interval

PROMS SATURDAY MATINEE 3
Spotlight on … Stevie Wishart

Composer, performer and musicologist Stevie Wishart began her career in electronic and contemporary music composition before studying medieval music. She was particularly drawn to the works of Hildegard of Bingen, which she has since recorded extensively with her group Sinfonye. 'Hildegard was so individualistic,' says Wishart, 'particularly in the way she set her words so expressively and even programmatically, which was so progressive for her time.'

'I was immediately struck on discovering medieval music by what was – and what wasn't – in the notation, in comparison with the intense detail of most modern scores.' No notation survives, though, for any of the four Hildegard texts that Wishart has chosen to set in her new work, *Out of This World*. 'I think of *Out of This World* as a sonic tapestry of frayed threads from hundreds of years ago, woven into a new pattern. For this work I imagined a choir full of contrasts and vocal personalities, which is why I really wanted to work with the BBC Singers.'

Completing the programme are two works that also set medieval texts. 'I liked the suggestion of including these Britten and Birtwistle songs,' says Wishart, 'so there is that common literary thread running throughout the concert.'

Broadcast
RADIO Live on Radio 3
ONLINE Live and 'listen again' options at bbc.co.uk/proms

WEEKEND PROMMING PASS • BEAT THE QUEUES AND SAVE MONEY (SEE PAGE 158)

SATURDAY 27 AUGUST

Proms Plus Family Orchestra and Chorus
1.00pm–3.00pm, Royal College of Music
A Mozart- and Beethoven-themed Family Orchestra and Chorus session for enthusiastic musicians of all abilities and instruments. See pages 92–99 for details of how to sign up.

Proms Plus Literary 5.45pm, Royal College of Music
Dynamic cellist Matthew Barley is the third guest in this four-part series in which musicians from this year's Proms season introduce their favourite works of fiction and poetry. Susan Hitch hosts.
Edited version broadcast on BBC Radio 3 during tonight's interval

Proms Plus Late Elgar Room, Royal Albert Hall
Informal post-Prom music and poetry. For details see bbc.co.uk/proms

7.30pm–c9.50pm

Anders Hillborg
Cold Heat   14'
UK premiere

Mozart
Piano Concerto No. 27 in B flat major, K595   31'

INTERVAL

Beethoven
Symphony No. 3 in E flat major, 'Eroica'   50'

Maria João Pires *piano*

Tonhalle Orchestra Zurich
David Zinman *conductor*

Premiered earlier this year by David Zinman and the Berlin Philharmonic, Anders Hillborg's *Cold Heat* leavens high-art finesse with the rampaging pulse and flow of street music. Quite a contrast with the autumnal poise of Mozart's final piano concerto, tonight featuring Maria João Pires, whose Late Night Chopin recital was a highlight of last year's Proms. After the interval, one of the great pinnacles of Western art music, a work inspired by the ideals of the French Revolution. Beethoven famously struck out the dedication to Napoleon Bonaparte when the latter declared himself Emperor but the heroic musical drama of the 'Eroica' stands for all time.
See 'New Music', pages 68–75

PROM 57
Spotlight on ... Maria João Pires

Few present will forget Maria João Pires's Late Night Chopin recital last year. The hall was packed to the rafters while she created an atmosphere of intense intimacy, as if sharing the inner poetry of Chopin's Nocturnes with a few friends.

With that in mind, there is no doubt she will achieve her aim in this year's concert, when she plays Mozart's introspective final piano concerto. 'It's a meditative piece. And the challenge – the beautiful challenge – is to get 5,001 people meditating together.'

This will be the Portuguese pianist's sixth appearance at the Proms. 'I have the best memories of playing at the Proms, because the atmosphere in the hall is unique and the mood almost magic: one does not feel alone on stage but very much together with the audience.' This concerto is a work she has played all her life. Has her approach to it evolved? 'To be honest, I have a feeling that it has not evolved very much, because the piece does not allow it. It's so simple and pure that one has to prepare one's own mood to suit the piece, rather than try to influence the music. David Zinman has, among his many qualities, a natural instinct that allows him to let the music speak for itself, and this makes him such a wonderful conductor of Mozart.'

Broadcast
RADIO Live on Radio 3
ONLINE Live and 'listen again' options at bbc.co.uk/proms

SUNDAY 28 AUGUST

Proms Plus Sing 2.00pm–4.00pm, Royal Albert Hall
Come and join professional singers to create a performance of parts of Mendelssohn's *Elijah* in only two hours. Ideal for enthusiastic amateur singers aged 16-plus. See pages 92–99 for details of how to sign up.

Proms Plus Intro 5.15pm, Royal College of Music
The seventh in the series of introductions to the music performed in Proms Choral Sundays. Andrew McGregor explores Mendelssohn's *Elijah* with recorded extracts and with live music examples from members of the Gabrieli Consort & Players. Ideal for anyone wanting to explore classical music.
Broadcast live on BBC Radio 3

7.00pm–c9.50pm

Mendelssohn
Elijah *(sung in English)*   128'

Rosemary Joshua *soprano*
Sarah Connolly *mezzo-soprano*
Robert Murray *tenor*
Simon Keenlyside *baritone*

Taplow Youth Choir
Ulster Youth Chamber Choir
Chetham's Chamber Choir
North East Youth Choir
Wrocław Philharmonic Choir
Gabrieli Consort
& Players
Paul McCreesh *conductor*

Mendelssohn's ever-popular Old Testament oratorio remains ripe for reassessment. We can be sure that Paul McCreesh will have re-examined the work in what will be the culmination of a large-scale project like the one that led up to his revelatory 2009 Proms performance of Haydn's *The Creation*. Out go certain old-fashioned conventions; in come period instruments, a raft of enthusiastic choirs and a sensational line-up of soloists. *See 'Choral Sundays', pages 62–65; 'Featured Artists', pages 78–81*

There will be one interval

Paul McCreesh

Broadcast
RADIO Live on Radio 3
ONLINE Live and 'listen again' options at bbc.co.uk/proms

MONDAY 29 AUGUST

1.00pm–c.2.00pm

Proms Chamber Music at Cadogan Hall

Graham Fitkin

L   10'
London premiere

Egberto Gismonti/Geraldo Carneiro

Bodas de prata and Quatro cantos   10'

Rachmaninov

Cello Sonata in G minor   34'

Yo-Yo Ma *cello*
Kathryn Stott *piano*

Yo-Yo Ma is not only one of the great cellists of our time but has also become one of the most important figures on the American cultural scene. His recent Proms, in 2004 and 2009, have followed connections to his innovative cross-cultural Silk Road Ensemble projects. Now, in the first of two appearances this season, he resumes his recital partnership with Kathryn Stott. Graham Fitkin's *L* was composed in 2005 for Yo-Yo Ma's 50th birthday and he will unveil Fitkin's new Cello Concerto later in the week (see Prom 61). Rachmaninov's Cello Sonata is a lyrically expressive work which is nevertheless one of the repertoire's great challenges, for cellist and pianist alike.

There will be no interval

Yo-Yo Ma and Kathryn Stott

Broadcast
RADIO Live on Radio 3
ONLINE Live and 'listen again' options at bbc.co.uk/proms

WEEKEND PROMMING PASS *(SEE PAGE 158)*

MONDAY 29 AUGUST

Proms Plus Family Orchestra and Chorus
1.00pm–3.00pm, Royal College of Music
Join professional musicians and musical families for a taste of Hollywood. Bring your instrument and create a new moment of cinematic magic. If you're aged 7 or over and want to make music with other members of your family, no matter how much experience you have, come and join the fun! See pages 92–99 for details of how to sign up.

Proms Plus Intro 5.45pm, Royal College of Music
Tonight's conductor John Wilson explores the themes of tonight's Prom and the unique partnership of song and dance during the Golden Age of film musicals. Presented by Louise Fryer.

7.30pm–c9.35pm

Hooray for Hollywood

A celebration of the Golden Age of Hollywood film musicals

Maida Vale Singers
John Wilson Orchestra
John Wilson *conductor*

John Wilson

The appearances of John Wilson and his hand-picked, high-octane orchestra have been among the most sensational Proms events of recent years. Joined by a formidable line-up of today's vocal stars, they give what one critic has described as 'the auditory equivalent of a steam-clean' to another cache of show-stoppers. 'Hooray for Hollywood' takes us from the dawn of the talkies and the birth of the movie musical through to the 1960s. An extended sequence pays special tribute to the RKO films of Fred Astaire and Ginger Rogers, who was born 100 years ago. See 'Hooray for Hollywood', pages 88–89

There will be one interval

Broadcast
RADIO Live on Radio 3
ONLINE Live and 'listen again' options at bbc.co.uk/proms
TV Recorded for broadcast on BBC Two on 3 September

TUESDAY 30 AUGUST

Proms Plus Literary 5.45pm, Royal College of Music
William Golding, Nobel Prize-winner, author of *Lord of the Flies* and *Rites of Passage*, was born 100 years ago. His biographer John Carey and award-winning writer Andrew O'Hagan celebrate the centenary of one of Britain's greatest post-war novelists.
Edited version broadcast on BBC Radio 3 during tonight's interval

7.30pm–c10.05pm

Mozart

Piano Concerto No. 25 in C major, K503   33'

INTERVAL

Bruckner

Symphony No. 8 in C minor   85'

David Fray *piano*

Netherlands Radio Philharmonic Orchestra
Jaap van Zweden *conductor*

In a previous life, as the youngest-ever concertmaster of the Royal Concertgebouw Orchestra, tonight's conductor (making his Proms debut in that role) played almost all the Bruckner symphonies under some of the great interpreters of an older generation. More recently, at the helm of this versatile Dutch radio orchestra, he has been preparing and recording his own cycle to great acclaim. The Eighth remains a particular challenge, one of the most momentous 'darkness to light' journeys in the whole symphonic repertoire. Before the interval, a Proms debut from the quietly iconoclastic French pianist David Fray, who has already collaborated on disc with van Zweden in the imposing concerto he performs tonight.

David Fray

Broadcast
RADIO Live on Radio 3
ONLINE Live and 'listen again' options at bbc.co.uk/proms

WEDNESDAY 31 AUGUST

Proms Plus Portrait 5.45pm, Royal College of Music
Graham Fitkin, in conversation with Tom Service, discusses his
Cello Concerto for Yo-Yo Ma and introduces performances
of his chamber works *Sciosophy*, *Hurl* and *Sinew* by musicians
from the London Sinfonietta Academy Ensemble.
Edited version broadcast on BBC Radio 3 after tonight's concert

7.30pm–c9.45pm

Graham Fitkin
Cello Concerto   c27'
BBC commission: world premiere

INTERVAL

Beethoven
Symphony No. 9 in D minor, 'Choral'   70'

Yo-Yo Ma *cello*
Christine Brewer *soprano*
Karen Cargill *mezzo-soprano*
Toby Spence *tenor*
Iain Paterson *bass-baritone*

BBC Symphony Chorus
BBC Symphony Orchestra
David Robertson *conductor*

Featured artist Yo-Yo Ma takes
centre stage with a new work
conceived especially for him
by a composer who prizes
clarity and a straightforward
approach. After the interval,
the BBC SO's Principal Guest
Conductor, David Robertson,
directs the traditional annual
Proms performance of
Beethoven's Ninth, perhaps
the richest, most provocative

Christine Brewer

statement in the symphonic canon. An impressive
team of soloists joins the BBC Symphony Chorus
to project the finale's optimistic vision of hard-won
triumph over adversity. See 'New Music', pages 68–75

Broadcast
RADIO Live on Radio 3
ONLINE Live and 'listen again' options at bbc.co.uk/proms

THURSDAY 1 SEPTEMBER

Proms Plus Intro 5.45pm, Royal College of Music
Andrew McGregor and musicians from the Israel Philharmonic
Orchestra offer an illustrated guide to the works in tonight's
programme with recorded and live musical examples. Ideal
for anyone wanting to explore classical music.

7.30pm–c9.30pm

Webern
Passacaglia, Op. 1   11'

Bruch
Violin Concerto No. 1 in G minor   24'

INTERVAL

Albéniz
Iberia – Triana; El Puerto; Fête-Dieu à Séville   16'

Rimsky-Korsakov
Capriccio espagnol   15'

Gil Shaham *violin*

Israel Philharmonic Orchestra
Zubin Mehta *conductor*

Zubin Mehta is back at the Proms with an orchestra
he has been conducting for 50 years and which
awarded him the title of Music Director for Life in
1981. He begins with one of his signature works,
the groundbreaking but still traditional score Webern
chose to call his Op. 1. The brilliant Gil Shaham
played two concertos last season, stepping in at the
eleventh hour to perform the Berg as well as the
Barber. Tonight he returns with Bruch's most enduring
contribution to the genre. After the interval we head
south for Albéniz's Impressionistic evocations of Seville
and Cadiz, followed by Rimsky-Korsakov's vibrant
orchestral original based on Spanish folk melodies.

PROM 62
Spotlight on … Zubin Mehta

It's 30 years since the Israel Philharmonic gave
Zubin Mehta the title of Music Director for Life,
and half a century since he first worked with the
IPO. Not only that, but both he and the orchestra
celebrate their 75th birthdays this year. Mehta
has been appearing at the Proms with the IPO for
more than three and a half decades, bringing his
dynamic interpretations of the Austro-German
classics four times since 1974.

    This season he's offering a concert of two
contrasting halves, showing the many facets
of this remarkable orchestra. 'It has had a very
Central European sound from the outset,' remarks
Mehta, 'with the inclusion of many musicians
from the former Eastern Bloc. The sound has
remained largely the same because they did not
arrive as a group of 50 musicians but came in
one by one and acquired our style of playing.'

    The first half of the concert pairs Bruch's
ever-popular G minor Violin Concerto
with Webern's Passacaglia, in which febrile
Romanticism melts into nascent Expressionism.
Gil Shaham – 'a member of our family', as
Mehta describes him – is the soloist in the
concerto. Afterwards, the authentic Iberianisms
of Albéniz are reflected in the 'imagined' Spain
of Rimsky-Korsakov's *Capriccio*.

Broadcast
RADIO Live on Radio 3
ONLINE Live and 'listen again' options at bbc.co.uk/proms

WEEKEND PROMMING PASS • BEAT THE QUEUES AND SAVE MONEY (SEE PAGE 158)

FRIDAY 2 SEPTEMBER

Proms Plus Intro 5.15pm, Royal College of Music
Fraser Trainer and musicians offer an illustrated guide to the works in tonight's programme with recorded and live musical examples. Ideal for anyone wanting to explore classical music.

7.00pm–c9.15pm

Liszt
Der Tanz in der Dorfschenke
(Mephisto Waltz No. 1)   12'

Mahler
Blumine   7'

Liszt
Totentanz   15'

INTERVAL

Mahler
Symphony No. 1 in D major   55'

Dejan Lazić piano

Budapest Festival Orchestra
Iván Fischer conductor

Dejan Lazić

Hungary's foremost music ambassadors continue the Liszt celebrations with two of the composer's more macabre pieces, separated by the floral intermezzo Mahler originally intended to be part of his First Symphony. That titanic work, first performed in Budapest under the baton of the composer, is guaranteed to raise the roof. Before the interval, in his second appearance this year, Dejan Lazić champions Liszt's powerfully original *Totentanz*, in which the *Dies irae* is reimagined as a virtuoso piano piece with orchestral support. See 'A Lust for Liszt', pages 24–27; 'Featured Artists', pages 78–81

SAME-DAY SAVER
Book for both Proms 63 and 64 and save (see page 158)

Broadcast
RADIO Live on Radio 3
ONLINE Live and 'listen again' options at bbc.co.uk/proms

FRIDAY 2 SEPTEMBER

10.00pm–c11.00pm

Audience Choice

Budapest Festival Orchestra
Iván Fischer conductor

Among the many achievements of Iván Fischer and the Budapest Festival Orchestra has been the introduction of new types of non-standard concert: one-hour family 'cocoa concerts' for young children, 'one forint concerts' where the conductor can reach out and talk to a larger crowd, and 'surprise' concerts where the programme is not announced. Tonight the audience will be asked to choose what they would like to hear played from the range of possible options in the orchestra's capacious music library.

There will be no interval

PROMS 63 & 64
Spotlight on … Iván Fischer

Iván Fischer has lately been immersed in Mahler, with a string of revelatory recordings and performances, and looks forward to conducting the First Symphony at the Proms. 'My reward is the beauty of the music. I have the best position in the hall. It is a privilege to listen to this masterpiece.'

He interleaves Mahler's music with that of Liszt, a composer to whom he feels almost a family connection. 'Liszt was my great-grandmother's piano teacher. I have hundreds of family stories about him but, unfortunately, none about the *Totentanz*, which we'll be playing with Dejan Lazić!' He almost runs out of adjectives to describe the Croatian pianist, with whom he's collaborated many times. 'He's creative, extraordinary, full of insight, colourful, detailed, poetic, intelligent, pointed, romantic, masterly…'

Reflecting on the two composers, he concludes that they are 'like chalk and cheese. Liszt means "flour" in Hungarian; Mahler means "painter" in German. But the combination will work well!' The Budapest Festival Orchestra returns to the stage at 10.00pm for a radical Late Night Prom, in which the audience will choose the repertoire. Fischer pretends to be a little apprehensive: 'The audience will choose works from a long list. We will be scared to death because they may choose the most difficult ones. Please have mercy!'

Broadcast
RADIO Live on Radio 3
ONLINE Live and 'listen again' options at bbc.co.uk/proms

SATURDAY 3 SEPTEMBER

3.00pm–c4.30pm

Proms Saturday Matinee at Cadogan Hall

Tippett
The Windhover   2'

Plebs angelica   4'

Sir John Tavener
Popule meus   14'
UK premiere

Tippett
Little Music for Strings   11'

Sofia Gubaidulina
The Canticle of the Sun   42'

Natalie Clein *cello*

BBC Singers
Britten Sinfonia
David Hill *conductor*

Natalie Clein

The BBC Singers are joined by the Britten Sinfonia and former BBC Radio 3 New Generation Artist Natalie Clein in a programme that opens with the music of an individualistic master who first worked with the BBC Singers in 1944. Sir John Tavener's *Popule meus* meditates upon the rejection of God by modern man, with the solo cello steadfast against the temptations of the secular world as hurled out by the timpani. In her 80th-birthday year, Sofia Gubaidulina is represented by the atmospheric *The Canticle of the Sun*, a setting of St Francis of Assisi in which the silences can seem as important as the notes. *See 'New Music', pages 68–75*

There will be no interval

Broadcast
RADIO Live on Radio 3
ONLINE Live and 'listen again' options at bbc.co.uk/proms

Prom 65

WEEKEND PROMMING PASS • BEAT THE QUEUES AND SAVE MONEY *(SEE PAGE 158)*

SATURDAY 3 SEPTEMBER

Proms Plus Literary 5.15pm, Royal College of Music
Tasmin Little, creator of the groundbreaking 'Naked Violin' project, completes the series of events in which musicians from this year's Proms season introduce a personal choice of readings from their favourite fiction and poetry.
Edited version broadcast on BBC Radio 3 during tonight's interval

Proms Plus Late Elgar Room, Royal Albert Hall
Informal post-Prom music and poetry. For details see bbc.co.uk/proms

7.00pm–c9.15pm

Elgar
Overture 'Cockaigne (In London Town)'   15'

Michael Berkeley
Organ Concerto   20'
London premiere

INTERVAL

Rachmaninov
Rhapsody on a Theme of Paganini   25'

Kodály
Háry János – suite   24'

Marc-André Hamelin *piano*
David Goode *organ*

BBC National Orchestra of Wales
Jac van Steen *conductor*

Elgar's colourful tour of Old London Town prefaces a concerto from Michael Berkeley, 'inspired,' he says, 'by my impressionable days as a chorister at Westminster Cathedral'. Marc-André Hamelin returns in Rachmaninov's dazzling Rhapsody, while the brilliant *Háry János* suite relates the unlikely exploits of a veteran hussar during the Napoleonic era. *See 'New Music', pages 68–75; 'Featured Artists', pages 78–81*

Jac van Steen

PROM 65
Spotlight on … David Goode

The 20th century spawned a profusion of repertoire for solo organ but the organ concerto has tended to escape the gaze of composers. Not so Michael Berkeley, whose intensely dramatic concerto – 'a work of "ritual",' he says – receives its London premiere this summer.

David Goode performed the work with the BBC National Orchestra of Wales and Jac van Steen in 2008, and sees the concerto as 'a significant part of the modern repertoire for organ. It's dramatic and technically quite complicated in a number of places. You need to work hard at the notes – but it's intriguing also to play note-clusters, where you also decide how they're going to sound. They're designed to become more and more haphazard, to sound gradually less precise – although, of course, that involves some degree of precision!'

What are the work's other challenges? 'Putting the organ part together with the orchestra is tricky as there's a greater distance between us, compared with most instrumental concertos. Also, the use of space is very creative, including three trumpets who process around. But the huge scale of the Royal Albert Hall should work particularly well for the piece.'

Broadcast
RADIO Live on Radio 3
ONLINE Live and 'listen again' options at bbc.co.uk/proms

WEEKEND PROMMING PASS • BEAT THE QUEUES AND SAVE MONEY (SEE PAGE 158)

SUNDAY 4 SEPTEMBER

4.00pm–c5.00pm

Overture in the Baroque Style (improvisation) *5'*

J. S. Bach
Chorale Prelude 'Nun komm,
der Heiden Heiland', BWV 659 *4'*

Thierry Escaich
Evocation III (on 'Nun komm,
der Heiden Heiland') *5'*
UK premiere

Reger
Chorale Prelude 'Jauchz, Erd, und
Himmel, juble hell', Op. 67 No. 15 *3'*

Franck
Chorale No. 2 in B minor *14'*

Liszt
Adagio in D flat major, S759 *5'*

Triptych on Themes by Liszt (improvisation) *15'*

Thierry Escaich *organ*

Thierry Escaich

The second of this year's organ recitals is given by the mercurial organist of St-Étienne-du-Mont in Paris, a composer and improviser of renown who is new to the Royal Albert Hall and its mighty instrument. His programme contrasts chorales by Bach, Reger and Franck, recalls the spirit of Bach in his own *Evocation III*, and concludes with an extended improvisation in homage to Liszt. See 'A Lust for Liszt', pages 24–27

There will be no interval

Broadcast
RADIO Live on Radio 3
ONLINE Live and 'listen again' options at bbc.co.uk/proms

SUNDAY 4 SEPTEMBER

Proms Plus Sing
1.00pm–3.00pm, Royal College of Music
If you love powerful choral music and would like to be immersed in the work from tonight's Prom by singing some of it yourself, then come and join professional singers to rehearse a performance of movements from Beethoven's *Missa solemnis*. Ideal for enthusiastic amateur singers aged 16-plus. See pages 92–99 for details of how to sign up.

Proms Plus Intro 5.15pm, Royal College of Music
The last in the series of introductions to the music performed in Proms Choral Sundays. Sara Mohr-Pietsch explores Beethoven's *Missa solemnis*, with recorded extracts and with live music examples from members of the London Symphony Orchestra. Ideal for anyone wanting to explore classical music.
Broadcast live on BBC Radio 3

7.00pm–c8.40pm

Beethoven
Missa solemnis *90'*

Carmen Giannattasio *soprano*
Sarah Connolly *mezzo-soprano*
Paul Groves *tenor*
Matthew Rose *bass*

London Symphony Chorus
London Symphony Orchestra
Sir Colin Davis *conductor*

Sir Colin Davis tackles a work whose uncompromising nature makes it as great a challenge as anything in the choral repertoire, whether you regard it as a statement of the composer's belief in the spiritual potential of man or his faith in a supreme being. 'A musician must make affirmations,' says Davis. 'If a musician cannot believe in music as a universal ideal, what is he left with? We may be encircled by gloom but music gives us a chance to throw what Meredith calls "that faint thin line upon the shore". … Beethoven is a man at war with himself but a man who is determined to win.' See 'Choral Sundays', pages 62–65; 'Featured Artists', pages 78–81

SAME-DAY SAVER
Book for both Proms 66 and 67 and save (see page 158)

There will be no interval

Broadcast
RADIO Live on Radio 3
ONLINE Live and 'listen again' options at bbc.co.uk/proms
TV Live on BBC Four

MONDAY 5 SEPTEMBER

1.00pm–c2.00pm

Proms Chamber Music at Cadogan Hall

Mozart
Violin Sonata in A major, K526 *22'*

Bartók
Violin Sonata No. 1 *34'*

Christian Tetzlaff *violin*
Lars Vogt *piano*

Christian Tetzlaff   Lars Vogt

Featured artist Christian Tetzlaff is joined by his regular duo partner Lars Vogt for a recital that travels from Mozart's last major work for violin and piano, completed just before the premiere of *Don Giovanni*, to Bartók's First Violin Sonata, composed in 1921. The Hungarian composer, a Tetzlaff favourite, here stretches tonality in a sonata which provides a visceral, richly rewarding listening experience while pushing its players' techniques to their limits. See 'Featured Artists', pages 78–81

There will be no interval

Broadcast
RADIO Live on Radio 3
ONLINE Live and 'listen again' options at bbc.co.uk/proms

MONDAY 5 SEPTEMBER

Proms Plus Literary 5.45pm, Royal College of Music
Poet and former Children's Laureate Michael Rosen and presenter Ian McMillan introduce the winning entries in the first ever Proms Poetry competition. For competition details go to Proms Plus events at bbc.co.uk/proms
Edited version broadcast on BBC Radio 3 during the interval of Prom 69

7.30pm–c10.20pm

Braunfels
Fantastic Appearances of
a Theme of Hector Berlioz   47'

Beethoven
Piano Concerto No. 4 in G major   35'

INTERVAL

Tchaikovsky
Symphony No. 5 in E minor   45'

Hélène Grimaud piano

Pittsburgh Symphony Orchestra
Manfred Honeck conductor

The Pittsburgh Symphony Orchestra visits the Proms for two concerts with its current Music Director. Tonight they are joined by a charismatic Proms favourite who made her debut here in 2001, playing the same concerto. Before revisiting Beethoven's introspective insights, there is the Proms premiere of a gorgeously flamboyant orchestral extravaganza from one of those German composers whose flourishing careers were knocked off course by the advent of the Third Reich. Tchaikovsky's equivocal triumph brings down the curtain.

Hélène Grimaud

Broadcast
RADIO Live on Radio 3
ONLINE Live and 'listen again' options at bbc.co.uk/proms

TUESDAY 6 SEPTEMBER

Proms Plus Intro 5.45pm, Royal College of Music
Petroc Trelawny introduces members of the Pittsburgh Symphony Orchestra and discusses their work, the current climate for American orchestras and the challenges they face.

7.30pm–c9.50pm

Wagner
Lohengrin – Prelude, Act 1   9'

Wolfgang Rihm
Gesungene Zeit   24'

INTERVAL

Mahler
Symphony No. 5 in C sharp minor   73'

Anne-Sophie Mutter violin

Pittsburgh Symphony Orchestra
Manfred Honeck conductor

For the second of their two concerts, the Pittsburgh Symphony Orchestra preface Mahler's turbulent and heart-wrenching Fifth Symphony with lyrical music by one of the most distinguished and prolific of contemporary German composers. It has been 35 years since Anne-Sophie Mutter's breakthrough debut at the age of 13. Her willingness to champion the music of our own time has been one of the defining qualities of a violinist renowned for her flawless technique and impassioned playing style.

Manfred Honeck

PROM 69
Spotlight on … Anne-Sophie Mutter

Contemporary music has always formed a vital strand of Anne-Sophie Mutter's repertoire. In a Proms career stretching back to 1986 she has explored the new – ranging from Berg to Lutosławski and Previn – as often as she has revisited the Romantic repertoire that forms the bread and butter of a violinist's portfolio.

This season she gives the first Proms performance of *Gesungene Zeit* ('Time Chant') by Wolfgang Rihm, composed for her in 1992. 'It's still a very contemporary-sounding piece – it's held up very well,' she says. 'Rihm's violin-writing is always remarkable for its singing quality: *Time Chant* is a never-ending aria.' Currently giving the first performances of a new violin work by Rihm, she identifies this *cantabile* approach to the violin as a recurring feature in his music: 'He seems to be attracted by that one strong component of a beautiful instrument.'

Mutter is pleased to be performing the music of our time at the Proms. 'I am always impressed by the huge amount of young people standing and taking in the music. England has always been a great place to play contemporary music – the Proms in particular – so I'm excited to share this music with an audience that is open-minded enough and interested enough to go on the journey without any sort of prejudice!'

Broadcast
RADIO Live on Radio 3
ONLINE Live and 'listen again' options at bbc.co.uk/proms

WEDNESDAY 7 SEPTEMBER

Proms Plus Intro 5.15pm, Royal College of Music
Proms Director Roger Wright is joined by Chris Cotton, Chief Executive of the Royal Albert Hall, to look back over the 2011 season and take questions from the audience. Presented by Petroc Trelawny.

7.00pm–c9.05pm

Bridge
Isabella   13'

Sir Harrison Birtwistle
Concerto for Violin and Orchestra   25'
UK premiere

INTERVAL

Holst
The Planets   50'

Christian Tetzlaff *violin*

Holst Singers
BBC Symphony Orchestra
David Robertson *conductor*

David Robertson

Frank Bridge is at his most romantic and Lisztian in the Keats-inspired *Isabella*, given its world premiere at the Proms by founder-conductor Henry Wood. Sir Harrison Birtwistle's concerto, his first for a string instrument, was commissioned by the Boston Symphony Orchestra for Christian Tetzlaff and unveiled by him in March to rave reviews. The composer himself studied the clarinet, although he says, 'I had some violin lessons at school, so I have a memory of the physical feel of the instrument, in a sense. It's rather like remembering how to bowl a leg break in cricket, even if I couldn't do it now.' Holst's planetary survey displays astonishing verve in its orchestration and in the radicalism of much of its content for its time. *See 'Out of the Shadows', pages 48–49; 'New Music', pages 68–75; 'Featured Artists', pages 78–81*

Broadcast
RADIO Live on Radio 3
ONLINE Live and 'listen again' options at bbc.co.uk/proms

WEDNESDAY 7 SEPTEMBER

10.15pm–c11.30pm

Tribute to Stan Kenton

Claire Martin *vocalist*

BBC Big Band
Jiggs Whigham *conductor*

Enjoy a late-night centenary tribute to Stan Kenton, whose orchestra, during the late 1940s and early 1950s, was the biggest jazz attraction in the world, embracing in its ranks many soloists and arrangers who went on to have brilliant careers of their own. One of the most creative of all bandleaders, Kenton's penchant for complex and highly structured work could run counter to the expectations of critics and audiences alike. Still, he kept on moving between dissonance and convention, and tonight the BBC Big Band celebrates his legacy, including some of his classical arrangements, with guest vocalist Claire Martin.

There will be no interval

SAME-DAY SAVER
Book for both Proms 70 and 71 and save (see page 158)

Stan Kenton

PROM 71
Spotlight on … Claire Martin

Making her Proms and Royal Albert Hall debut, award-winning jazz singer (and Radio 3 presenter) Claire Martin calls this Late Night Prom a dream come true. Anita O'Day, June Christy and Chris Connor – three women who inspired Martin to become a singer – were close associates of Stan Kenton, and it was through their work that she got to know his music so intimately.

Martin describes Kenton's arrangements as exciting, unpredictable and even controversial; he was a magnet for young, up-and-coming talent (tonight's conductor, Jiggs Whigham, was a protégé) and revered for his innovative line-ups, which included strings and more unusual jazz instruments such as euphoniums. 'His style has been called "The Wall of Sound" – it's going to be breathtaking in a venue like this,' Martin says. 'And the BBC Big Band is the cream of the British jazz scene. It's a band of bandleaders, it's a jazz juggernaut!

'Big-band jazz as an art form needs and deserves to be more celebrated. This is a rare chance to hear some of the greatest arrangements with a great line-up of players. This year's Late Night Proms series is going out with a bang!'

Broadcast
RADIO Live on Radio 3
ONLINE Live and 'listen again' options at bbc.co.uk/proms

THURSDAY 8 SEPTEMBER

7.30pm–c9.50pm

Sibelius
Finlandia   8'

Tchaikovsky
Violin Concerto   35'

INTERVAL

Rachmaninov
Symphonic Dances   36'

Ravel
La valse   12'

Janine Jansen *violin*

Philadelphia Orchestra
Charles Dutoit *conductor*

One of the world's great orchestras comes to the
Proms with a programme of familiar classics that
takes in Rachmaninov's bracing swansong, written
for Philadelphia. A regular visitor in recent years,
Janine Jansen joins the orchestra for the ever-popular
Tchaikovsky concerto she recorded recently in fresh
and unashamedly romantic style. These works are
bookended by Sibelius's patriotic rallying cry and
Ravel's apotheosis
of the waltz, a piece
whose unstoppable
whirling may have
been intended as
a metaphor for the
fate of European
civilisation. *See
'French Connections',
pages 36–39*

Janine Jansen

PROM 72
Spotlight on … Charles Dutoit

Founded in 1900, the Philadelphia Orchestra
is well known for its lush, vibrant string sound –
so it's no coincidence that the ensemble's Proms
programme contains several works to highlight
this. 'The sound of the Philadelphia Orchestra
is highly recognisable,' agrees Chief Conductor
Charles Dutoit. 'It's very dark and full and rich
and creamy – and my task, like that of any
conductor, has been to keep this traditional
sound alive, which comes from the time of
previous conductors Leopold Stokowski and
Eugene Ormandy.'

This distinctive sound is clearly heard
in Rachmaninov's *Symphonic Dances*, says
Dutoit. 'The work is one of the warhorses of
the orchestra's repertoire, and they really play
it superbly. Rachmaninov wrote the piece for
them in 1940, and dedicated it to the orchestra
and Eugene Ormandy.'

Rachmaninov's final composition, the work
is in three sections, with the central movement
formed from 'a very lugubrious waltz, which is
very, very dark and sad, and terribly Russian, in
a way,' explains Dutoit. 'Ravel's *La valse* is also
a very dark piece too – it's not just a showpiece
like many people think – so these two waltzes
are actually very close in mood and feeling.'

FRIDAY 9 SEPTEMBER

7.30pm–c10.25pm

Weber
Der Freischütz *(French version, 1841,
with recitatives by Berlioz; concert performance)*   135'

Andrew Kennedy *Max*
Sophie Karthäuser *Agathe*
Gidon Saks *Kaspar*
Virginie Pochon *Ännchen*
Matthew Brook *Kuno*

Monteverdi Choir
Orchestre Révolutionnaire et Romantique
Sir John Eliot Gardiner *conductor*

Sir John Eliot Gardiner
and his team have recently
been staging Berlioz's rarely
performed take on Weber's
Der Freischütz at the Opéra
Comique in Paris. As
originally composed, the
work has spoken dialogue
in German but, for the Paris
production of 1841, Berlioz
replaced the dialogue with
recitative as well as adding

Sir John Eliot Gardiner

the ballet expected by French audiences at the time.
This is the most familiar part of his revision today,
an orchestration of Weber's *Invitation to the Dance*.
Tonight's rendition of the complete opera in Berlioz's
reconfiguration is its first outing at the Proms.
See 'Aiming for Freedom', pages 52–55

There will be one interval

SATURDAY 10 SEPTEMBER

Proms Plus Sing 5.15pm, Royal College of Music
Start your Last Night celebrations in singalong style with vocal coach and musical director Stuart Barr. Blow the cobwebs off *Rule, Britannia!*, *Jerusalem* and music by Richard Rodgers, and create your own Last Night human orchestra. No need to book – just turn up!

7.30pm–c10.45pm

Last Night of the Proms 2011

Sir Peter Maxwell Davies
Musica benevolens   c4'
Musicians Benevolent Fund commission: world premiere

Bartók
The Miraculous Mandarin – suite   20'

Wagner
Götterdämmerung – Immolation Scene   18'

Liszt
Piano Concerto No. 1 in E flat major   19'

INTERVAL

Chopin
Grande Polonaise brillante, Op. 22   9'

Susan Bullock

Grainger
Mo nighean dubh (My Dark-Haired Maiden)   4'

Britten
The Young Person's Guide to the Orchestra   20'

Rodgers, arr. Jackson
The Sound of Music – 'Climb ev'ry mountain'   4'
Carousel – 'You'll never walk alone'   3'

Elgar
Pomp and Circumstance March No. 1
in D major ('Land of Hope and Glory')   8'

Arne
Rule, Britannia!   8'

Parry, orch. Elgar
Jerusalem   4'

The National Anthem   2'

Lang Lang *piano*
Susan Bullock *soprano*

BBC Symphony Chorus
BBC Symphony Orchestra
Edward Gardner *conductor*

Tradition meets high jinks once again as Edward Gardner conducts his first Last Night of the Proms. For this grandest of grand finales there are two very special guests. Since her first Proms appearance in 1995, Susan Bullock has emerged as Britain's leading dramatic soprano, specialising in what she calls 'the large ladies' of the repertoire. None is more challenging than Brünnhilde, whose Immolation Scene concludes Wagner's epic *Ring* cycle. Also featured is a classical music superstar, as popular in the West as in his native China. Lang Lang plays Liszt at his most dazzling on this, his sixth visit to the Proms.

Bartók's thrilling suite provides a blast of exotic orchestral colour. Arne, Parry and Elgar bring down the curtain in traditional fashion. But first the Master of the Queen's Music pays tribute to the Promenaders' fundraising efforts on behalf of the Musicians Benevolent Fund in his new work. See 'A Lust for Liszt', pages 24–27; 'New Music', pages 68–75; 'Featured Artists', pages 78–81

PROM 74
Spotlight on … Lang Lang

Having performed at the First Night of the Proms in 2003 and appeared in three subsequent seasons, Chinese pianist Lang Lang is thrilled to be playing not only at the Last Night but also earlier in the evening at Proms in the Park in Hyde Park. 'The Last Night of the Proms is probably the biggest event on earth for classical music, and it's a tremendous pleasure to be performing in it,' he says. 'I think it's phenomenal that such an event exists, and concerts like this show there's a brilliant future ahead of us for classical music.'

Lang Lang performs Liszt's Piano Concerto No. 1 – music by a composer with whom he's had a long relationship. 'When I was a kid, it was listening to Liszt – his *Hungarian Rhapsody No. 2*, in fact – that made me want to learn the piano,' he says. 'Liszt is like a god to me: he's a devil, he's an angel, he's a human being – he has everything! He somehow turns the piano into another instrument and makes it sound like a whole orchestra. He's a very special composer, especially in this 200th-anniversary year.

'This concerto is a very dynamic, virtuosic piece; it fizzes like a sparkling wine. It's so energetic but it's also very poetic – for me, it's not just about flashy show, as there are also a lot of deep thoughts and rich colours to explore.'

Broadcast
RADIO Live on Radio 3
ONLINE Live and 'listen again' options at bbc.co.uk/proms
TV First half live on BBC Two, second half live on BBC One

BBC Proms IN THE PARK

The Last Night magic, live in the open air!

Katherine Jenkins   Russell Watson   Lang Lang   Josh Groban

The BBC Proms in the Park experience offers a live open-air concert with high-profile artists and presenters, culminating in a BBC Big Screen link-up to the Royal Albert Hall and a firework finale in the park. So gather together your friends, pack a picnic and get ready for a fabulous night out.

Further Last Night celebrations around the UK will be announced. Please check bbc.co.uk/promsinthepark for details.

Last Night celebrations will also be shown on BBC Big Screens across the UK. For more details of locations, and for confirmation of timings, visit bbc.co.uk/bigscreens

Highlights of the Hyde Park concert will be included as part of the live coverage of the Last Night on BBC One and BBC Two, while digital TV viewers can choose to watch the Royal Albert Hall Last Night or a Proms in the Park concert via Red Button.

SATURDAY 10 SEPTEMBER, HYDE PARK, LONDON

Katherine Jenkins *mezzo soprano*
Russell Watson *tenor*
Lang Lang *piano*

with special guest **Josh Groban**

Royal Choral Society
BBC Concert Orchestra
Keith Lockhart *conductor*

Keith Lockhart

Join in the Last Night celebrations in Hyde Park with a host of internationally-acclaimed musical stars, including Katherine Jenkins, Russell Watson and Josh Groban, accompanied by Proms in the Park favourites the BBC Concert Orchestra under their Principal Conductor Keith Lockhart. And celebrated pianist Lang Lang makes a special appearance on the Hyde Park stage before hot-footing it to appear at the Last Night in the Royal Albert Hall – on the same night!

To get the musical party under way, presenter Ken Bruce introduces a range of artists including The Overtones and the cast of the new West End musical *Rock of Ages*.

For further details of all BBC Proms in the Park events, and additional concerts in London's Hyde Park over the Last Night weekend, visit bbc.co.uk/promsinthepark

Gates open 4.00pm; entertainment from 5.30pm

For details of how to order a picnic hamper for collection on the day, or to find out about VIP packages and corporate hospitality, visit bbc.co.uk/promsinthepark

Tickets £32.50 (under-3s free) – now available
Online via bbc.co.uk/promsinthepark
By phone from See tickets on 0844 412 4630†
(a transaction fee of £2.00, plus a booking fee of £1.35 per ticket applies); from the Royal Albert Hall on 0845 401 5040* (a booking fee of 2% of the total value, plus £2.10 per ticket applies)
In person at the Royal Albert Hall Box Office (Door 12, no transaction fee)
By post see page 157

Please note: *in the interest of safety, please do not bring glass items (including bottles), barbeques or flaming torches.*

† Calls cost up to 5p/min from a landline (min connection fee of 8p may apply). Calls from mobiles may cost considerably more.

with thanks to

THE ROYAL PARKS

Broadcast
RADIO Live on BBC Radio 2
ONLINE Live and 'listen again' options
TV Live via the red button on BBC Television

How to Book

Booking opens online, by telephone and in person on Saturday 7 May at 9.00am

A booking fee of 2% of the total value, plus £1.00, applies to all bookings, except those for Proms in the Park (*see page 161*) and those made in person at the Royal Albert Hall. Special arrangements apply to Last Night of the Proms tickets, owing to high demand (*see page 159*). Tickets may also be requested by post.

ONLINE

Book online at **bbc.co.uk/proms** from 9.00am on Saturday 7 May.

With the **Proms Planner**, accessible via bbc.co.uk/proms, you can create and amend your personal Proms Plan at your leisure before tickets go on sale, at any time from noon on Thursday 14 April until midnight on Friday 6 May. Once completed, your personal Proms Plan is ready for you to submit from 9.00am on Saturday 7 May. Because of the expected high demand when booking opens, using the Proms Planner means that you may be more successful in securing your preferred tickets, as your booking is likely to be processed more quickly.

How to use the Proms Planner

- From 12 noon on Thursday 14 April select 'Plan your Proms tickets' at bbc.co.uk/proms. (You will be redirected to www.royalalberthall.com.)

- Select 'Create my Proms Plan', either create an account (or log in if you are an existing user) and start choosing the concerts you would like to attend, along with the number of tickets and seating area. You can make changes to your Proms Plan at any time until midnight on Friday 6 May.

  Please note: this is a request system and there is no guarantee that the tickets you select in your Proms Plan prior to booking opening will be available once booking has opened.

- From 9.00am on Saturday 7 May visit www.royalalberthall.com and log in to your Proms Plan. In the case of exceptionally high demand, you may be held in an online waiting room before you are able to log in: you will be informed how many people are in front of you in the queue. *You must submit your Proms Plan in order to make a booking.*

- Your Proms Plan will now have been updated to reflect live ticket availability and you will be given the chance to choose alternatives should your selected tickets have become unavailable.

- Confirm your online booking by submitting your Proms Plan and entering your payment details.

- Your booking will be immediately confirmed by email.

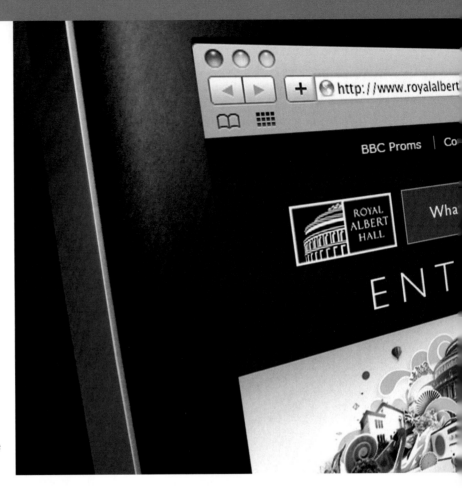

Why use the Proms Planner before booking opens?

- **Convenience** At any time from 12 noon on Thursday 14 April until midnight on Friday 6 May you can plan which Proms you would like to attend, and amend your selection.

- **Best chance for tickets** Creating your Proms Plan in advance speeds up the booking process and increases the likelihood of securing your preferred tickets when booking opens.

Please note: it is not possible to book entire boxes online. If you would like to book a full box, call the Box Office on 0845 401 5040* from 9.00am on Saturday 7 May.

If you have any queries about how to use the Proms Planner, call the Royal Albert Hall Box Office on **0845 401 5040***.

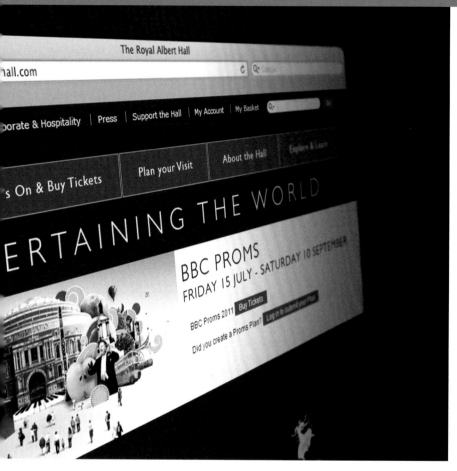

BY TELEPHONE

From 9.00am on Saturday 7 May, call the Royal Albert Hall Box Office on **0845 401 5040*** (open 9.00am–9.00pm daily).
A booking fee of 2% of the total value, plus £1.00, applies. For Proms in the Park booking fee information, see page 161.

IN PERSON

From 9.00am on Saturday 7 May, visit the Royal Albert Hall Box Office at Door 12. (The Box Office is open 9.00am–9.00pm daily.)
No booking fee applies to tickets bought in person.

BY POST

The postal booking form has been discontinued. If you wish to apply for tickets by post, please write to BBC Proms, Box Office, Royal Albert Hall, London SW7 2AP with the following details:

- your name, address, telephone number(s) and email address (if applicable)
- the concerts you wish to attend
- number of tickets required
- preferred seating section, preferably with alternatives *(see seating plan on page 160 and ticket prices on page 161)*
- applicable discounts *(see pages 158 & 164)*
- a cheque, payable to 'Royal Albert Hall' and made out for the maximum amount; or your credit card details, including type of card, name on the card, card number, issue number (Maestro only), start date, expiry date and security code (last three digits on back of Visa/Mastercard or last four digits on front of American Express).

Your details will be held securely. Postal bookings will be processed from 9.00am on Saturday 7 May when booking opens.

A booking fee of 2% of the total value, plus £1.00, applies. For Proms in the Park booking fee information, see page 161.

TICKET TIPS

Don't give up!

If you are unable to get tickets for a popular Prom, **keep trying** at bbc.co.uk/proms or the Royal Albert Hall Box Office, as returns often become available. In addition, many boxes and some seats at the Royal Albert Hall are privately owned, and these seats may be returned for general sale in the period leading up to the concert. The Royal Albert Hall does not operate a waiting list.

If you can't sit, stand

Up to 1,400 Promming (standing) places are available in the Arena and Gallery on the day for every Prom at the Royal Albert Hall. If you arrive early enough on the day of the concert, you have a very good chance of getting in. For more details, see pages 18–21.

Special Offers

Same-Day Savers

Book seats for more than one concert on the same day, and save £4.00 per ticket for the later concert. This discount is available through all booking methods, including online and via the Proms Planner. When booking online, it will be applied automatically at the checkout stage.

This offer applies to performances at the Royal Albert Hall only. Please note that Prom 20 (free Horrible Histories Prom) is excluded from this offer, and it is not valid for Arena, Gallery and Circle (Restricted View) price bands. *See page 161 for price-band information.*

Kids Go Half-Price

The Proms are a great way to discover live music and we encourage anyone over 5 years old to attend. Tickets for under-16s can be purchased at half price in any seating section for all Proms except the Last Night (Prom 74). This discount is available through all booking methods, including online and via the Proms Planner.

Note that the second Human Planet Prom at 11.00am on Sunday 24 July (Prom 12), and the free Horrible Histories Prom at 11.00am on Saturday 30 July (Prom 20) are both great ways of introducing young children to concert-going.

Great Savings for Groups

Groups of 10 or more can claim a 10% discount (5% for C-band concerts) on the price of Centre/Side Stalls or Front/Rear Circle tickets (excluding the Last Night). See page 161 for price-band information.

Please note: *group bookings can only be made by phone or in person at the Royal Albert Hall. They cannot be made online or by post. To make a group booking, or for more information, call the Group Booking Information Line on 020 7070 4408.*

Proms Chamber Music Series Pass

Attend all eight Proms Chamber Music concerts for just £30.00 with the Proms Chamber Music Series Pass (see page 163).

Weekend Promming Pass

Beat the queues at the weekend and save money! Promming is an essential part of the character of the BBC Proms. In addition to discounted tickets, the Weekend Promming Pass offers guaranteed access up to 20 minutes before start-time to the Arena or Gallery standing areas for all concerts in the Royal Albert Hall on Fridays, Saturdays and Sundays (excluding Proms 12, 73 and 74). Passes can be purchased online, by phone or in person at the Royal Albert Hall Box Office from 9.00am on Saturday 7 May, and planned online via the Proms Planner from 12 noon on Thursday 14 April. Passes can only be purchased up to 6.00pm on the day they start (5.30pm on 12 & 19 August and 2 September). Prices vary for each weekend depending on the number of concerts covered – see box below.

Note that Weekend 2 *excludes* Prom 12 (the second Human Planet Prom), Weekend 3 *includes* Prom 20 (free Horrible Histories Prom) and Weekend 7 (covering the August Bank Holiday) *includes* Prom 59. There is no pass covering Proms 73 and 74. Weekend Promming Passes are not valid for concerts at Cadogan Hall.

Passes are non-transferable and signature ID may be requested upon entry. Purchase of a Weekend Promming Pass does not guarantee entry to the Last Night, but tickets may be counted towards the Five-Concert Ballot *(see opposite)* in conjunction with further Passes or Day Ticket stubs.

Please note: *you may purchase a maximum of four passes per weekend. Weekend Promming Passes are subject to availability.*

For details of Whole- and Half-Season Tickets, see page 161.

Weekend Promming Pass prices		
Weekend 1	Proms 1–4	£17.50
Weekend 2	Proms 10, 11 & 13	£12.50
Weekend 3	Proms 19–22	£12.50
Weekend 4	Proms 29–32	£17.50
Weekend 5	Proms 38–41	£17.50
Weekend 6	Proms 47–50	£17.50
Weekend 7	Proms 56–59	£17.50
Weekend 8	Proms 63–67	£22.50

The Last Night of the Proms

Owing to the huge demand for Last Night of the Proms tickets, special booking arrangements apply.

The majority of tickets for the Last Night of the Proms will be allocated by ballot to customers who have bought tickets to at least five other Proms concerts at the Royal Albert Hall. A further 200 tickets will be allocated by the Open Ballot (see far right).

The Five-Concert Ballot To be eligible to enter the Five-Concert Ballot, you must book tickets for at least five other concerts. (The free Horrible Histories Prom [Prom 20], concerts at Cadogan Hall and Proms in the Park do not count towards the Five-Concert Ballot.) You can apply to buy a maximum of two tickets for the Last Night. (Whether you book one or 11 tickets for five concerts, you will be offered a maximum of two tickets for the Last Night if successful in the Ballot.) If you are successful in the Ballot, you will not be obliged to buy Last Night tickets should your preferred seating section not be available.

Please note: you must tick the Ballot opt-in box when booking online, or inform the Box Office that you wish to enter this Ballot when booking by telephone, in person or by post.

If you require a wheelchair space for the Last Night of Proms you will still need to book for five other concerts but you need to phone the Access Information Line (020 7070 4410) and request that you are entered into the separate ballot for wheelchair spaces by Tuesday 24 May. This ballot cannot be entered online. The Five-Concert Ballot closes on Tuesday 24 May and you will be informed by Wednesday 1 June whether or not you have been successful. If you are successful, **please note that your Last Night Tickets will not be issued until Friday 2 September.** We regret that, if you are unsuccessful in the Five-Concert Ballot, no refunds for other tickets purchased will be payable.

General availability for the Last Night

Any tickets not allocated by the Five-Concert Ballot or the Open Ballot will go on sale on Friday 8 July. There is exceptionally high demand for Last Night tickets, but returns occasionally become available, so it is always worth checking with the Box Office.

Please note: for all Last Night bookings, only one application (for a maximum of two tickets) can be made per household.

Promming at the Last Night

Day Prommers and Weekend Promming Pass-holders who have attended five or more other concerts (in either the Arena or the Gallery) can buy one ticket each for the Last Night (priced £5.00) on presentation of their used tickets (which will be retained) at the Box Office. A number of tickets will go on sale on Tuesday 19 July; a further allocation will be released on Tuesday 16 August; and a final, smaller allocation on Wednesday 31 August.

Season Ticket-Holders Whole Season Tickets include admission to the Last Night. A limited allocation of Last Night tickets (priced £5.00) is also reserved for Half-Season Ticket-holders, and will be available to buy from the Box Office from Tuesday 19 July (for First Half Season-Ticket holders) and Tuesday 16 August (for both First and Second Half-Season Ticket-holders). A final, smaller allocation available for both will go on sale on Wednesday 31 August.

Queuing All Prommers (Day or Season) with Last Night tickets should queue on the South Steps, west side (Arena), or the top of Bremner Road, left side (Gallery). Whole Season Ticket-holders are guaranteed entrance until 20 minutes before the concert. Whole Season Ticket-holders who arrive less than 20 minutes before the concert will be asked to join the back of the queue on the South Steps, east side (Arena), or the top of Bremner Road, right side (Gallery).

Sleeping Out Please note it is not necessary for Prommers with Last Night tickets to camp out overnight to secure their preferred standing place inside the Hall. Ticket-holders may add their name to a list which will be held at the Stage Door at the Royal Albert Hall from 4.00pm on Friday 9 September. They then need to return to the queue in list order by 10.00am on Saturday 10 September.

On the Night A limited number of standing tickets are available on the Last Night itself (priced £5.00, one per person). No previous ticket purchases are necessary. Just join the queue on the South Steps, east side (Arena), or the top of Bremner Road, right side (Gallery), and you may well be lucky.

Last Night of the Proms 2011 Open Ballot Form

One hundred Centre Stalls seats (priced £82.50 each) and 100 Front Circle seats (priced £55.00 each) for the Last Night of the Proms at the Royal Albert Hall will be allocated by Open Ballot. The Five-Concert Ballot rule does not apply: no other ticket purchases are necessary. Only one application (for a maximum of two tickets) may be made per household.

If you would like to apply for tickets by Open Ballot, please complete the official Open Ballot Form on the back of this slip and send it by post only – to arrive no later than Thursday 30 June – to:

BBC Proms Open Ballot
Box Office
Royal Albert Hall
London SW7 2AP

Note that the Open Ballot application is completely separate from other Proms booking procedures. Envelopes should be clearly addressed to 'BBC Proms Open Ballot' and should contain only this official Open Ballot Form. The Open Ballot takes place on Friday 1 July and successful applicants will be contacted by Thursday 7 July.

This form is also available to download from bbc.co.uk/proms; or call 020 7765 2044 to receive a copy by post.

Please note: if you are successful in the Five-Concert Ballot, you will not be eligible for Last Night tickets via the Open Ballot.

Last Night of the Proms 2011 Open Ballot Form

Title _____ Initial(s) _____

Surname _____

Address _____

_____

_____

Postcode _____

Country _____

Daytime tel. _____

Evening tel. _____

Mobile tel. _____

Email _____

Please indicate your preferred seating option‡

☐ I wish to apply for one Centre Stalls ticket (£82.50)

☐ I wish to apply for two Centre Stalls tickets (£165.00)

☐ I wish to apply for one Front Circle ticket (£55.00)

☐ I wish to apply for two Front Circle tickets (£110.00)

‡We cannot guarantee that you will be offered
tickets in your preferred seating section. You will not
be obliged to buy tickets outside your preference,
but we regret we cannot offer alternatives.

The personal information given on this form will not be used for any
purpose by the BBC or the Royal Albert Hall other than this ballot.

Choose Your Seat

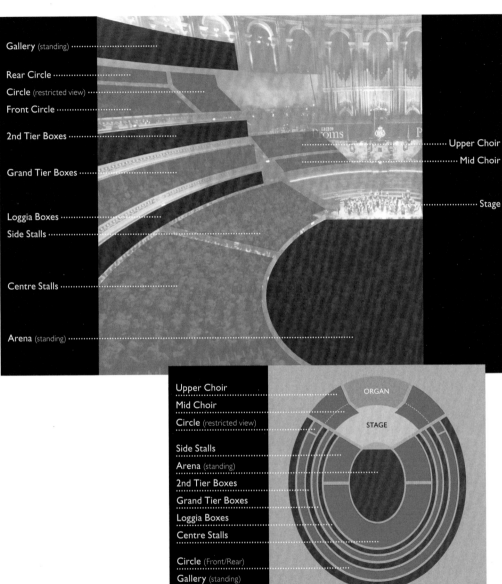

Gallery (standing)

Rear Circle

Circle (restricted view)

Front Circle

2nd Tier Boxes

Grand Tier Boxes

Loggia Boxes

Side Stalls

Centre Stalls

Arena (standing)

Upper Choir

Mid Choir

Stage

Upper Choir
Mid Choir
Circle (restricted view)
Side Stalls
Arena (standing)
2nd Tier Boxes
Grand Tier Boxes
Loggia Boxes
Centre Stalls
Circle (Front/Rear)
Gallery (standing)

ORGAN

STAGE

Chris Christodoulou/BBC

Ticket Prices

Seats

Concerts fall into one of seven price bands, indicated above each concert listing on pages 116–154.

	A	B	C	D	E	F	G
Centre Stalls	£28.00	£36.00	£46.00	£16.00	£19.50	£82.50	
Side Stalls	£24.00	£32.00	£42.00	£16.00	£19.50	£80.00	
Grand Tier Boxes 12 seats, price per seat	£36.00	£44.00	£55.00	£16.00	£19.50	£90.00	
	(AS MOST GRAND TIER BOXES ARE PRIVATELY OWNED, AVAILABILITY IS LIMITED)						
Loggia Boxes 8 seats, price per seat	£32.00	£40.00	£50.00	£16.00	£19.50	£85.00	
2nd Tier Boxes 5 seats, price per seat	£20.00	£25.00	£35.00	£16.00	£19.50	£72.50	
Mid Choir	£18.00	£21.00	£30.00	N/A	N/A	£60.00	
Upper Choir	£16.00	£19.00	£26.00	N/A	N/A	£55.00	
Front Circle	£15.00	£18.00	£22.00	£12.00	£15.00	£55.00	
Rear Circle	£12.00	£14.00	£18.00	£12.00	£15.00	£45.00	
Circle (restricted view)	£7.50	£8.50	£13.00	N/A	N/A	£25.00	

ALL SEATS £12.00 (UNDER-16s £6.00)

Promming

Standing places are available in the Arena and Gallery on the day for £5.00 (see pages 18–21)

Season Tickets	**Dates**	**Arena**	**Gallery**
Whole Season (Proms 1–74)	15 July – 10 September	£190.00	£190.00
Half-Season Tickets			
First Half (Proms 1–37)	15 July – 11 August	£110.00	£110.00
Second Half (Proms 38–73)	12 August – 9 September	£110.00	£110.00

A booking fee of 2% of the total value plus £1.00 applies to all bookings, other than those made in person at the Royal Albert Hall.

Unwanted tickets may be exchanged for tickets to other Proms concerts (subject to availability). A fee of £1.00 per ticket will be charged for this service. Call the Royal Albert Hall Box Office (0845 401 5040*) for further details.

BBC Proms in the Park, Hyde Park, London, Saturday 10 September

All tickets £32.50 (under 3s free)

Bookings for Proms in the Park tickets only will incur a booking fee of 2% of the total value, plus £2.10 per ticket. No fee is payable if booking in person at the Royal Albert Hall.

Other Information

Disabled Concert-Goers
See page 164 for details of special discounts, access and facilities.

Privately Owned Seats
A high proportion of boxes, as well as 650 Stalls seats, are privately owned. Unless returned by owners, these seats are not usually available for sale.

Season Tickets
Season Tickets and Proms Chamber Music Series Passes can be booked online, by phone or in person at the Royal Albert Hall Box Office from 9.00am on Saturday 7 May, and planned online via the Proms Planner from 12 noon on Thursday 14 April. Please note that two passport-sized photographs must be provided for each season ticket or pass before it can be issued.

Proms at Cadogan Hall
For booking information on the Proms Chamber Music series, see page 163.

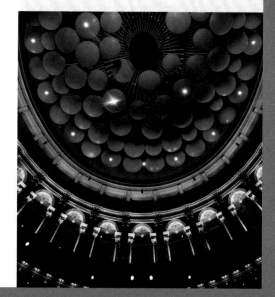

Chris Christodoulou/BBC

Royal Albert Hall
Kensington Gore, London SW7 2AP *(see map, page 165)* www.royalalberthall.com

Make the most of your visit and enjoy the full Royal Albert Hall experience. With 13 bars, three restaurants, box catering and a large array of products on offer, there is a wide range of food and drink for you to choose from.

Food and Drink at the Royal Albert Hall
All food and drink at the Royal Albert Hall is now provided by "rhubarb" food design, who can provide everything from a light bite before the show, to a three-course fine-dining celebration.

Restaurants
Coda is a stylish destination restaurant offering an elegant fine-dining experience with a modern British menu.

The **Elgar Room** offers a relaxed atmosphere ideal for any social gathering, be it cocktails while sharing tapas-style platters, or a three-course set menu with a bottle of wine. The Elgar Room will be open late on 15, 22 and 30 July, 5, 13, 20 and 27 August and 3 September for informal Proms Plus Lates events – see bbc.co.uk/proms for more information.

Café Consort is an all-day brasserie-style restaurant and offers a range of light meals and snacks, as well as being fully licensed.

Post-concert food and drinks are also available in all three restaurants on selected dates. Further details will be sent with your tickets and will also be available at www.royalalberthall.com.

The restaurants open two hours before the performance, except the Café Consort, which opens two and a half hours beforehand. Tables should be booked in advance. Visit www.royalalberthall.com or call the Box Office on 0845 401 5040* to make your reservation.

Contemporary chic at the Café Consort

Bars are located on all but the Gallery level, offering a full range of drinks, sandwiches, confectionery and ice cream. The Moët & Chandon Champagne Bar, Asahi Bar, Spitfire Bar, North Circle Bar, East Arena Foyer and the porch bars at Doors 3 and 9 all open two hours before each concert. All other bars open 45 minutes before each concert.

Interval orders can be arranged from any bar. Please ask any member of bar staff.

Box Catering
If you have seats in one of the Royal Albert Hall's boxes you can pre-order catering with "rhubarb" – choose from freshly made sandwiches and snacks to canapé selections, sushi boxes, and the finest vintage champagne. Please call 020 7959 0579 for details.

Please note: the consumption of your own food and drink in the Hall is not permitted. In the interests of health and safety, only cold drinks in closed plastic containers are allowed into the auditorium. Glasses and bottles are permitted in boxes, as part of box catering ordered through "rhubarb".

Car Parking
A limited number of parking spaces, priced £8.00 each, is available from 6.00pm (or one hour before weekend matinee concerts) in the Imperial College car park, which has entrances on Prince Consort Road (open Monday to Saturday until 7.00pm; closed on Sundays) and Exhibition Road. These can be booked online, by phone or in person at the Royal Albert Hall from 9.00am on Saturday 7 May, and planned online via the Proms Planner from 12 noon on Thursday 14 April. Please note that, if attending both early-evening and late-night concerts on the same day, only one parking fee is payable.

Doors open 45 minutes before the start of each concert (earlier for restaurant and bar access) and 30 minutes before each late-night concert. Tickets will be scanned upon entry. Please have them ready, one per person.

Latecomers will not be admitted into the auditorium unless or until there is a suitable break in the music. There is a video screen in the Door 6 foyer with a digital audio relay.

Bags and coats may be left in the cloakrooms at Door 9 (ground level) and at basement level beneath Door 6. A charge of £1.00 per item applies (cloakroom season tickets priced £20.00 are also available). Conditions apply – see www.royalalberthall.com. For reasons of safety and comfort, only small bags are permitted in the Arena.

Security
In the interests of safety, bags may be searched upon entry.

Children under 5 are not allowed in the auditorium out of consideration for both audience and artists.

Dress Code
Come as you are: there is no dress code at the Proms.

Mobile phones and other electronic devices are distracting to other audience members. Please ensure they are switched off.

The use of cameras, video cameras and recording equipment is strictly forbidden.

Tours of the Royal Albert Hall run every day and last approximately one hour. To book and to check availability, please call 0845 401 5045* or visit www.royalalberthall.com. Tickets cost £8.50 per person, with a number of concessions available.

A selection of **Proms and Royal Albert Hall gifts and souvenirs** is available inside the South Porch at Door 12. Proms merchandise can also be purchased at the Door 6 foyer during performance times.

Cadogan Hall

5 Sloane Terrace, London SW1X 9DQ *(see map, page 160)* www.cadoganhall.com

Proms Chamber Music at Cadogan Hall

Treat yourself to an hour of chamber music each Monday lunchtime during the Proms. Cadogan Hall is the venue for another season of Proms Chamber Music, with a range of artists and programmes that complements the orchestral concerts at the Royal Albert Hall. Brahms is celebrated by his gently autumnal Clarinet Quintet in a concert which also includes the premiere of a new work by Sally Beamish for the Elias Quartet. Liszt's virtuosity and musical mastery are summed up in his Piano Sonata in B minor, played by Khatia Buniatishvili alongside Prokofiev's tumultuous Seventh Sonata. Frank Bridge is celebrated by his famous pupil Britten in a newly rediscovered set of piano variations and shows his own indebtedness to Brahms in a youthful Piano Quintet, while oboist Nicholas Daniel joins the Aronowitz Ensemble for the young Britten's ardent *Phantasy*. The season's French music focus is given a Baroque twist and a dash of Italian flavouring by Christophe Rousset and Les Talens Lyriques. Henri Dutilleux's *Sonatine* forms the centrepiece of a recital by Emmanuel Pahud which also showcases sonatas by Martinů and Prokofiev. Two other featured artists give chamber recitals: Yo-Yo Ma, who includes a work composed for him by Graham Fitkin; and Christian Tetzlaff, who performs Bartók's rhapsodic and virtuosic First Violin Sonata. And, to launch the series, harpsichordist Mahan Esfahani presents one of the greatest keyboard works of all time: Bach's magnificent 'Goldberg' Variations.

All Proms Chamber Music concerts are broadcast live on BBC Radio 3 and repeated the following Saturday at 2.00pm.

Doors open at 12 noon; entrance to the auditorium is from 12.30pm.

Proms Saturday Matinees at Cadogan Hall

Proms Saturday Matinees continue this season at Cadogan Hall with a focus on contemporary music. The London Sinfonietta presents a birthday tribute to Sir Richard Rodney Bennett and return with a new work by Georges Aperghis. The BBC Singers are joined by Sinfonye and Stevie Wishart for her new settings of texts by Hildegard of Bingen, and also perform works by Tippett and Gubaidulina, while the Britten Sinfonia and cellist Natalie Clein give the UK premiere of a new work by Sir John Tavener.

Doors open at 2.00pm; entrance to the auditorium is from 2.30pm.

Cadogan Hall Ticket Prices

Stalls: £12.00
Centre Gallery: £10.00
Day Seats (Side Gallery): £5.00

Tickets can be bought online, by phone or in person from the Royal Albert Hall from 9.00am on Saturday 7 May (0845 401 5040*) and from Cadogan Hall from Saturday 14 May (020 7730 4500).

Tickets can be bought on the day of the concert – from Cadogan Hall only – from 10.00am.

£5.00 Tickets on the Day

At least 150 Side Gallery (bench) seats will be available for just £5.00 each from 10.00am on the day of the concert. These tickets can only be bought at Cadogan Hall. They must be purchased in person and with cash only, and are limited to two tickets per transaction.

£30.00 Proms Chamber Music Series Pass

Hear all eight Proms Chamber Music concerts for just £30.00, with guaranteed entrance to the Side Gallery until 12.50pm (after which Proms Chamber Music Series Pass-holders may be asked to join the day queue).

Passes can be purchased from 9.00am on Saturday 7 May online, by phone or in person at the Royal Albert Hall. Two passport-sized photographs must be provided.

Please note: Proms Chamber Music Series Passes cannot be purchased from Cadogan Hall.

Proms Chamber Music Series Passes are not valid for Proms Saturday Matinee concerts at Cadogan Hall and are subject to availability.

Royal College of Music

Prince Consort Road, London SW7 2BS *(see map, page 165)* www.rcm.ac.uk

Proms Plus

Proms Plus pre-concert events will be held in the Amaryllis Fleming Concert Hall at the Royal College of Music.

All Proms Plus events are free of charge and unticketed (seating is unreserved), with the exception of the First Night live *In Tune* event on Friday 15 July, where free tickets will be available from BBC Studio Audiences (bbc.co.uk/tickets or 0370 901 1227†). Places must be reserved in advance for all Proms Plus Family Orchestra & Chorus events, Proms Plus Sing events and the Proms Plus Literary poetry workshops (visit bbc.co.uk/proms or call 020 7765 0557).

Please note: all Proms Plus events are subject to capacity and we advise arriving early for the more popular events. Latecomers will be admitted but, as many of these events are being recorded for broadcast, you may have to wait until a suitable moment. The event stewards will guide you.

For Prommers who join the Royal Albert Hall queue before the Proms Plus event, make sure you take a numbered slip from one of the Royal Albert Hall stewards to secure your place back in the queue.

If you have special access requirements, see the Royal College of Music information overleaf.

†Standard geographic charges from landlines and mobiles will apply.

Chris Christodoulou/BBC

Access at the Proms

Tickets and Discounts for Disabled Concert-Goers

All disabled concert-goers (and one companion) receive a 50% discount on all ticket prices (except Arena and Gallery areas) for concerts at the Royal Albert Hall and Cadogan Hall. To claim this discount call the Access Information Line on 020 7070 4410 (from 9.00am on Saturday 7 May) if booking by phone. Note that discounts for disabled concert-goers cannot be combined with other ticket offers. Tickets can also be purchased in person from 9.00am on Saturday 7 May at the Royal Albert Hall. The Box Office is situated at Door 12 and has ramped access, an induction loop and drop-down counters. Ambulant disabled concert-goers can also book tickets online from 9.00am on Saturday 7 May and use the online Proms Planner from 12 noon on Thursday 14 April. Please note that the 'select your own seat' facility will not be available to customers booking online at this time – customers will be offered 'best available' seats within the chosen section. Wheelchair spaces cannot be booked online or via the Proms Planner.

Royal Albert Hall

Full information on the facilities offered to disabled concert-goers (including car parking) is available online at www.royalalberthall.com. Information is also available through the Access Information Line on 020 7070 4410 (open 9.00am–9.00pm daily).

The Royal Albert Hall has up to 20 spaces bookable for wheelchair-users and their companions. There are two end-of-aisle places in the Side Stalls and two in the Centre Stalls – these places are priced as such; front-row platform places either side of the stage are priced as Side Stalls seats; rear platform places are priced as Front Circle seats. Spaces in the Front Circle are priced as such.

Four additional wheelchair spaces are available in the Gallery for Promming. These cannot be pre-booked.

Customer lifts at the Royal Albert Hall are located on the ground-floor corridor at Doors 1 and 8. The use of lifts is discouraged during performances.

Hard-of-Hearing and Visually Impaired Concert-Goers

The Royal Albert Hall has an infra-red system with a number of personal receivers for use with and without hearing aids. To make use of the service, collect a free receiver from the Door 6 Information Desk. Patrons are welcome to use this facility to listen in to the BBC Radio 3 broadcast.

If you have a guide dog, the best place to sit in the Royal Albert Hall is in a box, where your dog may stay with you. If you are sitting elsewhere, stewards will be happy to look after your dog while you enjoy the concert. To organise this, please complete an online Accessibility Request at www.royalalberthall.com or phone the Access Information Line on

The BBC Proms: access for all

020 7070 4410 (open 9.00am–9.00pm daily) in advance of your visit. Following the success of the first ever signed Prom last year, Dr Paul Whittaker, Artistic Director of Music and the Deaf, returns to guide you through the free 'Horrible Histories' Prom on Saturday 30 July. The concert promises to be a great way to introduce children to concert-going. Please book your free tickets (from Friday 8 July) via the Access Information Line (020 7070 4410) and request the designated seating areas with the best visibility of the signer.

BBC Proms Guide: Non-Print Versions

Audio CD and Braille versions of this Guide are available in two parts, 'Articles' and 'Concert Listings/Booking Information', priced £3.00 each. For more information and to order, call RNIB Customer Services on 0845 702 3153*.

BBC Proms Guide: Large-Print Version

A text-only large-print version of the Proms Guide is available, priced £6.00. To order, please call 020 7765 3246.

Programme-Reading Service

Ask at the Door 6 Information Desk if you would like a steward to read your concert programme out to you.

Large-Print Programmes & Texts

Large-print concert programmes can be made available on the night (at the same price as the standard programme) if ordered not less than five working days in advance. Complimentary large-print texts and opera librettos (where applicable) can also be made available on the night if ordered in advance. To order any large-print programmes or texts, please call 020 7765 3246. They will be left for collection at the Door 6 Information Desk 45 minutes before the start of the concert.

Cadogan Hall

Cadogan Hall has a range of services to assist disabled customers, including provision for wheelchair-users in the Stalls. There are three wheelchair spaces available for advance booking and one space reserved for sale as a day ticket from 10.00am on the day of the concert. For further information, please call 020 7730 4500.

Royal College of Music

The Amaryllis Fleming Concert Hall at the Royal College of Music has six spaces for wheelchair-users. Step-free access is available from Prince Consort Road, located to the left of the main entrance. For further information, please call 020 7591 4314.

Chris Christodoulou/BBC

Getting There

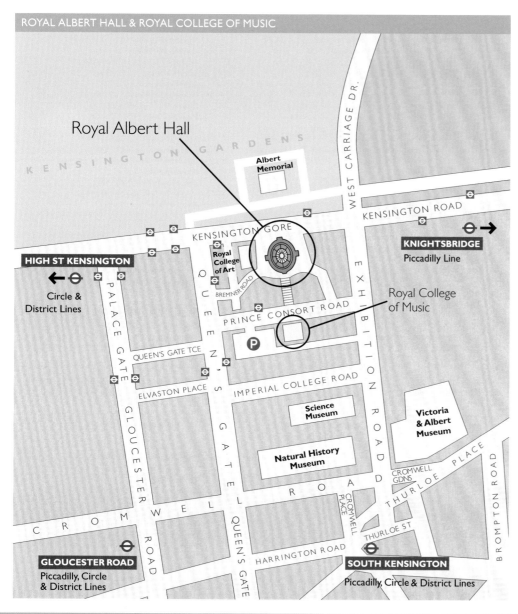

ROYAL ALBERT HALL & ROYAL COLLEGE OF MUSIC

Royal Albert Hall

KENSINGTON GARDENS

Albert Memorial

WEST CARRIAGE DR.

KENSINGTON ROAD

KENSINGTON GORE

KNIGHTSBRIDGE
Piccadilly Line

Royal College of Art

HIGH ST KENSINGTON

Circle & District Lines

BREMNER ROAD

PRINCE CONSORT ROAD

Royal College of Music

EXHIBITION ROAD

PALACE GATE

QUEEN'S GATE TCE

QUEEN'S GATE

ELVASTON PLACE

IMPERIAL COLLEGE ROAD

Science Museum

Victoria & Albert Museum

Natural History Museum

CROMWELL GDNS

CROMWELL PLACE

THURLOE PLACE

BROMPTON ROAD

GLOUCESTER ROAD

CROMWELL ROAD

QUEEN'S GATE

HARRINGTON ROAD

THURLOE ST

SOUTH KENSINGTON
Piccadilly, Circle & District Lines

GLOUCESTER ROAD
Piccadilly, Circle & District Lines

The following buses serve the Royal Albert Hall and Royal College of Music (via Kensington Gore, Queen's Gate, Palace Gate and/or Prince Consort Road): 9/N9, 10 (24-hour service), 49, 52/N52, 70, 360 & 452. Coaches 701 and 702 also serve this area.

The following buses serve Cadogan Hall (via Sloane Street and/or Sloane Square): 11, 19, 22, 137, 170, 211, 319, 360, 452 & C1. For 24-hour London travel information, call 020 7222 1234 or visit www.tfl.gov.uk.

Bicycle racks are near Door 11 of the Royal Albert Hall. (Neither the Hall nor the BBC can accept responsibility for items lost or stolen from these racks.) The Royal Albert Hall has limited cloakroom space and may not be able to accept folding bicycles. Barclays Cycle Hire racks are positioned outside the Royal College of Art, the Royal College of Music and in Cadogan Place.

Please note: the Royal Albert Hall is no longer within the Congestion Charge zone.

For car parking at the Royal Albert Hall, see page 162.

CADOGAN HALL

KNIGHTSBRIDGE
Piccadilly Line

CADOGAN PLACE

SLOANE STREET

ELLIS STREET

DOYLEY STREET

VICTORIA
Victoria, Circle & District and Mainline station

WILBRAHAM PLACE

Cadogan Hall

Cadogan Hall

SLOANE TERRACE

SEDDING STREET

CLIVEDEN PLACE

SYMONS STREET

SLOANE SQUARE

Royal Court Theatre

Peter Jones

SLOANE SQUARE
Circle & District Lines

Index of Artists

Index of Works

BBC Proms 2011

Director Roger Wright, Controller BBC Radio 3 and Director BBC Proms
Personal Assistant Yvette Pusey
Editor, BBC Radio 3 and BBC Proms Edward Blakeman
Concerts and Events Manager,
   BBC Radio 3 and BBC Proms Helen Heslop
Events Co-ordinator, BBC Proms and BBC Radio 3 Helen White
Events Co-ordinator, BBC Radio 3 and BBC Proms Hélène Frisby
Concerts and Events Assistant Sarah Pantcheff
Concerts Assistants Elizabeth Assmann, Lizzie Coxhead

Head of Marketing, Publications and Learning Kate Finch
Communications Manager Victoria Bevan
Assistant Publicist Madeleine Castell
Publicity Assistant Rosanna Chianta
Marketing Manager Emily Caket
Marketing Assistant Megan Bridge
Learning Manager Ellara Wakely
Learning and Audience Development Co-ordinator Naomi Selwyn
Learning and Audience Development Administrator Catherine Jack

Management Assistant Tricia Twigg
Business Assistant Rita Jno-Baptiste

Editor, TV Classical Music Oliver Macfarlane
Series Production Manager Charlotte Gazzard

Interactive Editor, BBC Proms and BBC Radio 3 Gabriel Gilson
Senior Content Producer, BBC Proms website Andrew Downs

BBC Proms Guide 2011

Editor Edward Bhesania
Sub-editor David Threasher
Publications Officer Lydia Casey

Design Premm Design Ltd, London
Cover illustration Justin Krietemeyer/Premm Design

Publications Editor John Bryant
Published by BBC Proms Publications, Room 1045 Broadcasting House, London W1A 1AA

Distributed by BBC Books, an imprint of Ebury Publishing, a Random House Group Company, 20 Vauxhall Bridge Road, London SW1V 2SA
Advertising Cabbell Publishing Ltd, London (020 8971 8450)
Printed by APS Group. APS Group holds ISO 14001 environmental management, FSC and PEFC accreditations

© BBC 2011. All details were correct at time of going to press.

ISBN 978-1-84990-263-2